Catherine Howard

Catherine Howard

LACEY BALDWIN SMITH

AMBERLEY

Amberley Publishing Plc
Cirencester Road, Chalford,
Stroud, Gloucestershire, GL6 8PE

www.amberley-books.com

British Library Cataloguing in Publication Data.
A catalogue record for this book is available from the British Library.

ISBN 978 1 84868 214 6

Typesetting and Origination by diagraf.net
Printed in Great Britain

CONTENTS

GENEALOGICAL TABLE I

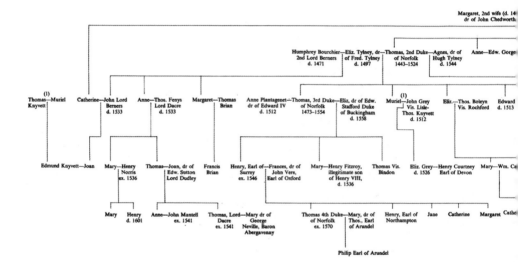

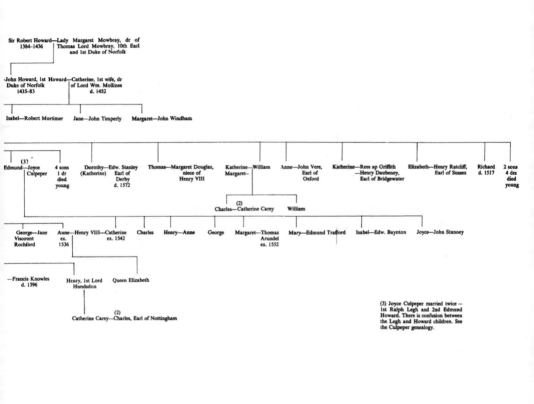

Sir Robert Howard—Lady Margaret Mowbray, dr of
1384-1436 | Thomas Lord Mowbray, 10th Earl
and 1st Duke of Norfolk

-John Howard, 1st Howard—Catherine, 1st wife, dr
Duke of Norfolk | of Lord Wm. Mollines
1435-83 d. 1452

Isabel—Robert Mortimer   Jane—John Timperly   Margaret—John Windham

(3)
Edmund—Joyce   4 sons   Dorothy—Edw. Stanley   Thomas—Margaret Douglas,   Katherine—William   Anne—John Vere,   Katherine—Rees ap Griffith   Elizabeth—Henry Ratcliff,   Richard   2 sons
        Culpeper   1 dr   (Katherine)   Earl of   niece of   Margaret—   Earl of   —Henry Daubeney,   Earl of Sussex   d. 1517   4 drs
                     died   Derby   Henry VIII   Oxford   Earl of Bridgewater   died
                     young   d. 1572   young

                                                                                        (2)
                                                                            Charles—Catherine Carey   William

George—Jane   Anne—Henry VIII—Catherine   Charles   Henry—Anne   George   Margaret—Thomas   Mary—Edmund Trafford   Isabel—Edw. Baynton   Joyce—John Stanney
Viscount   ex.   ex. 1542   Arundel
Rochford   1536   ex. 1552

-Francis Knowles   Henry, 1st Lord   Queen Elizabeth
 d. 1596   Hundsdon

                        (2)
            Catherine Carey—Charles, Earl of Nottingham

(3) Joyce Culpeper married twice —
1st Ralph Legh and 2nd Edmund
Howard. There is confusion between
the Legh and Howard children. See
the Culpeper genealogy.

AUTHOR'S NOTE

The truth is that this book is the product of many minds, and of much labour by a number of persons other than the author. I am particularly indebted to my colleagues Wallace Douglas, J. Lyndon Shanley and Frederick Stimson for their careful reading of the text, and to Walter Richardson for his many helpful suggestions. Though it would be inaccurate to describe this biography as being 'pure Neale', it does, nevertheless, reflect considerable Nealean influence and a vast amount of hard work by Sir John, who read and criticized the manuscript, for which I am deeply grateful.

CHAPTER 1

ALPHA AND OMEGA

At seven o'clock on the morning of 13 February, 1542, a young woman stepped out into the cold of the great courtyard of the Tower of London. Slowly she was escorted across the yard and carefully helped up the steps of the wooden scaffold. Only a small group of sightseers had gathered to watch the death of a queen; there was no weeping, no remorse, only chilly curiosity. The axe rose and fell, a life ceased, an episode came to an end, and the little band of privy councillors, ambassadors and citizens dispersed to their several duties.

Such indifference poses a problem: wherein lies the drama and tragedy of Catherine Howard's death? Is it to be sought for in the picture of vital youth so abruptly and mercilessly concluded? Possibly, but compassion for the unfulfilled promise of youth is dampened by the knowledge that her audience came not to mourn her death but to view it. Is the tragedy to be found in the brutality of an act of state necessity? Hardly, for few could find in the inner reaches of their hearts the conviction that Mistress Catherine Howard was undeserving of her fate. Possibly then the nature of her crime adds meaning to her death. The Queen was accused of having been a woman of 'abominable carnal desires' who had craftily and traitorously misled her royal spouse into believing she was 'chaste and of pure, clean and honest living'. Worse still, she had followed 'daily her frail and carnal lust' and had actually 'conspired, imagined, and encompassed' the final destruction of the King. Adultery can add zest to a narrative and treason lend stature to a life, but in the case of Catherine Howard the records reveal neither grand passion nor high ideals. Catherine's life was little more than a series of petty trivialities and wanton acts punctuated by sordid politics. It is, however, exactly here that one senses the ultimate tragedy. It is somehow shocking to our sense of justice to perceive the naked perversity of casual relationships that can transform juvenile delinquency into high treason.

There is a disproportion about Catherine's career that both repels and fascinates. She was a victim of inconsequentialities which somehow combined to produce a conclusion monstrously disproportionate to the myriad of petty causes. This book is an analysis of a life and a multitude of circumstances that culminated in violent death; a study of how chance and personality, morality and adultery, deliberate malice and good intentions, when operating within the limits set by environment, can create a single act in time – the swift descent of the executioner's axe.

Catherine's death is not simply a lesson in Tudor morality. It is an exercise in historical causation and encompasses the entire 'sink and puddle' of palace politics and backstairs bickering which throve so abundantly within the garden of Henry VIII's government. It stands as a grim reminder not only of the consequences of inadvertent folly, but also of the fact that all men are in some fashion victims of their age. Catherine's execution attains the level of grand tragedy only in terms of her milieu – that of the vast Howard dynasty and its ambitions in an age of scarcely veiled 'despotism', when men played the risky game of politics with their lives and women were hapless pawns in the complex scheme of dynastic ambitions. Catherine Howard's light-hearted idiocy was fatal only when fostered and distorted by family greed, royal absolutism, social callousness and violence, and a political theory that stripped the individual of all defence and left him alone and unprotected to face the truth that 'the King's wrath is death.' Only when taken in their entirety do the random events merge into a design, which at no point was ever predetermined or even necessary, but which tempts one to ask of that final tragedy enacted in the courtyard of the Tower of London: How else could it have ended?

CHAPTER 2

THE HOWARD DYNASTY

Catherine Howard's life is comprehensible only in terms of her family; she was born a Howard, a member of a clan whose predatory instincts for self-survival, urge towards tribal aggrandizement, a sense of pompous conceit, and dangerous meddling in the destinies of state, shaped the course of her tragedy. Her career begins and ends with the illustrious house of Howard, which had its origins back in the shadowy years of the fifteenth century.

Every age has its pushing young particles, families who are grasping after the golden apple of social respectability. But the early decades of the sixteenth century experienced something approaching a social revolution where upstart and adventurer, caitiff and villain, successfully rubbed shoulders with pedigreed nobles and peers of ancient lineage. No longer was it possible to discern a gentleman by dress alone, and one sixteenth-century snob inelegantly compared the social aspirants of his day to hatters' blocks, since they 'wear what is worthier than themselves.'[1] Lacking in social status and family inheritance, the new courtiers who garnished the Tudor court and the parvenu gentlemen who found favour in the eyes of a *nouveau riche* dynasty were quick to manufacture what they could not claim by blood. Imposing pedigrees could always be devised, so long as sufficient money and political influence were available to induce a quizzical society to accept what it knew to be fabricated. Brute force, not legitimacy, lucre not blood, had entrenched the Tudor monarchs

11

upon the throne of England, and when the royal person sanctioned the work of eager and artful genealogists there were few subjects so bold as to challenge the subsequent document. It took but a minimum of artistry to contrive a series of noble forbears, and the royal heralds were pestered with the questionable armorial assertations of obscure families whose sudden rise to political and social distinction made it mandatory that they be 'right worthily connected'.

In theory the College of Arms granted the privilege to bear arms and the dignity of a gentleman only to those 'of good name and fame and good renown' who could substantiate their gentle breeding with an annual rental of £10. In actual fact there was constant complaint that grants of arms were being issued 'to vile persons, bondsmen, and persons unable to take upon them any honour of noblesse'. The ancient order was constantly endeavouring to exclude those of more recent origin, and Hugh Vaughan, gentleman usher to Henry VII, was barred from jousting before the King by those of more credible ancestry because he 'was no gentleman nobled to bear arms'.[2] Not even his newly-conceived pedigree, properly sanctioned by the Garter King-of-Arms, was sufficient to win him recognition, until Henry decreed that his gentleman usher should joust with whom he pleased and should bear the arms issued him by the royal herald. Criticism was easily stifled when men became gentlemen by royal mandate. Only towards the end of the century did the social circulation begin to contract and claimants to gentle status have to prove their rights with more factual evidence.

Even the Howards, who joined in their veins the blood of the most honoured families of the realm, had once been viewed by those of more ancient descent as social upstarts. Until marriage and political power had secured their house, they were held as new and strange men, 'wild as a wild bullock'.[3] A fortunate marriage and a series of propitious deaths miraculously translated them from stolid East Anglia stock into the heirs to the dukedom of Norfolk. Unimpeachable as their pedigree was, the Howards, like others of their kind, were not above a certain amount of ancestry manipulation, and by the seventeenth century they were asserting Saxon and early

Norman blood as their heritage. The actual series of events, however, that elevated their house to noble pre-enunence commenced only in the year 1398, when Thomas, Lord Mowbray, tenth Earl and first Duke of Norfolk, was banished from the realm as a consequence of his political rivalry with Henry, Duke of Hereford, first cousin to Richard II. A year later, exiled and a vagrant in Central Europe, he died of what the chroniclers romantically describe as a broken heart, and the rights to the Dukedom passed to his four children – Thomas, who was conveniently executed five years later; John, who succeeded his brother; and two daughters, Isabel and Margaret. It is at this point that the Howards began the series of marriages that was to transform them into the most powerful dynasty of the sixteenth century, second only to the Tudors themselves, for Sir Robert Howard had the foresight to marry Margaret Mowbray. Auspicious as this union was, it could hardly have included ducal aspirations, since John Mowbray was presented with both a son and a grandson to carry on his name and title. Three generations passed, and suddenly in 1475 the last of the male Mowbrays died, and the rights to the barony and Dukedom were eventually bestowed upon the son of Sir Robert Howard and Margaret Mowbray.[4]

This Howard child proved to be an exceptional man. Most men acquired wealth and power during those closing years of the fifteenth century by wearing their honour upon their sleeve and putting their military reputation up for auction to the highest bidder. John Howard was different; it was through steadfast devotion to the Yorkist cause during the civil Wars of the Roses, that he earned the trust of both Edward IV and Richard III. Armed with a sword in one hand and a bag of gold in the other, he joined the Yorkist ranks in 1461; twenty-two years later that consistency was finally acknowledged when Sir John, as co-heir to the Mowbray estates and titles, became the first Howard Duke of Norfolk, while his son, Thomas, was created Earl of Surrey.

The Howard star so fortunately born of a propitious marriage a hundred years before now went into sudden and disastrous eclipse. Loyalty to the Yorkist crown had engendered fame and honour in success; in defeat it led to imprisonment and death. On 22 August 1485, the Yorkist faction was vanquished upon the high ground two miles from the market town of Bosworth. Richard III was left dead upon the field of battle, while the white rose of his family was trampled underfoot by the victorious army of Henry Tudor, Earl of Richmond. The Howards, father and son, were creatures of the Yorkist monarchy. Their dignity and estates had been bestowed as rewards for faithful service, and their rank and influence were but reflections of royal authority. As such they represented a new breed of nobility – the domesticated aristocrat. Unlike the Nevilles, the Percys, the Stanleys, and other baronial clans, they were tools of royalty, not custodians of ancient rights and feudal privileges. While Lord Thomas Stanley and his brother William maintained the doubtful tradition of king-making by a policy of cautious waiting that aimed at controlling the military balance between the opposing armies, Norfolk and his son fought for their liege lord, King Richard. The Duke was killed with his master, while Thomas was brought a prisoner to the Tower, his title and rights to the dukedom attainted by Act of Parliament, and his estates forfeited to the new sovereign.

The victory of the Earl of Richmond at Bosworth augured nothing but continued civil strife – a prolonging of that unsavoury feudal game which had commenced sixty years before as factional rivalry over who should whisper self-interested advice into the King's ear and had deteriorated into open civil war to decide which parry candidate should actually wear the crown. Behind the rival sovereigns stood the great baronial families, who sought to use the royal government to enlarge their estates, arrange their family alliances, assure their inheritance, and maintain their political and social influence. Thus the Wars of the Roses were marked more by the rifling of the royal coffers and the confiscation of land than by rapine and destruction. Bosworth was but another swing of the pendulum, and in the act of attainder against Thomas Howard, the supporters of the red rose of the house of Lancaster had what they wanted – the estates of their enemies. The old Duke of Norfolk was dead, while his son was little more than a political cipher, the fallen creature of a fallen monarch.

Consequently Thomas was allowed to keep his head, and even in the midst of deprivation he was not totally bereft of comfort. The new King was surprisingly generous and paid to the Lieutenant of the Tower forty shillings a week for the Earl's board and keep, and a further seven shillings and sixpence to maintain his three servants. Considering that the normal fee ranged between three and six shillings a week, it would appear that Thomas Howard lacked little except his freedom.[5]

At this juncture historical fact gives way to family fable – legends that have the ring of truth but may be little more than Howard efforts to revamp history more to the family's tastes. Presumably there were two occasions on which the attainted Earl came to the attention of Henry VII. The first story involves the Battle of Bosworth when Surrey was brought captive before the Conqueror. Henry Tudor is purported to have reproached his prisoner for having fought for that 'tyrant', Richard III; in answer, Thomas Howard said: 'He was my crowned King, and if the Parliamentary authority of England set the Crown upon a stock I will fight for that stock. And as I fought then for him, I will fight for you, when you are established by the said authority'.[6] Verisimilitude is a deceptive matter, and on the face of it Howard's words were uncharacteristic of his age and most certainly unwelcome to the ears of a new monarch who claimed his crown by God, by right and by conquest, and not by the authority of parliament. On the other hand, Henry VII recognized the legal dilemma involved, for how could the Earl of Surrey be attainted for high treason for supporting in battle his legal sovereign? A solution was discovered by the simple expedient of maintaining the fiction that the new reign had commenced the day before the Battle of Bosworth so that, legally, all those who had fought against Henry had in fact committed treason against their liege lord.

Might was quite capable of creating its own right, but once the throne had been secured, Henry VII may well have appreciated the value of fostering those who supported the crown, irrespective of the man who wore it. In the long run Thomas Howard was a more reliable and useful instrument of the monarchy than the two

Stanleys, whose actions at Bosworth had won Henry his crown but who operated in the tradition of the irresponsible right of aristocracy, as opposed to the divine right of kings. Nor was it accident that the Earl of Surrey was eventually liberated from his confinement in the Tower and became a devoted Tudor work-horse, while Sir William Stanley in 1494 ended his life on the scaffold, having connived at treason against the Tudor crown.

The second episode fits the same pattern of events. In 1487 the Earl of Lincoln, nephew of Edward IV and Richard III, staged one of the last efforts of the Yorkist faction to regain the throne. When the Earl landed in England, it first appeared as if the sides would be evenly matched, and before the decisive battle was fought, rumours were circulated that Henry Tudor had in fact met the Yorkist forces and been defeated. In the face of these reports, the Lieutenant of the Tower offered Thomas Howard his freedom. In an excess of what the Howard records prefer to regard as virtuous devotion, Thomas stoutly maintained that 'he would not depart thence unto such time as he that commanded him thither should command him out again.'

Fortunately for the Howards, this was one occasion in which a quixotic sense of honour, or more probably an acute sense of caution, coincided with self-interest; shortly afterwards Henry VII returned to London, following a smashing victory in which the Earl of Lincoln was left, like his equally unfortunate uncle, dead upon the field of battle. Henry was stronger than ever, and Thomas Howard was far safer within the confines of the Tower than abroad, the subject of Tudor wrath. As legend has it, Henry was so impressed by the 'true and faithful service' that Thomas had rendered his previous sovereign, and by his actions while a prisoner in the Tower, that he released the Earl after three and a half years of captivity and restored to him his title and estates.'[7] The King, however, with characteristic restraint, returned only the lands of Surrey's spouse. The Howards had to prove their devotion to the new dynasty many times over before such suspicious monarchs were ready to reward them with a complete restoration of their lands and titles. The dignity of Earl Marshal had to wait another eleven years, while the final and highest estate, the dukedom of Norfolk, was not restored until Thomas Howard and his sons had indicated their loyalty beyond a shadow of a doubt, and had successfully written off the sins of the family by their victory over the Scots at the Battle of Flodden Field in 1513. Then and only then did the family regain the position it had held a generation before in 1483.

Long before the Howards won back their ancient titles, the family had been systematically fortifying its political and social position through marital alliances with the most vigorous and distinguished families of the century. Marriages may be formed in heaven while politics remains the concern of this world, but under the Tudors, the two were intimately related. During the medieval past, the control of government rested largely with the independent baronial clans and over-powerful magnates, who at times successfully transformed the monarchy into a political football. Later, in the seventeenth century, factions within the House of Commons would determine national policy, but under the Tudors there developed within the framework of royal absolutism a variety of family politics in which matrimonial and political alliances marched hand in hand. The system retained noticeable feudal overtones in structure and organization, however the aim was no longer the custody of the royal person but simply the control of the approaches to the throne. The days had long since vanished when the earls of Northumberland and Warwick could muster private armies, intimidate royal justices, corrupt the laws of the realm to their own advantage, and demand as their feudal right entry into the royal council.

This did not mean, however, that the Tudor sovereigns could operate without the aristocracy. Society was hierarchical in form. Rank and title continued to involve economic, social and political privilege and obligation, and noblemen such as the Dukes of Norfolk and Buckingham still maintained complex family systems and extensive personal retinues. The Tudors aimed not at the annihilation of the peerage but merely at its domestication. They sought not so much to curtail aristocratic power as to destroy feudal independence. Aristocratic heads might roll and the lesser sort be elevated to positions of commanding authority, but dukes and earls still raised fighting men for the royal army, managed local government in the king's name, controlled the approaches to the sovereign, and administered governmental patronage. Consequently politics continued to be organized around men of rank and position, and political success remained as much a question of marriage as of proximity to the monarch. The union of Thomas Howard with the daughter of the Duke of Buckingham was a matter of supreme political importance. As long as men continued to think in family and pseudo-feudal terms, the Duke of Norfolk would never cease to agitate for the marriage of his sister to Edward, Earl of Derby, because, as one contemporary noted, it was 'an alliance essential to his family strength'.[8] The Tudors did not destroy the old system, they simply harnessed it, and Norfolk had to learn that the happy, carefree days of the fifteenth century – when a great baron could arrange such a match without regard to the royal assent – were over. In 1530 the mating of the Earl of Derby to a duke's sister, without royal licence, was branded as an 'abduction', and the Howard family had to seek the King's pardon and permission before completing the alliance.[9]

During the first decades of the century the old nobility clung tenaciously to the feudal standards of the past. Despite royal laws to the contrary, they retained liveried followers, tampered with the legal machinery of the realm, and supported vast, almost feudal establishments. Norfolk and his kind were no longer able to raise private armies, but a great baron's livery was often sufficient to protect a man from the consequences of his crimes and violence. Edward, Earl of Derby, numbered 220 men on his check-roll; John, Earl of Oxford, rarely moved abroad without a cavalcade of 200 horsemen. In 1562 the fourth Duke of Norfolk entered London at the head of 100 horsemen, dressed in the velvet of his livery, and with four heralds to announce his coming. Even that social upstart, Thomas Cromwell, mimicked the standards of the aristocracy by dressing his retainers in livery of grey marble.[10]

The King's government endeavoured to keep a wary watch upon its over-great magnates, and in 1516 the Earl of Northumberland was ignominiously sent to the Fleet prison and the Marquis of Dorset and the Earl of Surrey were put out of the council for keeping liveried retainers.[11] Not unlike governments today in regard to the income tax returns of the great financial and industrial barons of modern industry and banking, the Tudors required that noblemen post accurate lists of their liveried servants. The distinction between private and royal armies was dangerously unclear. Lord William Howard, brother of the Duke of Norfolk and Catherine's uncle, was expected to muster one hundred mounted men-at-arms and thirty archers for the King's army, but he would have been clapped into the Tower had he retained any for his private service.[12]

The great barons no longer dared to use their armed dependants to intimidate juries and royal judges or to maintain their friends and relations at courts of law, but they did not hesitate to utilize their local position to embrace juries and influence justice in civil cases. Catherine Howard's father, Lord Edmund, was indicted before the Court of the Star Chamber for having misused his position as Provost-Marshal of the county of Surrey. It was alleged against him that he had maintained his cousin Roger Legh against John Scotte in a matter of disputed land title. The Provost-Marshal was anything but a disinterested judge, since Roger Legh had turned over to him some eighty cartloads of wood cut from the land in controversy.[13] The Tudor monarchy was constantly trying to curb this tendency on the part of the nobility to transform the common law into a private preserve for their friends and kin. The fact remains, however, that justice was highly susceptible to influence, and in the shires the aristocracy could and did exercise a form of judicial patronage.

Behind the political, judicial and military influence of the nobility stood their economic strength. Their financial position had sorely deteriorated from that which had supported the extravagant existence of the previous two centuries, when the Duke of Lancaster boasted a yearly income of £12,000 and the Earl of Arundel could claim £66,000 in cash, a sum only slightly less than the entire royal revenue in a normal year.[14] But even so, their revenues were impressive. Thomas Howard's father-in-law, the Duke of

Buckingham, was reported to be worth 30,000 ducats annually, his brother-in-law, the Earl of Oxford, 25,000 ducats, and Thomas himself 20,000 ducats.[15] With such incomes the barons were able to maintain vast, feudal households. But whether they could have financed the princely palaces of the past is difficult to say. In 1343 the dowager Lady Elizabeth de Burgh had in her house 21 clerks, 18 lesser clerks, 93 esquires, 45 estate officials such as the bailiff and reeve, 51 gardeners, parkers and domestic minions, and 12 pages.[16] Certainly Cardinal Wolsey's establishment more than equalled this in an age when labour was both plentiful and cheap, for some 400 persons were numbered as his immediate servants. Henry, Earl of Northumberland, managed with a household of 166, while the Earl of Derby was served by 7 gentlemen-in-waiting and 140 servants, who consumed annually 56 oxen and 535 sheep.[17] In terms of the immense number of individuals financially and socially dependent upon the great magnates, their influence both at court and in the shires must have been considerable. It was not for nothing that the third Howard, Duke of Norfolk could control the election of ten members of the House of Commons from Sussex alone, or that another duke of Norfolk referred to such members as 'persons as belong unto him and be of his menial servants'.[18]

Ultimate political influence was centred at court, for it was here that the final source of royal patronage and office resided. Political and family rivalry revolved round the control of the King's council and the administration of the royal bounty. The sixteenth century was still a highly intimate society in which people, not institutions, and private cares, not public actions, were important. As yet there was no absolute distinction between the exchequer and the King's privy purse, or between a civil servant's sense of duty and his willingness to administer his office for personal gain. In a sense, almost everyone had his price, and though bribery and the operation of office for private profit may not have affected policy, a basic axiom of the era was that to the victor belonged the spoils of political office.

From the highest post to the most menial, the acceptance of 'gifts' was regarded as one of the perquisites of office. Favours, whether they involved decisions at law or the promotion of a friend or relation in government, were always made easy by a substantial gratuity, and it made small difference whether it was Lady Lisle sending a jar of marmalade to the King, or Thomas Cromwell accepting a toothpick and a gold whistle, four live beavers, and 18,000 slates for his roof. When society regarded office as being as much a private sinecure as a public trust, it was inevitable that the path to political success should be paved with the judicious distribution of gifts of every conceivable variety.

As in all ages, advancement in politics, or, more accurately, success at court, was predicated upon personal acquaintances and the ability to bestow favours. The best positions of all were those closest to the royal ear: the lord chancellor, who administered the king's conscience (usually for personal profit); the lord privy seal, who controlled a large portion of the royal patronage (again for a reasonable fee); and the lord chamberlain who not only managed the royal household but, more important, bestowed on deserving friends and clamouring relations minor offices which were often close to the king's person and were regarded as stepping-stones to a lucrative political career. The secret of success was in large measure dependent upon the attainment of royal notice, and the men who controlled the approaches to the royal presence consequently wielded enormous political power. Custody of patronage, irrespective of rank or dignity, was the key to party affiliations. Norfolk, Wolsey and Cromwell each had about him a host of personal followers who looked to their respective benefactor for promotion at court or in the shires. Appointments, such as the groom of the royal bedchamber, maid of honour to the queen, justice of the peace, or even commissioner of the sewers, held endless financial and social attraction even though they often involved onerous duties.

The measure of political success was the control of patronage, and a sign of the third Duke of Norfolk's political strength and influence was his ability to negotiate a loan from the royal treasury for his brother, Lord Edmund Howard. It was essential to the duke's control of his family and his status at court that Lord Edmund, along with other Howard dependants and relatives, should be placed on the commissions of the peace and of the sewers for Surrey; that Brians and Westons, Leghs and Howards, Holdens and Knyvets, all members of the duke's dynasty, should be listed in the Treasury Reports of 1539-41 as having received money for services rendered to the government; and that Catherine Howard's brothers should have been granted licence to import Gascon wine and Toulouse wood.[19]

Political empires, built upon the management of local and court patronage, tended in the sixteenth century to merge into family dynasties, since marriage and politics consisted of doing the best for oneself and one's family. Though blood relationships did not always conceal or mitigate personal rivalry and ambitions, they did at least tend to act as a form of political and party cement. The Howards are often accused of blatant family building and dynastic ambition, but one might as well condemn the peacock for insatiable vanity as criticize the dukes of Norfolk for family aggrandizement, for both characteristics are inherent in the species. Family alliances were tantamount to political existence, and the Imperial Ambassador recognized this fact when he suggested to his master that one way of influencing the Duke of Norfolk was to help him in his plans to marry his son to Henry VIII's daughter, the Princess Mary.[20] In this search for wives and husbands as the foundation for their political empires, the Howards were particularly successful, and they rival the House of Habsburg for the motto: '*Bella gerant alii: tu, felix Austria, nube* – Let others make war: thou, happy Austria, marry!' The Howards were blessed with the most important asset of a dynastic aspirant – a sufficient number of daughters who could be utilized to fulfil the matrimonial designs of the family. Generally speaking, a Howard lady 'who strikes the fire of full fourteen' was considered as being 'ripe for a husband'. The choice of the groom was solely a matter of family welfare and political expediency.

Even in eclipse the Howards showed a remarkable propensity for allying themselves with the most vigorous and successful of the parvenus. With unerring eye they selected the rising and often the most unscrupulous elements of the landed gentry as suitable husbands for their legion of daughters. One of Catherine Howard's half-sisters married Sir Edward Baynton, who lived to be vice-chamberlain to four of Henry's queens – not an inconsiderable record to escape unscathed four times from the matrimonial convulsions of that unpredictable monarch.[21] Included in the family web was Sir Francis Brian, whom even the 'devil's disciple" himself, Thomas Cromwell, referred to as the 'vicar of Hell'. Sir Francis was one of Henry's closest friends and was peculiarly successful in maintaining that friendship in the face of bitter political rivalry and the 'adulterous' activities of his two Howard cousins. He died in 1550 in Ireland under circumstances that even in the sixteenth century seemed to warrant an autopsy. The doctors could discover nothing, and sagely concluded that the knight had died of grief – a most uncharacteristic explanation which satisfied no one.[22]

Numbered among the Howard satellites were Sir Edmund Knyvet, the King's sergeant porter, Sir Francis Knollys, later to be vice-chamberlain and privy councillor to Queen Elizabeth, and Sir Thomas Arundel, the grandfather of the first Baron Arundel, and himself an important Tudor work-horse, who, like so many of his contemporaries, ended his career upon the scaffold.[23] The Culpeper family were important Howard allies both at court and in the country, and the Culpepers will play a considerable role in this story, since Catherine's mother was one of that clan, and another member was to go to his death as a consequence of Catherine Howard's matrimonial indiscretions.[24] Finally, both the Boleyns and the Norrises are to be numbered among the widening Howard galaxy. Catherine's first cousin was Anne Boleyn, Henry VIII's second wife, while her cousin by marriage, Sir Henry Norris, was executed in 1536 for his presumed intimacy with the ill-starred Anne. All of these were the new men and women of the century, individuals who had sampled the heady intellectual wines of the Renaissance, many of whom had travelled in Italy or France, and who were more at home in the gaudy costumes of the court than in the bulky plate of feudal armour. The Howards did well to fortify the ancient blood of the Mowbrays with the strength and vigour of the *nouveaux riches*, the men of the future and not of the past.

The family did not content itself with creatures of the royal bounty and social upstarts; the stiff and uncompromising pride of the feudal past was also allied to their family pattern. Catherine's aunts, who are to be reckoned by the dozen, were all married to peers of highest station, most of whom could claim the dubious distinction of having played at the risky game of treason, and who could count their rightful share of impaled heads above the tower gate of London Bridge. The Howards could boast alliance with earls of Sussex, Bridgewater, Oxford, and Derby. More distantly they were connected with John Grey, Viscount Lisle, Lord Dacre of the South and John Bourchier, Lord Berners. Even more distinguished, Thomas Howard, the third Duke of Norfolk, was married to Elizabeth Stafford, the daughter of the Duke of Buckingham, a direct descendant of Edward III, whose blood rights to the throne cost him his head in 1521.[25] The oldest and the youngest blood of the century were united in the Howard veins, and both family and political position conspired to place the Duke, both as a grandee of the realm and as the head of a family empire, at the pinnacle of a veritable dynasty.

Like many houses of ancient lineage, the Howards were 'puffed up with insatiable pride' and their dynastic ambitions did not stop with the daughters of dukes and earls. As the representatives of the Mowbray line, they had little use for the Plantagenet blood of the dukes of Buckingham, for their Mowbray ancestors had laid claim to royal descent. As the descendants of kings and in their own dignity as dukes of Norfolk, the Howards regarded it as their just deserts to sit as councillors to kings, ride as earl marshals of the host, and supply husbands and wives to royal progeny. The sixteenth-century author Cornelius Agrippa once suggested that there were at least three roads to political advancement in his age. You could win a peerage in war, you could purchase it with money, or, in extremity, you could become 'a royal parasite, or marry a discarded mistress or illegitimate child of a prince'.[26] The Howards regained their dukedom on the battlefield of Flodden, but it was along the last road that they advanced farthest, for above all others, the Howards were the clan from which Henry VIII selected spouses for himself and his family.

Two of the third duke's nieces, Anne Boleyn and Catherine Howard, became Henry's queens, and though both ended their lives upon the scaffold, the former gave birth to a reigning monarch and England's greatest queen. But this was only the beginning. Norfolk's daughter was wedded to Henry's illegitimate son, Henry Fitzroy; his son was suggested as a worthy husband for the King's first-born child, the Princess Mary; his niece, Mary Boleyn, became the King's mistress, and his half-brother, another Thomas, was briefly, if disastrously, contracted in marriage to Henry's niece, Margaret Douglas, the grandmother of James I of England.[27]

Howard sons and daughters seemed to be everywhere, at every level of society, entrenched in almost every key position. It was no easy matter to keep such a family empire together, and the Howards were forced to pay a heavy price for their matrimonial pre-eminence. Alliance with sovereignty won for them the envy of less fortunate clans, while their cherished position of acting as a stud farm for royalty, was fraught with dangers. Lord Burghley is reported to have once remarked that 'marriage with the blood royal was too full of risk to be lightly entered into',[28] and though union with the Tudors brought political influence and social prestige, it was rarely accompanied by security or peace of mind. The alliance between the two houses was more than once to prove itself dangerous to the Howard interests. A sixteenth-century proverb observes that 'there is more to marriage than four bare legs in bed', and the full significance of that dictum becomes particularly obvious when dealing with royalty, for more than one Howard was to discover that a double standard existed for those of princely blood and those of more humble clay.

Both Anne Boleyn and Catherine Howard lost their heads because they failed in their essential function, both as Howards and royal wives; neither could cement the union with a male heir, and both ladies allowed the breath of adulterous scandal to touch their lives. As mere mortals they deserved death twice over for their double sins. The Howards learned to their cost that marriage to royalty is a public, not a private, affair. Lord Thomas, the Duke's half-brother, died in the Tower of London in 1536 for 'having tried in the presence of witnesses to contract a marriage' with Lady Margaret Douglas, the King's niece. Elopement and high romance may be permissible in the lesser sort, but for royalty, wedlock was strictly a business proposition, and Henry was justifiably annoyed at the thought of squandering such a valuable diplomatic pawn as a Tudor niece upon a mere subject, even though he was a Howard. Moreover, the royal uncle placed a dangerous interpretation upon the foolhardy actions of the young Howard gallant, and it was rumoured abroad that Thomas had been 'led and seduced by the Devil' and was obviously aspiring to 'the imperial crown by reason of marriage in so high a blood.'[29] The Lady Margaret seems to have had a persistent and fatal penchant for Howard striplings, and five years later she was again in disgrace for having had an affair with Catherine's brother, Charles.[30]

The Tudors were constantly on the watch that the Howards limit their ambitions to Tudor women and refrain from casting greedy eyes upon the Tudor crown. Henry Howard, first cousin to Catherine and heir to the dukedom, was relieved of his head in 1546 for having 'openly used, and traitorously caused to be depicted, mixed, and conjoined with his own arms and ensigns, the said arms and ensigns of the King.'[31] The heraldic pretensions of the Howard family were tantamount to an assertion that Howard blood was the equal of Tudor blood, and that a Howard might yet succeed a Tudor upon the throne. The folly of young Henry Howard was twofold, for not only did he arouse the most fundamental and predatory instincts of the Tudors, but he also exposed himself and his family to the enmity of personal and dynastic hatred. The Howards were envied by those who coveted their dignity, intrigued against by those who feared their power, and detested by those who abhorred their policy. Once the artful and persuasive whisper of the opposing faction had inflamed the King's natural suspicions, Henry Howard's fate was sealed. Social status, political influence, and marriage to royalty were coveted dignities, but the price came high: the Howards found themselves surrounded by a host of rivals who were only too willing to replace them in the blissful and lucrative light of royal favour.

At the moment of Catherine's birth the head of the Howard clan was Thomas, third Duke of Norfolk, who had been waiting none too patiently for over half a century to enter into his ducal dignity when his father, hoary and full of years, finally died in 1524. The Duke was a nobleman of limited mentality, few inhibitions, and inordinate ambitions, who succeeded regularly in transforming the banal into the burlesque. When Thomas blundered, he did so with magnificent stupidity; when he fought, he operated with terrifying efficiency; when he married, he espoused first the daughter of Edward IV and then the heiress of the greatest grandee of the realm, Edward Stafford, Duke of Buckingham; when he dreamed, he saw before him the dazzling spectre of the crown; and when he quarrelled with his wife, he ordered his servants to pin her to the floor, where they sat on her until she spat blood. The only thing that was in any fashion commonplace about the Duke was his intelligence, which was never able to penetrate the window-dressing of sixteenth-century diplomacy and politics. It is only too easy to paint Norfolk as a 'ponderous, cold-hearted, chicken-brained Duke, moving sluggishly in the mists of the feudal past like some obsolete armoured saurian'.[32] Thomas Howard represented a contradiction in terms – the domesticated feudal magnate. The third Duke stood midway between his father, who advocated the self-destroying creed of absolute duty to the monarchy and who would defend the crown irrespective of the man who wore it, and his son, who betrayed signs of family and feudal megalomania and whose long, arrogant face and stiffnecked pride were almost a symbol of what the Tudors felt most obliged to liquidate – the divine right of aristocracy. Sir Thomas Palmer once remarked of the Duke's brother and Catherine Howard's father, Lord Edmund Howard, that 'though he be a lord, yet he is not God.'[33] By the third and fourth generation the Howards tended to be increasingly forgetful of their purely mortal origins.

Uniting the county blood of the Howards with the ancient race of the Mowbrays, the Duke equivocated; he was never able to decide whether he was a strange new man whose dignity was simply a mirror of royal authority, or a feudal baron with his roots in the impenetrable past. He nurtured a positive phobia for Cardinal Wolsey, not because the cardinal monopolized political power about the King, but because he was a presumptuous upstart, the son of an Ipswich butcher, and the Duke boasted that he would some day eat that butcher's cur alive.[34] Yet the Venetian Ambassador observed that Thomas was 'liberal, affable and astute' and would associate with everybody, no matter what his origins.[35] Above all else Norfolk was a realist and, though his instincts were feudal both in politics and religion, he realized the political expediency of compromising with the powers that be, for he had learned the lesson of the proverb that 'enjoins our kissing the hand we are unable to cut off'.

Of all the facets of Thomas Howard's personality, the one most often exposed to criticism is his servility, which later generations have stigmatized as 'unbecoming his rank and station'. This indeed is the ultimate irony – to rebuke the feudal wolf for his good behaviour! Of all the great barons of Henry's reign, Norfolk had the most reason and the greatest occasion to try his hand at treason. Yet he remained true to a crown that struck down his father-in-law, executed two of his nieces, shocked his religious sensibilities, elevated men of no social consequence to high dignity and authority, and viewed the Duke himself with deep suspicion, lest the feudal wolf revert to its predatory nature.

At least twice he sacrificed personal popularity to accomplish his sovereign's nefarious plans. During the Evil May Day riots of 1517, the apprentices of London gave vent to their narrow nationalism and economic hatred by looting the homes and shops of foreign merchants and lynching Flemish and Venetian traders. Thomas and his brother Edmund and his father were called in to suppress the turmoil, and enforce brutal royal justice, while Henry VIII himself played the pleasing role of gracious pardoner after legal vengeance had been administered.[36] Again in 1536, Norfolk was called out of political exile as being the only man capable of curbing the feudal-religious uprising of the northern counties during the Pilgrimage of Grace that rocked the Tudor throne to its foundations. The Howards, as the heroes of Flodden Field against the Scots in 1513, were immensely popular in the northern shires, and had the Duke harboured treasonous thoughts he could easily have joined the insurgents. Thomas put aside any such ideas and became the willing instrument of Henry's vengeance that enjoined the Duke to 'cause such dreadful execution upon a good number of the inhabitants, hanging them on trees, quartering them, and setting their heads and quarters in every town, as shall be a fearful warning.'[37] The memory of the silent figures swinging from a hundred gibbets was more than enough to transform the Duke's popularity into bitter hatred, and the final paradox was attained when lordly Norfolk and low-born Cromwell were associated in the popular mind, which wished to see both strung up from the same gallows.[38]

The slight, dark-haired, swarthy man who held the ducal title may have been an unscrupulous dynast, greedy for personal power and family aggrandizement, but in Tudor times security rested on calculated servility and cautious recognition of the political facts of life. All the Howards had to dance nimbly the Tudor fandango, lest their suspicious sovereign reach down and pluck from them their family titles, or lest their political opponents interpret bristling dynastic pride as high treason. Retirement into secure political nonentity was impossible, for whether Thomas Howard desired it or not, the ducal dignity and feudal blood were always the magnetic centre for political organization and traitorous sentiments. Howard blood conjoined with Plantagenet descent made the Duke and his son possible successors to the throne should Henry VIII die without a male heir. During the crisis of Henry's divorce of Catherine of Aragon and the break with Rome, the Pope suggested that Catherine's daughter, the Princess Mary, might marry Norfolk's son and 'thus gain many adherents and overthrow her father'.[39] The faintest rumour of such a suggestion was enough to place the duke's head in jeopardy, and the Howards learned to move cautiously in the midst of plots and counterplots, any one of which might have cost them their lives. In 1536, during the rebellion of the north, it was hoped that Norfolk would join others of the feudal discontented, and the old nobility revealed to the Imperial Ambassador that they 'counted in case of need' on the Duke to 'support the cause of Faith and Church'. The Ambassador, however, shrewdly noted that 'owing to the said duke's versatile and inconstant humour' no one could 'rely on him'.[40] Norfolk was too experienced a campaigner and too agile a politician to risk his neck in defence of either faith or Church.

If Thomas Howard is to be classified at all, it is as the rough and ready military man, more at home in camp life than in that pavilion of Renaissance brilliance and wit which was Henry's court. Efficient and thorough, if unimaginative, he found the weight of medieval armour a lighter burden than the intricate game of court politics and international diplomacy. The King, his master, went straight to Norfolk's greatest weakness when he wrote: 'We could be as well content to bestow some time in the reading of an honest remedy as of so many extreme and desperate mischiefs.'[41] Like many military men, the Duke tended to be an alarmist who could offer a military remedy, but rarely a lasting political solution. An inveterate intriguer, but politically inept, he never won the recognition after which he grasped, because he was both too inconstant and too cautious. Taciturn and often tactless, his brusque and arrogant methods lost him valuable friends at court, while his constant aspiration 'for greater elevation', together with family insolence, antagonized both friend and foe. 'Never,' the Duke expostulated, was gold 'tried better by fire and water';[42] never did a man more loyally do his duty. One suspects, however, that Norfolk never attained his ambitions because his loyalty and service were offered more for the sake of reward than from a feeling of devotion to the Crown.

It is dangerous to underestimate Thomas Howard's abilities or his influence. He may have been constantly grasping after the realities of power and confusing it with its shadow, but he was never the foul-mouthed illiterate of history books. His brother William may have been a veritable 'block-head', but it is well to remember that the Duke's son, Henry, Earl of Surrey, was a major literary luminary, and his grand-niece was England's most accomplished sovereign. He may have belonged to an older tradition which considered that it was sufficient if a nobleman could blow lustily upon the horn and carry his hawk with experience, but he was far from being in a class with his ill-educated ducal colleagues who were almost illiterate. Thomas was proud of his son's 'proficiency and advancement in letters', while his own knowledge of French and Latin was better than might have been expected of an old soldier.[43]

Above all else, the third Duke of Norfolk was an Englishman with all the inherent characteristics of his breed and class – instinctively conservative, suspicious of newfangled ideas, and mistrustful of mincing society, foreign fashions, and unorthodoxy in religion. He once informed Cardinal Wolsey that he gave not 'a straw' for the cardinal's legatine and foreign powers, but that he honoured the man because he was an archbishop and cardinal of the Church 'whose estate of honour surmounteth any duke now being within this realm'.[44] A subject was to be known and esteemed for his social position within the English hierarchy, and not by some intruding authority of the Pope in Rome. The Duke could accept separation from the papacy because for him, as for other loyal subjects of the throne, the Holy See represented a corrupt and alien influence, but in all else he was essentially conservative. 'He had never read the Scripture nor ever would', and he suggested that England was a far merrier place before 'this new learning came.up'.[45] But for all that, the man was a realist, and when he was asked what he thought about priests having wives, he answered that 'he knew not whether priests had wives but that wives will have priests'.[46] The theological niceties of the issue were quite beyond him; they were the pastime of scholars and ecclesiastics and beneath the dignity of a nobleman. No matter what the duke's personal sympathies may have been for the Holy See, it was sufficient for Norfolk and his kind to support the decision of the King when Henry 'had distinctly declared his will more for one thing than for the other'.[47] This was Thomas Howard's creed, and he warned Sir Thomas More that 'By the mass, Master More, it is perilous, striving with princes. And therefore I would wish you somewhat to incline to the King's pleasure. For by God's body, Master More, *Indignatio principis mors est!*'[48] Tottenham Court would turn French before cautious Norfolk disobeyed his prince.

Crafty, servile, compromising, and versatile, Thomas learned his lesson well; so well that neither the family which was so much a portion of his life, nor the feudal past which was so much a part of his instincts, was allowed to stand in the way of obedience. The clothing of a complacent and obedient Tudor servant might sit ill upon the self-seeking, self-interested shoulders of this Howard duke, but at least the feudal wolf, whether Henry VIII believed it or not, had in fact been domesticated, and like any tamed wild animal, Norfolk was neither a very pleasant nor a very enviable creature.

Not only did personality and tradition place the Duke in an impossible position, but in terms of his leadership of the Howard clan and political faction at court, this senior member of the family spent a lifetime chasing after the unattainable. Though he was the titular head of the Howard dynasty, the Duke found it almost impossible to hold his family empire together. There was little to endear the tactless and inept magnate to his more polished and talented relatives. Married to the daughter of a descendant of Edward III, and his sisters espoused to members of the old nobility, Norfolk was by breeding and sympathy a member of the feudal aristocracy, and he tended to hold himself aloof from the newer men of the reign, even though they were associates of his own tribe. The younger and bolder set of the Boleyns, the Norrises, the Knyvets, and the Brians, may have been better educated and more cultured, but in the eyes of the ancient caste this was not necessarily the mark of a gentleman. The old maxim was often reiterated that 'a Prince may make a nobleman but not a gentleman.' The Howard dynasty was imposing enough on paper, but it was not what it might have been a century earlier – the vast feudal following of an independent magnate to whom the lesser sort owed personal fealty.

If Thomas Howard failed as a family patriarch, he was no more successful as a politician at court. There is something pathetically inconsequential, almost tragically futile, about the duke. Always fascinated by the lamp of power, he fluttered aimlessly about the source of light and authority, accomplishing little and occasionally burning himself rather severely. As Earl Marshal of the kingdom and the ranking peer of the realm, his traditional place was beside the King, both on the field of battle and in the Privy council. But what once belonged to the barons by feudal right, the Tudors now bestowed only as a reward for single-hearted service. Thomas Howard and his father had proved their loyalty and had in part wiped clean the sins of their ancestors, but the new devotion demanded by the Tudor monarchs was a self-destroying faith which could countenance no rivalry. The Howards could never quite overlook their ancient connections and traditions, and consequently Henry VIII hesitated long before rewarding or depending upon a family which claimed status and authority from a source outside the royal bounty. Norfolk was constantly complaining that he was not receiving his just deserts, and that he and his kind were being replaced in government by parvenus and upstarts, but the Duke was careful to limit himself to querulous outbursts about the 'thieves and murderers' who were placed in positions of high office.[49] Once, in 1536, Henry pointedly snapped back saying, 'If there be any ... of what degree soever he be, that will not serve as lowly, and as readily under the meanest person We can put in authority, as under the greatest Duke in our realm, We will neither repute him for our good subject nor ... leave him unpunished.'[50] Since there were only two dukes at the time, Norfolk took the hint and swallowed his annoyance. The decline of the old standards finally reached the point where one of Norfolk's own nieces, by virtue of her marriage to the sovereign, could scold him as if he were a 'dog, so much so that Norfolk was obliged to quit the royal chamber' in a towering rage, but all he dared do was call her a 'big whore' under his breath.[51]

This, then, was Thomas, third Duke of Norfolk and chief of his clan, a man who, in the words of the Warwickshire proverb, was like a bear, for 'the bear he never can prevail to lion it for lack of tail.' This was also the family to which the future Queen belonged, a family rigid in its pride and insatiable in its greed for political power. From the start, Catherine knew her duty: to further the interests of her uncle and tribe.

CHAPTER 3

HORSHAM AND LAMBETH

To an age accustomed to preserving its documents in bombproof shelters, it seems inconceivable that a queen of England should have neither baptismal record nor death certificate. Today, modern man is besieged with bureaucratic identifications, numerical tabulations and physical reports. From birth to death his path is inundated by a vast ocean of statistical data, testifying to the most intimate aspects of his life. For the age of Catherine Howard, however, the ravages of some four hundred years and the rather random documentation of a society uninterested in immortalizing itself in quadruplicate have left the historian with little upon which to recreate the life and character of even a queen. The gossamer thread of recorded history is often so delicate that it tends to vanish under the scrutiny of historical analysis. An occasional strand, an accidental vestige must suffice to reconstruct the mind and personality that spun the web of history.

The process of historical preservation is devious in the extreme; though Catherine's father, Lord Edmund Howard, remains a rather shadowy figure, scarcely perceptible through the darkness of history, there is clear evidence that the hapless gentleman suffered from kidney stones. In 1536 he wrote to his friend, Lady Lisle, thanking her for her medical prescription for, 'it hath done me much good, and hath caused the stone to break so that now I void much gravel.' Unfortunately for Lord Edmund, the remedy had more than the desired effect, and he complained that 'your said medicine hath done

34

me little honesty, for it made me piss my bed this night, for the which my wife hath sore beaten me, and saying, "it is childrens' parts to bepis their bed." In fact, the poor man was in such a state that he was unable to accept Lady Lisle's dinner invitation, and he concluded his excuses by suggesting his own antidote. It had been shown him, he said, that 'a wing or a leg of a stork ... will make me that I shall never piss more in bed, and though my body be simple, yet my tongue shall be ever good, and specially when it speaketh of women.'[1]

All this is by way of warning the reader that almost nothing is known about the early life of Catherine Howard: the date of her birth is open to speculation, her home is unknown, and except for the more lurid details of her childhood which have been preserved in connection with her trial, we know almost nothing about her early friends and environment. The historian can recreate, he can make judicious guesses, he can and often does indulge in wishful thinking, but the fact remains that except for the accident of being Queen Consort of England, Mistress Catherine would have joined the legion of men and women who lived and died without ever having left their mark on history – those who, in a sense, never lived at all, since they left no monument to their individuality.

Every life is the product of chance, and the secret of Catherine Howard's career lies in the accident of birth – that her father was born both a Howard and a younger son. Lord Edmund Howard was the third son of a man who sired twenty-three progeny of whom ten lived to marry and further populate the island with Howard sons and daughters. Except for aristocratic blood, Lord Edmund had little with which to commence the struggle of existence. It appears almost as if he were the victim of some ill-natured fairy, for everything conspired to frustrate his career. As one of the younger sons of a family that faced political annihilation as a consequence of the Battle of Bosworth, he was constantly plagued by poverty, and not even the reviving fortunes of his clan seem to have relieved him of his constant burden of debts. Impecuniousness could always be transmuted into opulence by means of royal favour, but Edmund Howard strangely failed to ingratiate himself with his sovereign. He was almost the same age as Henry VIII and might have become one of the King's cronies who accompanied their sport-loving monarch in his constant and restless quest for chivalric distinction and athletic prowess. Unfortunately, however, Henry evidenced signs of a marked distaste for this young Howard scion.

When the Howards distinguished themselves at the Battle of Flodden Field, and a grateful sovereign rewarded the Earl of Surrey with the dukedom of Norfolk, Edmund Howard was still denied entry into the warm and rewarding light of royal favour. Catherine's father stood on the right wing of the battle in command of 1,500 Cheshire and Lancashire men. Once again his luck held true to form, and Lord Edmund sustained the only serious defeat of the day when his soldiers were routed by the lord chamberlain of Scotland and his family banner trampled under foot. His personal bravery was beyond dispute; twice he fell and twice lie rose to fight again, but it took the opportune arrival of Lord Thomas Dacre to save the right wing from total annihilation. His father knighted the young man on the field of battle for his heroism, but the royal bounty was singularly niggardly. His father was elevated to the ducal title, but Edmund received merely a pension of three shillings and fourpence a day, which was abruptly terminated after three years.[2] Again, in August of 1537, when as a mark of popularity he was elected mayor by the assembly of the city of Calais, it was the King who quashed the election, and Thomas Cromwell wrote saying that 'the King will in no wise that my lord Howard be admitted to the mayoralty.'[3] Finally, just before his death in 1539, he was removed from his position as Controller of Calais with little certainty of any future post.

Why Henry was so reluctant to bestow honours upon the younger son of a family on which he had heaped the highest rewards of state, is something of a mystery, but there is no escaping the fact that Edmund Howard was never a favourite at court. Possibly he was too stiff and proud, for like many a younger son his only asset was his name and blood. Vainglorious and indigent, trained in little except the art of war, he lacked the intellectual agility and social polish to adapt himself to life at court. He belonged to that set in society that regarded the aspiring courtiers around the throne as jays 'chattering in a golden cage', and his family pride and class arrogance won him powerful enemies.

The only evidence that Lord Edmund was anything more than another incompetent aristocrat who harked back to the happy, carefree days of the fifteenth century, is the fact that in 1510 he entered the Middle Temple.[4] It would appear that he did not take kindly to the law, for in the following year he was back again at the more congenial pastime of jousting, in a tournament in honour of the birth of a royal son. In fact, what little he knew about the law he misused, for in 1516 he was hauled before Cardinal Wolsey and the Court of the Star Chamber for 'maintaining, embracing and bearing' his friends and relations at law and having undermined 'the good rule and execution of justice within the county of Surrey'.[5] Edmund Howard represented almost every characteristic that the Tudor government sought to exterminate – the irresponsible nobleman who sets himself above the law of the realm.

In 1519 he again found himself the subject of royal and official ire for having instigated riots in Surrey. The Howard influence at court was sufficient to obtain a royal pardon, but his friend and colleague, Lord Ogle, fared less well, and this unfortunate gentleman was turned over to the normal course of the common law, with the royal reminder that his actions had resulted in the murder of one of the King's subjects, 'which great offence is not only to us but to God.'[6] If we add to this that Catherine's father was suspected of harbouring pro-papal sentiments, then there is little wonder that he was distinctly *persona non grata* in court circles.[7]

As a consequence, Edmund Howard seems to have endured a penurious existence upon the periphery of wealth and status encircling the monarch. He often appears in the accounts of the more festive activities of Henry's reign, and in 1514 he was awarded £100 from the royal exchequer, 'to prepare himself to do feats of arms' in honour of the marriage of Henry's sister to the aged and ailing Louis XII of France.[8] Occasionally he was utilized by the government for less glamorous if more essential duties, when he was placed on various commissions of the peace, and for three years he received a salary of twenty shillings a day for 'taking thieves'.[9] He profited briefly when his family fortunes at court were enhanced by the patronage controlled by his niece, Anne Boleyn, who exercised her dangerous influence over Henry's affections from 1528 to 1536. He was offered the post of Controller of Calais in April of 1531 and four years later, through the instigation of the Queen and his brother, the Duke of Norfolk, he succeeded in inveigling his reluctant monarch into presenting him with the goods and chattel of Master Skell, a condemned felon.[10] In the end, fate dealt the final irony, for he died only a few months before his daughter Catherine had accomplished what he himself had signally failed to do – win the royal affection.

Not only did this ill-starred gentleman have to struggle against a chilly reception at court, but he was constantly confronted with the dreary fate in store for a younger son. It is sometimes argued that English history owes much to that peculiar social system of primogeniture, whereby the eldest son takes all, for it forced the scions of noble and landed families either to make their own fortunes or to marry someone else's, and it ensured a steady flow of well-connected young men into the paths of commercial enterprise and empire-building. Salutary as this social system may have been as a historical phenomenon, it was not altogether a happy lot for those born into it. One young gentleman towards the end of the century analysed the situation, by writing that the estate of a younger brother 'is of all stations for gentlemen most miserable, for if our father possess 1,000 to 2,000 *l.* yearly at his death, he cannot give a foot of land to his younger children in inheritance.' Yet for all the obvious iniquities of such a system, the writer admits in a singularly broad-minded fashion that it 'doth us good someways, for it makes us industrious to apply ourselves to letters or to arms, whereby many times we become my elder brothers' masters, or at least their betters in honour and reputation'.[11]

Unfortunately, Edmund Howard neither took kindly to letters nor became his elder brother's master. Instead, poverty and misadventure dogged his footsteps. Nor was he the man to accept his misfortune with

the stoic optimism of the previous writer. In 1527 he grovelled before
Cardinal Wolsey, announcing that he was 'utterly undone' and that his
debts were such that he dared not 'go abroad, nor come at mine own
house, and am fain to absent me from my wife and my poor children,'
for fear of being cast into a debtor's prison. He implored Wolsey to
give thought to his miserable condition and his ten starving children,
and begged that the great man employ him in the projected voyage
of discovery to Newfoundland. Then in tragic words he summed up
the plight of his kind by saying 'if I were a poor man's son, I might
dig and delve for my living', but because of his noble dignity he could
not labour without bringing great reproach and shame to himself and
all his blood.[12] Even when he did finally attain a government position
at Calais, he continued to be plagued with financial difficulties and
found the Controller's salary of £80 per annum too little to maintain a
household worthy of a Howard and a government servant.

Chronic poverty rarely enhances the character, and Lord Edmund
has come down to us through history as a pitiful and not very stalwart
personality – cringing, begging, and threatening his way to a few extra
pennies. The verse awarded him as one of the heroes of Flodden Field:

And Edmund Howard's lion bright, Shall bear them bravely in the fight,[13]

has been more than eclipsed by his flood of pleading letters and futile
efforts to win a financially secure niche in governmental circles. In 1527
his monetary affairs were so desperate that he was actually forced to
send his wife to plead in his name before the Cardinal, since he himself
did not dare show his face abroad lest he be caught and imprisoned
for debt.[14] Five years later a well-meaning, if not over-perceptive, friend
made the mistake of going surety for Lord Edmund, and for his efforts
found himself wrested by his friends' creditors.[15] Nor was the reputation
of Catherine's father any better among his own kin; Sir John Legh
carefully wrote into his will that 'if the Howards trouble the Executors
they are to have nothing.' The Leghs seem to have been darkly suspicious
of Edmund, and Dame Isabel Legh, his mother-in-law, went to great
pains to curtail his control over his wife's patrimony by insisting that

her daughter receive the bulk of her estates only on 'condition that her husband redeem all lands [that are] the inheritance of my daughter in the county of Kent from her father, Richard Culpeper, and her brother, Thomas Culpeper, so that the lands descend to her heirs.'[16] This may, of course, be dismissed as mother-in-law trouble, but considering Lord Edmund's general insolvency, it seems unlikely. Catherine's father was constantly seeking and never attaining, and the full tragedy of his life is testified by his own hand in a letter he wrote to the low-born Thomas Cromwell. He said that he had heard from his brother, Lord William, that Cromwell had promised to advance his petition to the King. He acknowledged that he owed all to the Vicar-General and would never forget such kindness, for he was so 'smally friended' and so 'beaten in the world' that he knew what a treasure it was to have a faithful friend.[17]

Only in the field of matrimony did Edmund excel, and like so many of his clan he seems to have inherited his family's astute eye for selecting women of breeding and wealth. Considering his lack of prospects, Edmund did extraordinarily well, for he married three times and each wife brought land and riches into the itching Howard grasp. His first and only fruitful marriage was with Jocasta Culpeper, the wealthy widow of Ralph Legh, and co-heir of Sir Richard Culpeper of Aylesford, Kent. Mistress Jocasta can hardly be described as a youthful charmer, since she was considerably senior to her second husband and must have been nearing thirty at the moment of her marriage. Moreover, Edmund married an entire family, since his wife had at least two, and possibly as many as five, children by her previous husband. What this newest Howard bride lacked in appearance, however, she made up in substance, for both the Leghs and the Culpepers were extensive landowners in Kent, Surrey, and Sussex.[18]

There is considerable controversy over the year in which the marriage took place.[19] As with so many other events surrounding Catherine and her family, the truth remains obscure. Probably they were espoused about the year 1514, since it is highly improbable that Edmund, merely as the third son of the Earl of Surrey, could have snared such an eminently respectable and affluent lady. The translation of his father to the dukedom in 1513 must have made a considerable difference to Jocasta's matrimonial interests in this impecunious gentleman, with nothing but blood and family to his credit. Lord Edmund was free to marry twice more; first Dorothy Troyes, another wealthy widow with a family of eight; and second, after 1532, Margaret, widow of Nicholas Jennings.[20] Except for the recurrent theme of wealthy widows and marriage settlements to stay the sagging finances of the Howard groom, there is little of interest about these final marriages. It is with Jocasta Culpeper that the life of Catherine Howard begins.

The only statement that can be made with any degree of certainty about Catherine's birth is that she was one of the youngest children of a family of ten, and that she was born before 1525, most probably in 1521 (see Appendix). Where she was born and reared is still a total mystery. Some sources indicate London, others suggest the Howard residence at Lambeth, while still others favour Oxenheath in Kent,[21] the home of Catherine's maternal uncle, William Cotton. The only really authenticated fact is that Catherine spent her childhood with her step-grandmother, the Dowager Duchess of Norfolk, who divided her time between her estates at Horsham in Sussex and the Howard suburban residence at Lambeth.

At this juncture some writers cannot refrain from shedding tears over the cruel fate of a young girl whose mother died while she was still in the first decade of life, and whose father was an impoverished if aristocratic ne'er-do-well, who abandoned his daughter to her own devices in the vast entourage of that Norfolk matriarch, the 'testy old' Dowager Duchess. In the imaginative, if singularly inaccurate, language of Miss Strickland, it was 'indeed an evil hour for the little Katharine when she left the paternal roof, and the society of the innocent companions of her infant joys and cares, to become a neglected dependant in the splendid mansion of a proud and heartless relative.[22] Possibly by modern standards her lot left something to be desired, but in the opinion of her own society, it was customary to farm out children to the establishments of rich friends and relations where they could learn the ways of polite society and proper respect for their elders and betters. In an age of little formal education, such houses as that of the Dowager Duchess supplied the discipline and training of a boarding school where the offspring of the well-connected could escape what was considered to be the enervating influence of a mother's love. Catherine's first cousin, Mary Boleyn, was sent as a maid-in-waiting to the establishment of Margaret of Austria, while Anne Boleyn accompanied Mary Tudor to the court of Louis of France. Lord Edmund Howard did not do as well for his progeny, but it was neither his poverty nor the death of his wife that induced him to board his children with his stepmother, it was simply part of the educational process. There in the draughty halls and dormitories at Horsham or Lambeth, and under the titular custody of the Dowager Duchess, the children of innumerable Howard relations and dependants were conditioned to the realities of sixteenth-century life.

It may be charitable to excuse Mistress Catherine's rather wanton activities as the fault of her heartless step-grandmother, who forced her 'to associate with her waiting-women' and 'compelled' her to sleep in communal sleeping apartments with 'persons of the most abandoned description' who took 'fiendish delight in perverting the principles and debasing the mind of the nobly-born damsel who was thrown into the sphere of their polluting influence'.[23] There are only two things wrong with this touching thesis. First, Catherine herself was regarded as a pseudo-servant, or rather an apprentice learning the secret of good manners and accomplishments. It was important for children to know that they were expected to 'rise when their elders and betters' entered the room, stand while their superiors sat, and curtsy to the Duchess 'in token of humility and subjection'. These were considered to be social graces best inculcated by treating children as indentured domestics and keeping them from idleness.[24] Menials were customarily viewed as being part of the family, and there tended to be little distinction between those of gentle and humble birth. Anyone who served in the household appeared on the account books as servants, and this applied to the chaplain, the chamberlain, and the secretary, as well as to the scullery urchin. It made little difference that more often than not, the dowager's ladies-in-waiting were as well-born as their mistress and that her steward might be a close relative. As for the children, they were expected to help their elders' dress, to wait at table and to fetch and carry on command, and when they failed in their social and educational duties they were beaten with as much vigour as any village maid.

Secondly, on closer inspection, Catherine appears to have been no better born than those 'abandoned persons' who presumably took such 'fiendish delight' in systematically corrupting her innocent mind. Her brothers and sisters were all under the Dowager's care at various times, and the children of her aunt, the Countess of Bridgewater, were her constant associates.[25] It emerges that her bedmates, those immoral temptresses, were her cousins, for both Katherine and Malyn Tylney were relatives of the Duchess, while Dorothy Baskerville, Margaret Benet, and Alice Restwold were of lesser but eminently respectable landed stock. As for her paramours, one was a neighbour, the other a distant kinsman. Henry Manox, who taught her to play on the virginal, and possibly a good deal else, came from a neighbouring gentry family, and Francis Dereham was a cousin. Both gentlemen formed part of the Howard *ménage* – the former as music teacher to the Howard children, and the latter as one of the Duke's pensioners and later as a member of the Dowager's service at Lambeth.[26] Even that 'drab' Elizabeth Holland, who carried the doubtful title of laundress and was for years the Duke's mistress, was sister to the Duke's secretary and related to Lord Hussey of Sleaford.[27]

The effect of sending children away from home at an early age was fatal to any sense of family solidarity, since the progeny of the upper classes might live to manhood without laying eyes on their parents, and the relationship between father and son was often one of bitter enmity and rivalry. Even when the educational process took place in the home, the pedagogical maxim of the age was spare the rod and spoil the child. Not for nothing did one mother mention as a normal occurrence that her daughter had been beaten 'twice in one day and her head broken in two or three places'.[28] Children were generally regarded as being important financial assets, and it was in no way remarkable that Sir John Fastolf sold the marriage rights of his stepson to Sir William Gascoigne for 500 marks and then bought them back again.[29] In a very real sense, children were considered as being the goods and possessions of their parents, to be disposed of as their elders saw fit. Romance and courtly love may have been suitable for chivalric tales of the past, but neither was in the least concerned with marriage. Throughout the sixteenth and seventeenth centuries, society was generally convinced that love marriages led only to trouble, and one lady quite honestly asked whether there was 'any thing thought so indiscreet, or that makes one more contemptible' than marrying for love.[30] Land and financial settlements were the considerations at stake, and slight value was placed upon the wishes or sentiments of the bride or bridegroom. The Duke of Norfolk's daughter was married at fourteen to a lad of fifteen; the Duke of Suffolk's brother, a boy of eighteen, was espoused to a widow of fifty; and young Master Robert Barre, aged three, had to be lured with an apple to get him into the church, to celebrate his engagement to Elizabeth Rogerson.[31]

Child marriages were the constant custom of the age, and most of Catherine's relatives were married young. Her mother, at the age of twelve, had taken as her first husband a man who belonged to a previous generation;[32] and the Earl of Surrey had his marriage arranged for him at thirteen and was betrothed by the age of fourteen.[33] It is true that this was beginning to exceed the legal limits, since the law prohibited the marriage of boys under fourteen, and legally the 'flower of a female's age' was twelve.[34] But as Bishop Latimer complained, a society that regarded marriage primarily as the joining of 'lands to lands, and possessions to possessions' paid scant heed to either the physiological or psychological factors involved.[35] When it was rumoured that Sir Brian Stapleton had been offered 1,200 marks in ready gold and land worth 100 marks for the hand of his son and heir 'and yet he trusteth to have more',[36] one could hardly expect anxious parents to have waited until their progeny reached the legal age. This, of course, did not necessarily mean that girls of twelve, or even the 'forward virgins' of fourteen, were exposed to the doubtful care of their spouses, and they often lived at home until eighteen lest they endanger themselves through childbearing. As far as the parents were concerned, the essential aspect of wedlock had been established, for once the marriage settlement was signed then the estates involved were fixed and settled by law. When we come to Catherine Howard's youthful escapades and her marriage to a sovereign, it might be well to remember how the Howards regarded the subject of marriage and the contemporary view: the girl 'who strikes the fire of full fourteen, today [is] ripe for a husband.'

The education and training of a young lady or gentleman of good birth was geared to these considerations. 'A good housewife is a great patrimony', and the honest wife, who also had an honest income of her own, was even more highly treasured. It was not necessary that a young lady be accomplished in the arts.[37] That both Queen Elizabeth and Queen Mary were highly educated ladies is the royal exception, and not the common rule. Catherine Howard had few intellectual accomplishments, and it was considered unnecessary that she should. It was a 'gentleman's calling to be able to blow the horn, to hunt and hawk', and to leave learning to the 'clodhoppers' who made scholarship a substitute for birth.[38] For a young gentlewoman, it sufficed if she was of honest, humble and of a wifely disposition. As late as 1598, Robert Cleaver could write that parents had only four duties that they owed their children – to instruct them in the fear of God, to instil in them a love of virtue and a hatred of vice, to keep them from idleness, and (the most important of all) to rear them to acknowledge the strict authority of the father, whose judgment must be obeyed at all times, especially in matters of matrimony.[39] It was this last duty that was most often discussed, and Roger Ascham bewailed that 'our time is so far from that old discipline and obedience' that not only young gentlemen but even girls dared to marry 'where they list and how they list' without respect to 'father, mother, God, good order and all'.[40]

Though Ascham's condemnation may have been justified as far as court circles were concerned, the country families still maintained that the 'principal commendation in a woman [is] to be able to govern and direct her household, to look to her house and family', and 'to know the force of her kitchen'.[41] It was to learn such honest and wifely duties that Catherine was sent to live with her step-grandmother. The finer accomplishments of life were not needed to enhance her eligibility as the wife of some country squire within the Howard circle, or some strategic courtier who might be useful to the family interests. No one, least of all Catherine, had any notion that she would be consulted when the time for connubial selection arrived, or that a Howard daughter would be thoughtlessly thrown away on just any hopeful aspirant to her hand.

For Catherine and the other maids of the Dowager's household, it was sufficient if they learned obedience and the inner mysteries of domestic organization. It is magnificently ironic that it should have been the Duchess's efforts to bring a touch of refinement into her granddaughter's life that resulted in the first of those fatal acts for which Catherine eventually paid with her life. What began as playing on the virginal and the lute under the tender care of Mr Henry Manox ended in clandestine meetings in the dark places under the chapel stairs. In the other, if less dangerous arts, Catherine seems to have been neither an especially apt nor a well-trained pupil, but she was certainly not the illiterate and neglected damsel of the history books. She was as well-educated as most of the ladies of the period, and could both read and write, which is more than can be said for other ladies-in-waiting at Henry's court.[42]

Catherine, however, never transcended the narrow educational and intellectual horizons of her kind. Reared under the strict and conservative influence of the old Duchess, she was orthodox in religion and naively credulous. She learned her paternosters, but was quite content to leave matters of theology and interpretation to those who knew better, happily mixing ceremonial punctiliousness with a firm belief in supernatural omens and signs. Catherine's world was crowded with blue crosses above the moon, flaming horseheads and swords, and church steeples demolished by the Devil's hand.[43] It mattered little, however, whether this Howard girl could write courtly love sonnets, appreciate theological niceties, or even sign her name, for when the moment came, Henry was not looking for a second Anne Boleyn who could match his own amorous love-letters. With Catherine he was seeking a less vicarious experience.

Born into a family of ten children, reared in the peripatetic household of a father who constantly sponged on both friend and relation, and accustomed to the rough and ready existence of sixteenth-century childhood, Catherine was probably prepared for almost everything that she might encounter at the Duchess's country house at Horsham – except perhaps its size. Agnes, Dowager Duchess of Norfolk, who presided over the manors of Horsham and Chesworth in Sussex[44] and the school for young relatives in her household, was herself something of an anachronism. Stiff-necked, testy and old-fashioned, she harkened back to the Wars of the Roses and the irresponsible anarchy of the old nobility. Rigidly religious, balancing the sins of her youth with a hair-shirt in the twilight of her life, the old Dowager was under it all a kind-hearted if short-tempered matriarch. She had most of the strength and shortcomings of her generation. She rarely went to court except on business or command, and she must have represented almost everything that Henry and the new men of the age most disliked. Her acid tongue, her stubborn defence of Henry's first wife, Catherine of Aragon, her studied disregard for the refinements of high society, and her total disdain for courtly etiquette must have made her distinctly unpopular at court. But under this starched and feudal façade lay both shrewdness and knowledge of the ways of the world, and despite her outward religious orthodoxy, there remained a good deal of amused toleration of the antics and escapades of youth. Officially frowning upon what went on in her 'maidens' chambers' at night, the Dowager probably knew a good deal more about such 'goings-on' than Catherine and her companions gave her credit for. She knew full well where a certain Mr Francis Dereham was prone to spend his evenings, and more than once she was heard to exclaim: 'I warrant you if you seek him in Catherine Howard's chamber ye shall find him there.'[45] All she required was that the younger generation should not flaunt their love-affairs in her face, and when she stumbled upon Catherine and Dereham kissing in the corridor she flew into a rage, boxed her granddaughter's ears and upbraided Dercham for his liberties. Yet for all the Duchess's vinegary words and violent fashions, she seems to have liked the full-blooded adventurer, and when Catherine finally grew weary of Dereham's attentions she found a perverse pleasure in reminding Mistress Howard of her early fascination.[46]

Life was too short and too complex for her to be burdened with the morals of her household, and all she asked was that the lusty youth conform to outward appearances. Her time was filled with the multitude of tasks related to the running of a vast and disorganized estate. As one of the richest widows in the realm, she was chronically being hounded by poor relations, and her son, Lord William, was constantly plaguing her for money and an advance upon his inheritance. In an age when banking facilities were almost non-existent, the old lady resorted to the proverbial sock (she confessed in later life that she had some £800 in cash hidden about the house), and rapidly acquired a reputation for being something of a miser.[47] But the care of money was not her only consideration. In the paternalistic society of the sixteenth century, her responsibilities reached out into the surrounding countryside, where she cared for her sick neighbours and prescribed 'treacle and water imperial' as a sure cure for all their ailments. The Duchess was evidently something of an apothecary, for she suggested to Cardinal Wolsey that 'vinegar, wormwood, rosewater and crumbs of brown bread is very good and comfortable to put in a linen cloth to smell unto your nose.'[48] This was her remedy for the various noxious odours that pervaded the Tudor world.

Most important and time-consuming of all was the management of her own household. How many people were involved in such an organization it is impossible to say, and very likely the old lady of Norfolk was not sure herself. Considering the size of other noble establishments, there may have been well over a hundred persons, ranging in a carefully graduated hierarchy from the dirty and naked scullery-boys who scrubbed the cauldrons in the great kitchen to the most important household officials, such as the steward, the chamberlain and the cellarer. Whether the Dowager had a house at both the manors of Horsham and Chesworth is not clear, but the Chesworth house itself consisted of five great rooms below stairs – not counting such 'necessary rooms' as the kitchen, pantry, and storage places – and five rooms upstairs, plus a garret. Then there were the malt-house, the barn, the stable, the cow barn, and four acres of orchards and gardens plus 'divers fish ponds'. At one time there had evidently been a moat, while the park of 223 acres harboured a herd of 100 deer.[49] Like other large estates, Horsham and Chesworth were self-sustaining organizations, splitting their own wood for the insatiable Tudor fireplaces, carding their own flax, weaving their own clothes, and producing food for guests and retainers. Hams had to be smoked, bacon cured, vegetables preserved, fruit stored, ale brewed, bread baked, for the whole household, and goose-down collected for the mistress's bed. Agnes Howard was in charge of all this, and though she had her steward, her secretary, and her cellarer to assist her, the ultimate responsibility for the establishment rested on her shoulders.

It was into such a household that Catherine, aged approximately ten, entered, so as to become versed 'in the worthy knowledges which do belong to her vocation' – that of a prospective housewife to a Tudor gentleman.[50] Life at Horsham must have been the epitome of luxurious discomfort. Early Tudor mansions were cold, damp, and dirty. The stone floors of the draughty halls remained bare, except for rushes that were rarely changed as often as they should have been, and the cavernous fireplaces did little to cut the chill. The sanitary facilities were both primitive and infrequent, and at best a house the size of the Dowager's would boast but a single 'house of easement' which was usually in cellar or the corner of the courtyard; occasionally, however, they were supplied with double seats. Chamber-pots were usually furnished in the various 'privy chambers', and their contents were disposed of with careless and dangerous abandon.

Such an establishment was not only labyrinthine and self-sufficient, it was also crowded and intimate to a degree unimaginable to modern society. Privacy was almost unknown; eating was a formal and communal function; and not even the Duchess herself slept alone. The sixteenth century was not particular where or with whom it slept, and the usual arrangement consisted of dormitories divided between men and women. Only in the most elevated and distinguished cases did married couples sleep together, and more often than not two couples shared the same bed. It is difficult to conceive of a society in which the bed was a household luxury, where chairs were scarce and kings ate at collapsible trestle tables. In the early part of the century, even in the homes of the rich and powerful, linen was a rarity, and a down mattress or a feather bed was a possession worthy of mention in one's last will and testament. Probably only the Duchess and a few honoured visitors were esteemed deserving of such luxury. For Catherine and her dormitory-mates a straw mattress and dagswain blanket with 'a good round log under their heads' sufficed, while pillows were kept for women in childbirth.[51] Moreover, society made little distinction in assigning beds, and where children were concerned, servants and noble progeny were indiscriminately mingled.

So far the life of Catherine Howard in Sussex has been merely a historical reconstruction – the surroundings of any girl given a similar position in society. Historical reality commences in the year 1536 when Catherine had reached the 'fire of full fourteen' and Henry Manox, the son of the Duchess's neighbour, George Manox, was summoned to Horsham to instruct the children of the house in the art of playing the virginal and the lute.[52] Henry Manox, like so many others of the Dowager's entourage, occupied a tenuous position somewhere between that of a servant and a gentleman; nor was he the only member of his family to be in service at Horsham, since his cousin, Edward Waldgrave, was one of the gentlemen-in-waiting to the old lady of Norfolk. He may have been something of a cad, but he certainly was not the systematic corrupter of innocent youth portrayed by some historians. In a society which left children to their own devices behind the back stairs, it is not surprising that Manox flirted with his pretty, auburn-haired pupil, who seems to have shown no sign that she in any way resented his advances or was ignorant of his designs.

Catherine was obviously not swept off her feet. On the contrary, it was the music teacher who was captivated, and he begged her, if indeed she loved him, to let him 'perceive by some token that you love me'. Catherine's rejoinder made it cruelly evident that she was acutely aware of the social gulf that existed between a duke's niece and the son of a simple landed family. 'What token should I show you?' she answered. 'I will never be naught with you and able to marry me you be not.' Manox persisted and begged for a few intimate (very intimate) caresses, to which the lady replied that she was willing to oblige on condition that he 'desire no more'. They arranged a courting place, and several days later met secretly in the Duchess's chapel chamber 'in the dark evening', where Manox bid Catherine 'keep her promise wherewith she was content'. There, under the lengthening shadows of the vaulted arches, the young music teacher found this Howard daughter even more responsive than he had hoped, and he later confessed that 'he felt more than was convenient.'[53]

Where these intimate caresses behind the altar ended will never be known, but Manox later swore 'upon his damnation' that he 'never knew her carnally'.[54] Considering Catherine's earlier insistence that he should 'desire no more' than a token of her love, Manox was probably telling the truth. Moreover, the affair was abruptly interrupted by the outraged Dowager, who discovered them together in their secret meeting-place. This was the second time they had been caught together and the Duchess was thoroughly annoyed. What action she took is not recorded. She may have dismissed Manox from his tutorial post, for he reappears later in the household of Lord Bayment, but more probably she did nothing, viewing the episode as a meaningless escapade and charging that the two should 'never be alone together'.[55] Certainly their relations did not cease; they were merely made more diffifcult, since the young people had to use one of the maids as a go-between to carry tokens back and forth, and it was rumoured in the kitchen circles that the two were secretly engaged.[56]

While Catherine was exchanging love-tokens with Henry Manox, the Dowager Duchess removed her household to Lambeth, which lay only a few miles from London. At first the love affair continued unabated, since Manox found a position close by in the service of Lord Bayment. In the end, however, the new and exciting atmosphere of Lambeth began to take effect, and while Henry Manox became increasingly confident of his control over Catherine's heart, the young lady herself was rapidly outgrowing her infatuation for the virginal player.

Norfolk House lay abreast of the king's highway leading from Lambeth town and directly opposite the archiepiscopal residence of Thomas Cranmer. Its imposing gateway and paved courtyard, its vast chambers, gallery and oratory, and its great hall opening on to the gardens in the rear, were palatial in contrast to the country establishment at Horsham.[57] Moreover, it was right across the river from Westminster and the royal court, and Catherine was suddenly introduced to a cavalcade of eligible and fascinating young men who lived on the neighbouring estates, or accompanied her uncle the Duke on his frequent visits to his stepmother's house. The break came when one of the servants reported to Mary Lassells, the Duchess's chamberer, the rumour of an engagement between Manox and Catherine. Mistress Lassells did not mince words, and she proceeded to upbraid Manox for his impudence at aspiring to the hand of a Howard lady. 'Man, what mean thou to play the fool of this fashion,' she said. 'Know not thou that if my lady of Norfolk knew of the love betwixt thee and Mistress Howard, she will undo thee.' Then the chamberer gave a warning: 'She is come of a noble house and if thou should marry her some of her blood would kill thee.'[58]

The advice was sage, for sons of yeoman stock married Howards at their peril. Even so the young man refused to be intimidated and he replied scornfully, boasting of his intimacy with Catherine. 'Hold thy peace, woman,' he retorted, 'I know her well enough.' Then, in unmistakable words, he proceeded to recount exactly how well he did know her, and concluded with the statement that 'she hath said to me that I shall have her maidenhead though it be painful to her, not doubting but I will be good to her hereafter.'[59] Unfortunately for Henry Manox, he had overplayed his hand, for when Catherine was informed of his words she made it cruelly evident that she no longer had any use for him, and she did not hesitate to tell him so to his face. Manox was abashed and murmured as an excuse that he 'was so far in love with her that he wist not what he said'. Mistress Catherine was as quick to pardon as to anger, and she was seen the following Saturday walking with him in the Duchess's orchard, 'they two alone'.[60] Though she was incapable of holding a grudge, the affair from Catherine's point of view was over, for a far more exciting suitor than a mere country-bred music teacher now made his appearance.

Francis Dereham, a young gentleman of birth and substance, was one of the Duke's gentlemen-pensioners, one of those feudal vestiges of the days of liveried retainers whom a few of the great magnates still retained. He was young, he was handsome, and he was well bred, and Catherine Howard fell before his manifest charms. Exactly when Dereham began to haunt the Dowager's Lambeth residence is not recorded. He was merely one of the many young gallants who were attracted to the 'maidens' chamber', and at first his attentions were directed not towards Catherine but to Joan Bulmer, another of the young ladies of the household.[61] In theory, the door to the girls' dormitory was locked every night, but this evidently constituted only a trifling barrier. The lock could be picked, athletic lovers could climb the lattice, or the maidens themselves could steal the key from the Duchess's bedchamber, once she was safely asleep.

It was not Catherine's decision alone to turn the dormitory into a rendezvous for young lovers; there were other ladies equally interested in having a secret and uninterrupted hour with the gentleman of their choice, and years later Catherine stubbornly insisted that the door was unlocked 'as well at the request of me, as of others'.[62] Alice Restwold, her bedmate, seems to have been particularly adept at arranging entry into the women's quarters, while more than one lady-in-waiting was charmed to co-operate in making her bedchamber available to the eligible gallants of the neighbourhood. The only element in the least remarkable about the whole arrangement was the fact that word of what was going on did not percolate down to the Duchess sooner. The girls evidently took the view that what their elders did not know would not hurt them, and there seems to have been a singularly successful conspiracy of silence maintained for a considerable period of time. How many of the young men in service with the Duke or with the other noble households of the area availed themselves of the pleasure of an evening with the Dowager's maidens it is impossible to say, but the two names that have been preserved are those of Francis Dereham, esquire, and Henry Manox's cousin, Edward Waldgrave, esquire.[63]

It is not difficult to reconstruct what occurred during those months between 1537 and 1539 when Catherine became so fatally involved with her lover. The maidens generally retired early, while their admirers, loaded with delicacies left over from banqueting in the great hall below stairs, would insinuate themselves into the communal bedchamber. 'Wine, strawberries, apples, and other things to make good cheer' were served at these midnight sessions, and careful arrangements were worked out lest a suspicious Duchess make an unexpected visit, for there was always the 'little gallery' into which the young men could hide if taken unawares.[64] From clandestine feasting to secret love-making was only a short step, and Dereham and Waldgrave would lie upon their mistresses' beds, making the most of the quiet hours before dawn. That Catherine became Dereham's paramour is indisputable, but it is far from clear how long the alliance lasted. Later, Catherine insisted that they had been 'carnal lovers' for only a quarter of a year – presumably during the autumn and winter of 1538, but a rather exaggerated rumour reported that Dereham had been systematically corrupting the girl for five years, since she was thirteen.[65]

All the instruments of courtship were utilized; they exchanged intimate tokens of their love, Catherine receiving a shirt of fine linen in return for an armband for her lover's sleeve. Francis Dereham was a gentleman of considerable means and evidently could gratify his mistress's fancy, for he presented her with velvet and satin for her gown, a 'quilted cap of sarcenet' and an embroidered friar's knot to symbolize their love.[66] More than once they were caught kissing in the great gallery by the Dowager, who vented her annoyance in words and blows, and caustically asked whether they thought her home was Henry VIII's court. But the old Lady of Norfolk seems to have done little to obstruct their meetings.

Later, when the more intimate details of their relationship became public knowledge, one witness confessed that Mistress Catherine 'was so far in love' that they kissed 'after a wonderful manner, for they would kiss and hang by their bellies together as they were two sparrows.'[67] Nor, if the evidence is to be believed, were Catherine's heavy brocaded skirts any protection against Dereham's experienced advances, and on the occasions when he visited her in the communal bedchamber it was inevitable that abandoned caresses carried on in doublet and hose should end in 'naked bed'. Mr Dereham was such a constant visitor behind the heavy curtains of the bed that the other inmates of the dormitory knew exactly who he was, and would remark: 'Hark to Dereham broken winded.'[68] Some of the ladies, who were not so fortunate as to have their Derehams and Waldgraves, complained about being kept awake at night, while others, the married ones, were shocked. Alice Restwold later, if not quite accurately, claimed that she was disgusted by the whole affair and announced to a friend that 'she was a married woman and wist what matrimony meant and what belonged to that puffing and blowing' that went on in her bed.[69]

That Catherine knew exactly what she was doing is undeniable, and in response to the warning that she was taking a grave risk she retorted that 'a woman might meddle with a man and yet concieve no child unless she would herself.'[70] Before a more inhibited age passes judgment on a girl in her teens, it might be well to judge first the moral standards of her generation. Foreign observers were shocked by the moral laxity of the English, but exactly why they should have felt this way is something of a paradox, considering what went on in such places as the French court. Possibly it was because the English were not as adept at the game of courtly love and took their amours where they found them, in an easygoing, unembarrassed fashion, not bothering to garb their sex in a glitter of sonnets and formality. Such a code would have to wait until the golden age of Elizabeth, when an entire nation became enthralled by the fascinating game of courting its virgin queen.

Almost every foreigner commented in wonder and with distaste at the manner in which the English treated their women, and allowed them such unchaperoned freedom. Nicander Nucius remarked that 'one may see in the market and streets of the city married women and damsels in arts and bartering and affairs of trade, undisguisedly.' The English displayed, he added, 'great simplicity and absence of jealousy in their usages towards females. For not only do those who are of the same family and household kiss them on the mouth with salutations and embraces, but even those too who have never seen them.'[71] Nucius could not understand why such behaviour appeared 'by no means indecent' to the English, while another traveller, later in the century, concluded that England was 'a paradise for women, a prison for servants, and a hell or purgatory for horses'.[72]

Tudor women were regarded as valuable financial assets, sources of obvious pleasure, and the mothers of lusty children to ensure family succession. That old warrior the Duke of Norfolk did not hesitate to offer Thomas Cromwell, by way of hospitality, the wife of one of his minions with whom he could 'be sure of a welcome', and if the Vicar-General lusted 'not to dally' with the wife, why then Norfolk knew of 'a young woman with pretty proper tetins'.[73] Thomas Howard was not the man to bestow what he himself had failed to savour, and he infuriated his wife and shocked his stepmother by publicly flaunting his own mistress in their faces. What filled the Duchess with rancour, however, was not that Bess Holland was her husband's concubine, but that she was a 'churl's daughter' and laundress in her nursery. The outraged lady complained that when she had grown violent over the duke's infidelity, she was seized by common serving-girls and bound and sat upon till she spat blood. The Duchess complained bitterly that she was 'a gentlewoman, born and brought up daintily', and had been forced to flee her home in self-defence.[74] How much of this is true it is difficult to discern, for Elizabeth Howard tended to be more imaginative than truthful, and the Duke dismissed her claims as great and 'abominable lies'.[75]

The lady seems to have been willing to pass over the extra-marital activities of her husband, but what she could not forgive was that her own children ignored her plight. 'Never', she wept, had a woman conceived 'so ungracious an eldest son and so ungracious a daughter and so unnatural.'[76] These unsympathetic children were Catherine's first cousins. The elder of them, the Earl of Surrey, once suggested to his sister Mary that she should seek the King's 'fantasy' and strive to become his mistress, so as to foster the Howard interests at court. Mary Howard indignantly refused, claiming that she would rather cut her own throat than Consider the bed of that obese and dying monarch.[77]

The girl who vigorously and successfully defended her virtue was an exception in early Tudor England, and the Imperial Ambassador thought it unlikely that Henry's third wife could still be a virgin at twenty-five. 'You may imagine', he satirically remarked of Jane Seymour, 'whether being an Englishwoman, and having been so long at court, she would not hold it a sin to be still a maid.'[78] The educational theory may have been given lip service – that 'a woman who giveth a gift, giveth herself; a woman who taketh a gift, selleth herself,' but in actual practice ladies of Catherine's station both gave and received gifts to the full. All that was required was that a certain minimum of decorum be maintained and the necessary precautions taken. Only when the unmistakable signs of unfaithfulness were perceived did society feel constrained to take a stand, and when Mary Boleyn, after four years of widowhood, did the one thing a lady of breeding could not explain – that is, become pregnant – the Howard family was justifiably annoyed and disowned her, if only because of her foolish neglect.[79] In the circumstances it was just as well that Catherine Howard appears to have known something about the rudiments of birth control.

Nor is there any evidence that when Catherine's amour with Francis Dereham was finally brought to the attention of her elders, they were particularly shocked. The agent of revelation was that discarded and neglected gentleman, Henry Manox, who grew frantic at the thought of Dereham and Waldgrave's admission to pleasures of which he was deprived. In a burst of righteous indignation, he announced that the Duchess's household was being 'dishonoured' by such activities, and sanctimoniously he and his friend, Barnes, took it upon themselves to warn the Dowager. They composed a letter which they left in the old lady's church pew, suggesting that the Duchess inspect the activities of her gentlewomen. 'For if it shall like you,' they wrote, 'half an hour after you shall be abed to rise suddenly and visit their chamber, you shall see that which shall displease you.'[80] Agnes of Norfolk went through her usual verbal storming at her servants for their negligence, but evidently she did not associate the warning with Catherine Howard and dismissed it as being of no great significance. Unfortunately for Mr Manox, Catherine spotted the letter in her grandmother's pew and later stole it from her coffer and showed it to Dereham, who turned in a towering rage on Manox.[81] This seems to have been the end of the virginal player, for he shortly thereafter acquired a more suitable lady for a wife, and disappeared from the scene. Though the Dowager may have been unaware of the full extent of the relationship between the two lovers, Catherine's aunt, the Countess of Bridgewater, and her uncle, Lord William Howard, were not so blind. Lady Bridgewater, however, was more worried by the nightly banqueting than by anything else, and she wisely warned her niece that 'if she used that sort [of thing] it would hurt her beauty.'[82] Lord William's reaction was to blame Manox for stirring up needless trouble, and he made light of the affair saying: 'What mad wenches! Can you not be merry amongst yourselves but you must thus fall out.' Since Lord William was himself having an affair with one of Catherine's dormitory-mates, his position is quite understandable.[83]

Catherine was a mirror of her age. Scantily educated, plagued by few inhibitions, and impetuously passionate, she simply reflected the

standards of a society which accepted as natural a certain amount
of promiscuity. Moreover, Catherine's relations with Dereham by
no means fell outside the existing bounds of propriety. The two
lovers acted as if they were engaged, and in the eyes of the Church
they were in effect married – a fact that will become increasingly
important as the story unfolds. Whether Catherine recognized any
legal obligation to her young man is not clear, but Dereham obviously
felt he had some form of lawful right. On one occasion when the
two had been found cuddling in the gallery, he asked why he should
not kiss 'his own wife'. When one of the witnesses remarked that
it appeared as if 'Mr Dereham shall have Mrs Catherine Howard',
he answered, 'By St John you may guess twice and guess worse.'[84]
Even Catherine confessed that during those intimate months she
had been content to call him husband.[85] Though such an informal
agreement, consummated as it was by carnal knowledge, constituted
a form of marriage, both lovers must have realized that they were
reckoning without the final decision of the Dowager and the Duke.
Dereham seems to have been cognizant of this, for as the socially
inferior, he was constantly endeavouring to legalize their union, and
he persistently pestered Catherine with 'the question of marriage'.[86]

It is easy to forget in the midst of youthful romance the stiffnecked
pride of the Howard clan. Even as a maiden in her teens, Catherine
Howard had developed a keen sense of the social abyss which
existed between herself and Henry Manox, and now with Dereham
she must have realized that her family would hardly consider him
an eligible catch for a Howard lady. Love and marriage were two
entirely different things, and though she might have a good deal
to say about the former, it was up to the family to determine the
latter. Acutely conscious of her family name, Catherine was a victim
of that ingrained arrogance which assumes that a Howard lady
is destined for a more illustrious future than marriage to a simple
family retainer. She had learned well the code that demanded that
her personal desires conform to the will and political requirements
of her house. Already one might have predicted the unbending stand
the Queen would later take, when questioned about her relations

with Dereham. She stubbornly denied any form of marital contract between them, at a time when her life might have been saved by confessing that she had never been legally married to Henry VIII. That she slept with Dereham she admitted, but excused it as the result of youth, ignorance and frailty, and she steadfastly refused to acknowledge that she had ever accepted his pleas for matrimony.[87] Such a perverse and fatal stand is in part explicable only in terms of family pride – the refusal to admit even to herself that she had not been the wife of a king.

The parting of the two lovers came in the autumn of 1539 when the Duke's influence finally arranged an opening at court for Catherine as one of the maids-in-waiting to the most recent of Henry's wives. The monarch was getting ready to wed his fourth wife, the German princess of Cleves, and once again there was a scramble on the part of the noble families of the realm to place their nieces and daughters, cousins and friends, in the new queen's household. Anne of Cleves arrived with an extensive and Germanic retinue, complete with three laundresses. She shortly learned, however, that her role was that of an English queen and not a Rhenish princess, and that she was expected to surround herself with well-connected ladies of her adopted land. Consequently the twelve to fifteen 'Dutch maids' were dispatched home again, and the foreign princess was given a thoroughly English household.[88] Attendance upon the queen was highly coveted, and such offices as gentlewoman of the privy chamber, chamberer, cup-bearer, and maid of honour were carefully parcelled out according to political influence. The positions were particularly desirable since it had long been recognized that the King had a weakness for a pretty face and might listen to a petition spoken by soft lips. The Howard clan did well in this struggle for placement, and of the six maidens about the Queen two of them, Catherine and her cousin, Mary Norris, were both of the Duke's patronage.[89]

The story of the family efforts to place Mistress Howard at court is lost, but the methods cannot have been far removed from the conniving employed by Lady Lisle in establishing her daughter Kattherine Basset, in the household of Henry's newest wife. Lady

Lisle wrote to her cousin, the Countess of Rutland, for assistance in this matter, and the countess reported, saying that the king had placed a limit upon the number of maids to be allowed at court, but if Lady Lisle would 'make some means unto mother Lowe' she might accomplish her purpose.[90] Mrs Lowe held the title of 'mother of the Dutch maids', and the hint is transparent: a certain amount of judicious corruption would win Katherine Basset the precious post. Mistress Basset eagerly awaited the outcome of her mother's intrigues, and wrote to her parent urging her to send Mother Lowe 'my good token that she may the better remember me'.[91] Anne Basset, sister to Katherine, had already attained a place at court, and the Lisle family called upon her charms to win the King's approval of her sister's appointment. Anne, however, was not encouraging, and reported that she had spoken to the King and he had answered that he had not decided upon the final number or selection of maids, but that they would have to 'be fair and as he thought meet for the room'. Evidently Anne did not feel that her own efforts were sufficient, for she advised her mother to 'send to some of your friends that are about his grace to speak for her.'[92]

Once a foothold at court had been attained, nieces and daughters were expected to make the most of their favoured position. Not only was Anne Basset utilized in her mother's dynastic ambitions, but she was expected to maintain the family name and reputation fresh in the King's mind. 'I have presented', she wrote to Lady Lisle, 'your codiniac [quince marmalade] to the King's highness, and his grace does like it wondrous well, and gave your ladyship hearty thanks for it. And whereas I perceived by your ladyship's letter that when the king's highness had tasted of your codiniac, you would have me to move his grace for to send you some token of remembrance ... I durst not be so bold to move his grace for it no other wise.' Lady Lisle's schemes and aspirations were insatiable, and she instructed her daughter to seek the King's favour for a business friend of her husband's and to say a good word for a son of one of Lord Lisle's acquaintances. The unfortunate girl was too terrified to plague the monarch with these constant requests and petitions and implored her mother to excuse her, 'for I dare not be so bold to move the King's grace in no such matter, for fear how his grace would take it.'[93] As Henry grew older and more impatient, no one could forecast how he might react to these irritating appeals for tokens, pledges, and offices, but it was regarded as a reasonable assumption that he would receive them better from a pretty maid-in-waiting than from a member of his own generation.

If a Basset daughter was expected to further her family's interests, it is a fair conjecture that the Howards anticipated the same of Catherine Howard and Mary Norris. King Hal had already shown a marked preference for Howard charm and beauty, and though the family could hardly have hoped to place another daughter upon the throne of England, they could at least surround the sovereign with the fairest of their clan. Henry had pronounced, if unpredictable, tastes concerning female beauty; he had taken one Howard lady to bed as his mistress and made another his queen. If nothing else, Catherine, as well as Anne Basset, could present quince marmalade to her sovereign.

The voice of family duty and the dazzling prospects of the court ended any hopes that Dereham may have had about marrying a Howard daughter, and it thrust Catherine into a world far removed from the Duchess's household at Horsham or Lambeth. How Mistress Catherine viewed the new developments is not clear, for there are two versions of her leave-taking, told years later by the lovers themselves and narrated under the probing and hostile eyes of government interrogators. Dereham described a deeply emotional scene with Catherine, tears trickling down her checks, reluctantly obeying her family's command to leave Lambeth for a career at court, and Dereham swearing that 'he would not tarry long in the house' and that 'he should never live to say thou hast swerved.' Catherine's version is one of cold indifference – she announced that he 'might do as he list' for all she cared.[94] Probably both stories contain an element of truth. For Catherine, the parting was but the end of an episode in her life. The Derehams of her world belonged in Lambeth as the Manoxes of her life belonged in Horsham. For her, the future held marriage, adventure and distinction. Probably tears did trickle down her face, for despite Mistress Catherine's callousness and pride, she cannot be accused of impassivity. Moreover, girls are not prone to contemptuous dismissals when their paramours have presented them with £100 as a highly useful token of their enduring love.

Dereham was off to the Irish coast, in persuit of the commercial activities which lay somewhere between legitimate trade and piracy, and he presented the money to Catherine with instructions to keep it should he never return. It was only after Dereham had left that the girl began to realize the gulf between their stations in life, and that their paths had actually diverged. When they met again, Catherine had been at court almost a year, and Dereham confronted her with the rumour that another man, one Thomas Culpeper, was being considered as a possible husband. Catherine coldly retorted: 'Why should you trouble me therewith, for you know I will not have you.'[95] As usual, however, the young maid-in-waiting was incapable of prolonged anger, and just as she had willingly walked with the lovelorn Manox in her grandmother's orchard at Lambeth, so now she did not entirely forget Dereham. When she became queen she found room for her ex-lover as a private secretary in her regal household.

The girl who appears dimly through these early years was a bundle of contradictory passions and desires. She was pretty and giddy, unscrupulous and passionate, easy to anger but quick to forgive, capable of intense if mercurial emotions, but always and acutely aware of her Howard descent and family obligations. At nineteen, Catherine was probably no different from other girls of gentle blood whose greatest ambition was to be maid of honour to the new Queen. As yet, the future remained mercifully hidden. The only characteristics that in any fashion differentiated her from the other maidens of the court were her vitality, her diminutive stature, her Howard connections, and above all that fatal something that caught and held the royal eye.

The moment that Catherine left the security of Lambeth and Horsham, she entered a world of quickened tempo in which the

stakes were dangerously high, the risks immeasurably greater –
where the price of failure was death, and where the reward of talent
was beyond calculation. She was going to court as a member of the
Howard tribe in order to promote the interests of her family and
make for herself an advantageous marriage. The past belonged to
forgotten paramours – to Henry Manox and Francis Dereham; the
future was promised to the young gallants at court, to her cousins
the Norrises, the Arundels, the Culpepers, and the Leghs. Catherine
stood upon the threshold of a fairytale come true; that the wonderful
vision of the future should explode into a nightmare from which
there was no awaking, was due to Catherine herself, for she lacked
both the intuitive insight and the rational assumption to perceive
that 'slippery is the place next to kings.' Once she faltered, Catherine
would be forsaken by friends, family and society, to face alone the
truth that 'the king's wrath is death.'

CHAPTER 4

LONDON TOWN

Comet-like, brilliant yet transitory, Catherine Howard blazed across the Tudor sky. The light that so fiercely illuminated the dark places of history lasted only eighteen months, but the harsh flame of her passing silhouetted and exposed the monstrous realities of her age – the cruelty and violence of London, the predatory morality of the court, the dazzling magnificence of the Crown, and the complex character of the man she married, the King himself. These four underlie the ephemeral spleandour of her life and the tragedies that followed her career at court; and here a diversion from the main flow of events leading to the fateful days of February, 1542, is necessary. Catherine was something more than the product of her family; she was also a child of her age, the product of, and in the end victimized by, those vague postulates of social and political behaviour which, though rarely articulated, nevertheless set fetters upon men's minds and condition their actions. Catherine mirrored in her assumptions and ethical standards the violence that pervaded all levels of society, and especially the city of London and the royal court – the essential stages upon which the final acts of her life were played.

The city that lay downstream and across the river from the suburban residences, immaculate gardens and well-kept orchards of Lambeth was sprawling, disorderly and inelegant. London was slovenly but exciting, sordid but vital, callous yet deeply religious. No industrial Hercules had as yet swept clean its Augean stables, and the combination of soap factories and tanneries, slaughterhouses and muck-heaps made the metropolis more discernible to the nose than to the eye. The city was still dominated by its three medieval landmarks – the towering Gothic spire of St Paul's Cathedral; London Bridge with its cluster of shops, fortified towers and drawbridge; and finally that ancient bastion and symbol of royal authority, the Tower of London. The major streets were paved with sand, gravel and cobblestone, but the rabbit-warren of by-ways and alleys remained a mixture of dirt, rubble and mud. A single gutter or open channel divided the lesser roads, while a main throughway such as Westchepe and Cornhill had double drains dividing the road into three parts, with vendors' stalls located in the middle section. The mental picture of medieval streets, narrow and tortuous, noxious and noisome, is only partly correct. London had its broad avenues, and even as late as the reign of Henry VIII, Cheapside was still a place for jousting and tournaments – after unwilling merchants had been induced to move their portable stalls to make room for mounted knights.

The growth and life of the city were essentially accidental and random, the result of centuries of avarice and generations of thoughtless activity. Portable sheds tended to become cherished and vested rights; broad highways were transformed into narrow lanes by the encroachments of artisans anxious to sell their wares from permanent shops immediately contiguous to their homes; and roads grew higher and higher as each passing generation repaired cart ruts and mud holes with new layers of sand and stone, so that by 1595 the parish church of St Katherine was seven steps below street level. The city was constantly changing, incessantly moving, and by Catherine's day the old terms had already lost their meaning. Ironmongers' Lane no longer housed the iron trade; the hosiers had long since forsaken Hosier Lane to invade Cordwayner Street, while the drapers had removed to new quarters on Candlewick Street. Houses that had once been designed as modest single-floor structures, with a garret by way of sleeping accommodation, now rose three and four storeys. Their overhanging upper levels effectively obliterated both light and air, and the introduction of outside stone staircases added to the confusion of the teeming streets.

To a casual observer, the city represented a myriad of fascinating pictures: of hustling and hurried commotion, of carts and coaches, 'thundering as if the world ran upon wheels', of men, women and urchins 'in such shoals' that posts had to be set up to protect the houses lest the jostling crowds shoulder them down. London continued to live and work in the open, and her streets were a congestion of clamorous bargaining and primitive manufacturing. Laws had to be enacted ordering tailors and rag dealers to scour their cloth in the streets only at night, and butchers and fishmongers had to be restrained from turning the roads into sinks of entrails and scales. Chapmen, 'as if they were at leap frog', skipped from shop to shop; tradesmen, 'as if they were dancing galliads', were incessantly on the move; and street scavengers and takars, priests and apprentices, criminals and saints were all 'as busy as country attorneys' at an assize.[1] This was the rhythmic pulse of London, the throbbing heart of England.

The city lured rich and poor, gentleman and caitiff into the rat-infested haven of twisted streets and filthy cottages. London was not simply the residence of the monarch's perambulating court, but was also the centre of wealth, the home of fashion, the sink, and 'the storehouse and mart' of all Europe. 'What can there be in any place under the heavens,' exclaimed one loyal, 'that is not in this noble City either to be bought or borrowed?'[2] The economy of the entire southern part of the island was effectively oriented to the needs and pleasure of possibly 100,000 Londoners, and daily the roads leading into the metropolis were crowded with country folk bringing food, fuel, and fodder. The city walls afforded a sanctuary for all who sought justice or profit, labour or crime, fame or adventure. The army of lusty beggars, victims of the ever-increasing population of domesticated ruminants and farmlands turned into sheep-runs, were attracted by the hope of work, charity and larceny. Likewise, the veterans of Tudor wars found shelter from the unsympathetic arm of authority, which frowned, during peacetime, upon the activities of men trained to loot and kill.

Scattered indiscriminately among the stalls, the taverns, the hostels, and the cottages of the town were the establishments of the rich and mighty. Nothing so amazed and baffled the foreign traveller as this tendency for wealthy merchants and even gentlemen of ancient lineage to live in the midst of squalor and commotion. Actually, appearances were deceptive, and one observer noted that the larger houses, being 'built all inward' with their front rooms let out to shopkeepers, made but a poor impression upon those ignorant of the true magnificence that lay concealed behind shabby mercantile exteriors.[3] Behind the commercial façade lay spacious halls and broad gardens – a fact which helps to explain why the city was not periodically burned to the ground. In many ways, London was closer to a provincial town than to a modern metropolis, and the picture of narrow, noisome streets hides the existence of sizeable open spaces, which acted as effective if quite accidental fire-breaks. Fear of fire hung perpetually over rich and poor alike, and as early as 1189 the city had ordained that the first floor of all houses must be constructed of stone, and that slate or baked tile should take the place of thatched roofs. The Crown and the city aldermen waged a chronic but losing battle to enforce the building and zoning laws, but the growth and pressure of population was too great, and by Elizabeth's reign London was primarily a city of wood and plaster.[4] Possibly the only advantage of such jerry-built structures was the ease with which they could be pulled down by the grappling-hooks kept by each ward in case of fire, for the basic principle of fire-control in the sixteenth century was demolition, not extinguishment.

During the day London was a mosaic of clashing and primary colours. Hose and doublet tended to be gaudy if not over-clean; servants wore the brilliant livery of their masters; and that part of society which could neither read nor write advertised itself and its wares by armorial designs and heraldic beasts. Taverns, hostels and shops were all known by the swaying sign above the door, and the pressure for increasingly extravagant commercial self-expression,constrained the city elders to limit the length to which such signs could extend out into the street to seven feet. In a life which for most people continued to be short and savage, the harlequin design of clothing, the clash of vivid and basic hues, and the sumptuous splendour of pageantry were all necessary antidotes to an otherwise squalid and drab existence. The court, the church, and the city itself, supplied the populace with a constant round of entertainment and diversion. Holy days tended to become holidays, with maidens dancing in the streets and young apprentices practising with shield and cudgel. A royal entry into the city was a matter of meticulous planning and magnificent celebration, and even a funeral would lure from every nook and cranny the curious housewife, the idle artisan, the accomplished cut-purse, and the chronic scalawag.

The festival that London loved best was that of the 'marching watch', when the constabulary paraded through the streets on Midsummer's Eve. On these occasions the entire town participated in the spectacle, and rich and poor each contributed their share – the former their gold, the latter their insatiable thirst and empty bellies. Bonfires were lighted in the streets, and cakes and ale were handed out in abundance by men of substance who still held to the paternalistic notions of the medieval past. It was 'a goodly show', for every man's door was 'shadowed with green birch', decked with white lilies, and 'garnished upon with garlands of beautiful flowers'. Shopkeepers and artisans lit 'lamps of glass, with oil burning in them all the night', while others 'hung out branches of iron curiously wrought, containing hundreds of lamps alight at once'. The watch formed in front of St Paul's, then moved ponderously through Westchepe Street to Aldgate and finally back again via Fenchurch Street. The procession, as it it twisted its way through the city, ablaze with bonfires and torches, must have been an unforgettable sight of varied extravagance. Half the constabulary, dressed in gilt harness, scarlet cloaks and gold chains, held the place of honour, while their less fortunate colleagues continued to guard the city. Behind them followed minstrels and morris dancers, drummers and standard-bearers, sword-players and archers in coats of white fustian. There also was the lord mayor with his footmen and torch-bearers, and the twenty-four aldermen of the city, each with his servants.[5] Often pageants or floats, representing the work of a particular guild, were incorporated into the procession. Each float depicted a scene, some religious, some nationalistic. Satan was presented 'naked with a drawn sword so contrived that when he brandished it the serpent (on which he sat) vomited stinking sulphur fire-balls'; a spectacle that must have endangered the entire metropolis. In marked contrast was another float showing the Virgin Mary in the guise of a 'very beautiful little girl' surrounded by four boys who chanted their veneration. There were also St George and his dragon, scenes from the Last Judgment, and performing acrobats and animals.[6]

For all its display and magnificent pageantry, London remained a place of dark violence and callous crime. 'Wild rogues' in company with harlots and armed with picklocks, saws, hooks and ladders nightly roamed the streets, bent on vandalism, murder, and brutality. The little band of constables, which numbered but 240, was no match for the city's cut-purses, professional beggars, starving vagrants and excitable apprentices. The parishes and wards did their best to maintain order and discipline, but the gap between written legislation and actual law enforcement remained almost insurmountable. The red-light district in Southwark was carefully regulated by municipal ordinances, and the ladies who operated at such establishments as the Cardinal's Hat, the Cross Keys, the Boar's Head, and the Swan, were limited to a single customer a night and had to 'lie with him all night till the morrow'. Both the houses and the ladies themselves were regularly inspected, and, in theory at least, their area of operation was confined to Southwark.[7] Actually, however, the streets crawled with bawds and harlots, and any continuous efforts at either medical or financial control of the profession proved impossible.

The two most troublesome and unpredictable elements of the population were the students of the Inns of Court, and the apprentices of the city. Both were desperately poor, readily incited to senseless riots, and easily excited by stories of witches who cast their evil eye and devils who made merry in God's churches. Narrow, prejudiced, and intolerant of everything un-English, they made life miserable and at times dangerous for foreign merchants and travellers, who were unanimous in their distaste for the brutish London populace, which yielded 'to none other in disrespect, outlandishness, boorishness, savagery, and bad bringing up'.[8] For most of these students and apprentices, life was centred in London and their horizons penned in by ignorance and incredulity. City dwellers were sufficiently naive to believe that the charcoal which arrived daily on the Thames barges, was grown on trees in some distant part of the realm. The slightest argument or the most casual encounter could result in violence and crime, and hardly a night passed that some local brawl did not endanger the peace and sleep of the city. One June evening a typical riot was started when a tailor and a law clerk, 'both very lewd fellows', fell out over a harlot. The tailor called to his aid 'the prentices and other light persons' of the neighbourhood, and chased the clerk into Lyon's Inn. There, some three hundred ruffians broke windows and assaulted the students. Matters became worse and the rioting spread when a baker's son 'came into Fleet street and there made solemn proclamation for "clubs".'[9] This last was the cry which was the signal for every apprentice and scholar to grab a cudgel and throng through the streets looting and breaking into shops.

It was this turbulent and loutish character of the citizenry that earned London such an evil reputation. Reginald Pole described the populace as being made up of incorrigibly lazy rogues given 'to idle gluttony'.[10] Later in the century the Duke of Württemberg complained that 'street-boys and apprentices collect together in immense crowds and strike to the right and left unmercifully without regard to person; and because they are the strongest, one is obliged to put up with the insult as well as the injury.'[11] Estienne Perlin, who deplored all things English, was particularly critical of the common sort, who were 'proud and seditious, of an evil conscience, and unfaithful to their promises'. In his opinion, and in the opinion of many others, the London masses were nasty, dangerous, and 'extremely fickle, for at one moment they will adore a prince, and the next moment they would kill or crucify him.'[12] The Tudors perceived that the secret of their power resided in the devotion of these same rowdy, ignorant throngs, and they viewed with the darkest suspicion the actions of any demagogue who dared to covet London's volatile affections. Henry VIII and Elizabeth were accomplished masters in the art of catching and holding the imagination, and though both may have preferred the quiet and security of Hampton Court, Windsor, or Nonsuch, they remained at Westminster and London, for here resided the crucial audience towards which the magnificent pageantry of majesty was directed.

It is important to sense the flavour of Tudor London, to catch a sniff of its atmosphere, for in it lies the essence of sixteenth-century society. Elegance and pomp, ceremony and romance, from the perspective of some four hundred years, tend to obscure the realities of life – its cruelty, its viciousness, and its total lack of social inhibitions. Men were as quick to anger as to love; no one walked unarmed through the streets at night; and wise men rarely walked alone. Only the clergy faced such dangers unprotected, and even they might carry a stout club concealed beneath their clerical robes, for thieves and drunkards did not always respect the protection of God. Society suffered little from our modern plague of mental diseases, and there was little need and even less machinery to suppress basic human instincts. The unlit streets and the King's high roads approaching the city were the haunts of every sort of criminal. Crime was the livelihood of the jetsam of society-gentlemen who had ruined themselves and their families at cards and dice, serving-men 'whose wages cannot suffice so much as to find them breeches', discharged and disabled soldiers who knew no other profession, and evicted and starving peasants. With only 240 constables to protect the city from the multitude for whom society felt no social responsibility, and with emotions close to the surface of daily life, authority could do little except make frightful examples of those unfortunate enough to be caught. In the circumstances it is understandable that the watch fortified itself with strong ale or regarded 'every hour a thousand' while on duty, and when summoned to exercise police control answered, 'God restore your loss! I have other business at this time.'[13]

In contrast to law enforcement, law enactment was extensive, detailed, and ferocious, and though we can in part dismiss Estienne Perlin's description as nationalistic propaganda, there is nevertheless considerable truth in his words that 'in England the legal punishments are very cruel, for a man is put to death for a trifling offence; for a crime which in France would be only punished with a whipping, a man would here be sentenced to death.'[14] The laws of the realm were far from being so simple, but they were just as brutal as Perlin claims. Treason was the most heinous of all crimes, and with a fine appreciation of the rule that the punishment should fit the crime, society condemned the traitor to death by being 'laid on a hurdle and so drawn to the place of execution, and there to be hanged, cut down alive, your members to be cut off and cast in the fire, your bowels burnt before you, your head smitten off, and your body quartered and divided at the King's will.'[15] The chronicles are filled with the dreary spectacle of men being 'hanged, drawn, and quartered'. Poisoners were boiled alive, witches and heretics were burnt at the stake, and murderers were hanged alive in chains. As late in the century as 1595 men were still searching for ways to discourage crime – especially the forger, who, if left to his own devices, was a threat to any well-ordered society. In that year, the Lord Treasurer suggested a modification of the normal punishment for forgery. Since the usual burning of the letter F in the ear and on the hands tended to disappear, he argued that the culprits should be 'scarified on the balls of the cheeks with the letter F by a surgeon, and that some powder be put there to colour it, so that it would never vanish.' This improvement was not accepted and the offenders were merely given the usual sentence to 'stand on the pillory and lose their ears, if they have any, and be branded on the forehead with the letter F, and be condemned perpetually to the galleys.'[16]

The most common engine of justice was the gibbet, and any theft over a shilling could be punished by hanging. There seem to have been a number of curious exceptions to this: the man who stole a horse or a sheep was put to death, but he who absconded with an ox or a cow was granted his life, if it were his first offence. The singular logic behind this was that 'a horse or a sheep may be easily stolen, while an ox or a cow present great difficulty, surrounded as they are in their meadows by ditches.'[17] Again, the argument was that the punishment should in all cases fit the crime, and the easier the criminal act, the more important it was to discourage it by the severity of the penalty. Lesser offences were punished with lesser but equally distasteful consequences. The stocks were placed in highly conspicuous locations where drunkards, rioters, name-callers, bawds, and scolds could be exposed to public derision. Fraudulent merchants and slanderers were effectively curbed by the use of the pillory where the culprits stood, neck and wrists pinioned, and, on occasion, with their ears nailed to the board behind their heads. The fate reserved for false jurors was similarly unpleasant; in 1509 the three ringleaders of a false inquest were forced to ride about the city 'with their faces to the horse tails", and paper caps on their heads, and 'were set on the pillory in Cornhill, and after brought again to Newgate, where they died for very shame.'[18] Then there was the 'cocking stool', reserved for inveterate gossips and scandalmongers, whom society endeavoured to chasten by ducking in the nearest pond. Whipping, either at the whipping-post or at the rear of a cart, was the usual method of discouraging idleness and prostitution. In all, John Stow estimated that some 72,000 persons were executed during the reign of Henry VIII for criminal offences, while the number who suffered branding, mutilation, and humiliation is beyond reckoning. Even so, social thinkers felt that the laws were insufficiently enforced; crime remained unchecked, and one contemporary complained that this was the result of 'want of punishment by the day, and idle watch in the night'.[19] Others, such as Sir Thomas More, associated the harshness of the laws with the high crime rate, and argued that the constant use of the death penalty was an invitation to murder since, in the eyes of the thief, murder and robbery were equal in terms of the punishment.

Shocking as this picture is, two observations should be made before passing judgment upon Tudor criminal procedure. The infliction of pain and the carefully calculated cruelty were not the result of any sadistic desire for pleasure. Instead, they reflect the general level of brutality of the age and the conviction on the part of most people that the evil-doer deserved everything that society could inflict upon him. There is some evidence that men were slowly awakening to the knowledge that crime is a social phenomenon, but most denizens of the Tudor world were sufficiently close to their medieval heritage to view crime as a sign of sin. Man, not society, was held as the source of evil; society was still viewed as being of divine inspiration, and consequently it could not be held accountable for the wickedness that was everywhere so manifest in a city such as London. The individual was born into a divinely ordained system with certain prescribed duties, rights and obligations, and when he failed in those responsibilities, when he fell into vice and corruption, then society held him fully responsible for his actions. Pride, avarice and vanity were the breeders of crime, and as the tree was known by its fruits, so man would be judged by his actions.

The more vicious the act, the more evil and sinful the actor. Pride was always viewed as the most noxious of sins; and nothing burns quite so fiercely in a Christian hell as the sin of insatiable pride. What could be more arrogant than treason; who could be more 'puffed up with insatiable pride' than the traitor who sets his own egotism above the will of society? What could be more suitable than that he should be made to suffer for his sinful pride by any instrument society could devise? The source of crime, wrote one Tudor citizen, was to be found in 'the excess of apparel. Hose, hose! Great hose! Too little wages, too many serving men, too many tippling houses, too many drabs, too many knaves, too little labour, too much idleness.'[20] Here is an interesting mixture of the sociological and the religious view of crime, a blending of the modern thesis that crime stems primarily from economic distress and alcoholism, and the medieval notion that the personal sins of vanity and idleness are the culprits.

The ferocity of the laws also reflects the savageness of life itself. The world in which men lived was just as cruel, just as barbarous, as the laws of the realm. 'At any season,' lamented Bishop Fisher, one could see 'beggars or poor folks that be pained and grieved with hunger and cold, lying in the streets.'[21] When death, disease, torment and starvation are common phenomena, men learn to accept them as an inevitable part of life. Though the good bishop might preach compassion, for most men pity went little farther than speeding their criminal associates into the presence of their Maker. Condemned criminals were placed in carts, 'each one with a rope about his neck', and the hangman drove his doleful passengers:

> Out of the town to the gallows, called Tyburn [roughly where Marble Arch stands today], almost an hour away from the city. There he fastens them up one after another by the rope and drives the cart off under the gallows which is not very high off the ground; then the criminals' friends come and draw them down by their feet, that they may die all the sooner.[22]

It was not easy to show much inward compassion when the pitiful was everywhere, and every city had its share of those who lacked 'their arms, feet, hands, and other features of their bodies', or who had 'their arms broken or else the flesh eaten away with divers sores and infirmities'. How many, grieved Fisher, 'lie in streets and highways full of carbuncles and other uncurable botches'?[23] The citizens of London town lived under the shadow cast by the heads of traitors pinioned upon the pikes of the portcullis of London Bridge, and at times as many as thirty skulls were collected there as a grim reminder to those who harboured the thought of treason. A grisly boast evolved, a perverted Tudor sense of humour, for it became the mark of a gentleman to have at least one unfortunate relative or ancestor hanged and quartered and his head elevated for public inspection. In the circumstances there is little wonder that Henry Bullinger could write in 1541 that 'to say the truth, people did not inquire much, as it is no new thing to see men hanged, quartered, or beheaded, for one thing or another.'[24]

Indifference to the death and suffering of others was the mark of a society that itself lived upon the brink of eternity. The calm acceptance of the torment of the poisoner being boiled alive is understandable, for what was 'piteous' was not the sight of his agony (which was not far removed from that of soldiers and plague victims, who knew not the blessings of anaesthesia), but that his sinful heart should have brought him to such straits. It was almost as if life were too short for the luxury of moderation, and the manifest moral of a criminal dangling by the neck was too easily lost upon an audience whose senses were blunted to the sight of human anguish.

There was one aspect of Tudor life that could and did cut through the coarse veneer of indifference, and strike terror into the souls of men grown accustomed to cruelty. This was the twofold threat of bubonic plague and the sweating sickness – both silent, merciless dreads that gripped even the stoutest heart. Sir Thomas More recorded something of the senseless caprice of the plague, and the fear it could invoke, when he described the ironic death of his good friend, Andrew Ammonius:

> He thought himself well fortified against the contagion by moderation in diet. He attributed it to this that, whereas he met hardly anyone whose whole family had not been attacked, the evil had touched none of his household. He was boasting of this to me and many others not many hours before his death.[25]

How many victims these epidemics claimed is impossible to say, but in 1540 the French Ambassador reported that the parish records 'show that for a month past, 300 persons have died each week within the circuit of the town.'[26]

The shock of death which could transform in an instant 'thy beautiful face, thy fair nose, thy clear eyes, thy white hands, thy goodly body' into 'earth, ashes, dust, and worm's meat' constantly haunted the sixteenth-century mind.[27] Poets and preachers were at pains to emphasize the frailty of beauty, pride, and youth, which 'shall vanish quite within an hour as fire consumes the ice'. Nothing was more popular than the sermon that pictured the 'burning fire of hell' that awaits the unsuspecting and unprepared sinner struck down in the instant of life, or which lashed out against the vanities of the world. London was viewed by the righteous as a veritable sink of vice and pollution, the citadel of the Devil himself. Towards the end of the century, Thomas Nashe warned that 'we here in London, what for dressing ourselves, following our worldly affairs, dining, supping, and keeping company, have no leisure' to watch against sin.

Then he thundered an exhortation: 'In pranking up our carcasses too proudly, we lift up our flesh against God.'[28] Life was regarded by many conscience-stricken men of the century as being short and transitory, and the lustful pride of rich attire was evidence of the power of Satan and the 'dalliance of thy doom'. What indeed was beauty, Nashe demanded of his audience, other than 'a wind-blown bladder' which in life was 'the food of cloying-concupiscence' and in death 'the substance of the most noisome infection.'[29]

Ministers of God were not the only ones to decry the foolish vanity of this world and the wanton disregard for the everlasting life to follow. In a society in which men refrained from masking death behind the marble façade of the funeral parlour, almost every imagination was touched with a form of necrophilia. Under Henry VII the macabre 'Dance of Death' depicted upon the walls of the cloister of St Paul's continued to exercise a hideous fascination over men's thoughts. Even such a balanced individual as Sir Thomas More could not help but reflect upon the physical details of the act of death. With clinical accuracy he described the dying man as:

> Lying in thy bed, thy head shooting, thy back aching, thy veins beating, thy heart panting, thy throat rattling, thy flesh trembling, thy mouth gaping, thy nose sharping, thy legs cooling, thy fingers fumbling, thy breath shortening, all thy strength fainting, thy life vanishing and thy death drawing on.[30]

The cathedral spire had not given way to the skyscraper. Morally and financially, the Church had not been succeeded by the insurance company. Most men, both Catholics and Protestants, continued to live within the shadow of eternity, and of a Church that made the mystery of life and death both endurable and explicable.

Common suffering and insecurity can produce acts of supreme charity, but they can also breed callousness, fatalism and extravagance, and London had its share of all of them. Fear, despondency and depression had once dulled men's senses and chilled their souls, but by the third decade of the sixteenth century the emphasis had shifted, and the very imminence of death now made life all the more precious. A generation was born which was 'urged to dare all'. Verve, vitality and daring, however, are purchased at a price – the price of insensitive indifference to the fate of others and the icy stoicism that accepts the dictum: 'my lot today, tomorrow may be thine.' Even the plague was transformed by some into a source of profit; it struck down the rich and greedy, exposing their bodies to the indignities of desperate men willing to risk death to snatch rich apparel, and costly finery from disease-ridden corpses. As one hardened beggar put it: the rich man's loss 'is our luck; when they become naked, we then are clothed', for 'their sickness is our health, their death our life.'[31] The laws of the kingdom may have been ferocious, but the hearts of men were equally savage.

It should not be too difficult for the twentieth century, conditioned as it is by the memory of Buchenwald and Dachau, to appreciate the atmosphere of the society into which Catherine Howard stepped once she left the care of the Dowager Duchess. It might, of course, be argued that the picture painted in these pages is a portrait of the crawling, stinking masses and not representative of court and noble society, but Henry's household cannot be dissociated from the ethics of the age. Fine gentlemen and fair damsels may have been slightly more refined than the jostling crowds of London with their 'malevolent look of pigs deprived of their trough', but the difference was merely one of degree, not of kind. Polite society was almost as violent, almost as crowded and credulous, almost as brutal as the 'lesser sort'. Though a gentleman might hesitate to rob a plague-infested corpse of its riches, he eagerly plundered the estates of fallen ministers and luckless courtiers, and often he did not have the decency to wait until the victim was dead. Catherine's life and personality are only comprehensible in terms of the ethical atmosphere that encompassed all levels of society, from Henry VIII himself to the local executioner who lived with the knowledge that eventually his own criminal activities would destroy him.

Reflecting the city – at once its economic heart and social paradigm – was the royal and peripatetic court of the sovereign, where, in glittering microcosm, high society mirrored the macrocosm of the metropolis in showy ostentation, violence and stinking congestion. As one historian has put it, the mental picture of court life in the sixteenth century must include 'perpetual crowding, chronic disorder, and elaborate ceremony'.[32] To this trinity of characteristics must be added yet another – that of the unrestrained fury so distinctive of the street life of the city. It was this compulsive violence of mind and unsublimated sensualism of emotions that underlay the extravagance of decoration, brilliance of dress, excess of brutality, and intricacy of pomp and ceremony, all of which formed the dominant motifs of court society.

Henry's court was both a public and a private organization – the private retinue of kings and the public centre of government. It was a clumsy, pulsating mass of humanity, surrounding the royal person. Wherever the King was in residence, whether at Whitehall or Baynard's Castle, Hampton Court or Richmond, the court was in attendance. Ministers of state, servants of the Crown, social and political aspirants, patron seekers and vendors, parasites and sages, they were all drawn into the King's household.

Being the personal household of the King, the court was organized like any private residence. It was infinitely larger, vastly more chaotic, and teeming with intrigues and violence, but structurally it differed little from what Catherine had experienced either at Lambeth or at the Duchess's country estate at Horsham. The immediate area surrounding the sovereign, his privy chamber, was referred to as the 'above stairs' of the household. Over it presided the lord chamberlain, who attended to the personal wants of the king and organized the ponderous ceremony which encircled his royal person, protecting him and gracing his every action with the divine dignity that doth hedge about a king. 'Below stairs' was the domain of the lord steward, who was responsible for the domestic needs of the entire staff. Under him was an army of domestics ranging in importance from the controller, the four masters of the household, the master of the jewels, and the King's fool, down to the children of the squillery, the apprentice cooks of the kitchen, and the groom of the stool.[33]

The division between the two parts of the household was essentially that of the master's suite versus the servant's quarters, but the distinction between the two tended to become blurred on the upper levels. In many baronial homes the steward or chamberlain was often a relative of the family; so at court, the high officials of the house, though they performed duties below stairs, socially belonged to the upper household. Technically, the Duke of Norfolk, as lord treasurer, came under the jurisdiction of the Lord steward, but in actuality he had entree above stairs, as one of the ordinaries of the kings's privy chambers.

In theory, the professional activities of the lord steward were multitudinous and endlessly varied. He catered for the needs and peculiarities of the entire entourage. He saw to the feeding of strangers and to the 'exclusion of boys and vile persons'; he insisted that members of the court eat at the prescribed hour and place; he disbursed bouche of court or the daily ration of bread, beer, wine and faggots allotted to gentlemen and ladies and upperclass servants, according to their rank and service. Catherine, for instance, as one of the maids-in-waiting to the Queen, received not only room and dining privileges, but also shared daily with the other maids two loaves of coarse bread and three of white, four gallons of ale, and a half pitcher of wine. From the last day of October to the first day of April, the maids were issued three torches a week, six candles a day, six talshides of wood, and six bundles of faggots, amounting in value to over £24 a year.[34]

One of the lord steward's most vexing and complex tasks was the feeding of this hungry army of courtiers, maidens and domestics, in an age when both sexes ate prodigiously, at length, and with vast ceremony. The gastronomic well being of Englishmen in the sixteenth century was proverbial, and rarely did a foreign traveller refrain from commenting upon the fact that farmers and yeomen ate almost as well as gentlemen and nobles. In a period of three days, Elizabeth's court managed to consume 67 sheep, 34 pigs, 4 stags, 16 bucks (used to make 176 meat pies), 1,200 chickens, 363 capons, 33 geese, 6 turkeys, 237 dozen pigeons, 2,500 eggs and 430 pounds of butter,

plus a cartload and two horseloads of oysters.[35] Such abundance
was limited to State functions, but Henry VIII regularly spent over
£1520 a year on food for himself and his Queen, and the Duchess of
Norfolk commonly sat down to a table set for twenty and served as
her first course two boiled capons, a breast of mutton, a piece of beef,
seven chevets, a swan, a pig, a breast of veal, two roasted capons, and
a custard.[36] When Mr Henry Machyn, the undertaker, could polish
off with the help of eight friends half a bushel of oysters, a quantity
of onions, red ale, claret, and malmsey at eight in the morning,[37]
the extent of royal consumption, though still prodigious, no longer
appears disproportionate to that of the rest of society. The usual
royal fare consisted of such fattening delicacies as venison, mutton,
carp, veal, swan, goose, stork, capon, conies, custard, fritters, and six
gallons of beer and a sextet of wine to wash down what was only
the first course. Then followed jellies, cream of almond, pheasant,
hem, bittern, partridge, quail, cock gulles, kid, lamb, tarts, more
fritters, eggs, butter, and finally fruit with powdered sugar.[38] Not
content with mere quantity, the eye as well as the stomach had to
be satiated, and on special occasions dishes were transformed into a
riot of colour and form, representing heraldic, historic and classical
scenes. The rich man's table was loaded to overflowing and appetites
matched the supply, but it must be remembered that 'waste' was an
economic necessity. Everybody from the household servant to the
passing beggar was expected to make do with the leftovers.

For all its size, the court still retained something of its original
private and family atmosphere. The royal store-houses were still the
King's private storage rooms; the great dignitaries of State remained
the King's servants, and Henry's first wife, Catherine of Aragon,
continued to count her husband's linen. Ceremonial exclusiveness,
brittle ritual, and the divinity that invests a king, had not yet destroyed
all traces of the familiar informality of the medieval past. Henry VIII,
for all his massive dignity and consuming egotism, was strangely
accessible, and his restless and vital personality stamped every facet
of his household. The energy of the man was inexhaustible; at fifty
he kept the court alive with music and masquing, tennis and dancing,

archery and hunting, tournaments and hawking. Possibly some of the brilliance of Henry's early court – which one observer described as glittering with 'jewels and gold and silver, the pomp being unprecedented'[39] – may have become somewhat tarnished by 1539, but to a girl in her teens, both the monarch himself and his royal household must have appeared impressive beyond comparison.

The organization into which Mistress Catherine found her way was a strange and fascinating balance of opposites – an establishment which Erasmus lavishly described as being more a museum of genius than a royal residence, but which also sanctioned spitting on the floor, picking one's teeth in public, and eating with one's fingers. But the most profound dichotomy of all lay in the sumptuous elegance of the decor and the primitive discomforts of life within the gilded cage of the court. It was here in the magnificence of Tudor architecture and the richness and lushness of colour that the parvenu love of the extravagant and ostentatious joined hands with the medieval taste for the vivid and the picturesque. Sixteenth-century art broke out into a riotous profusion of azures, golds, reds and whites. The severe majesty of Gothic Perpendicular was shattered into a myriad of baroque fragments achieving the fairyland quality of a late medieval illumination. In part, this gaudy out pouring of colour and detail was pseudo-classical in form – terracotta medallions of Roman emperors pasted upon Gothic façades – but mostly it was garish ostentation, the luxuriant proof of the ability to pay and the fertility of the human imagination.

Much of the full impact of Tudor pretentiousness has vanished with the weathering and darkening of timber and the fading and flaking of brilliant paints, so that the effect has become one of gloomy panelled chambers and impressive but ill-contrived Gothic Perpendicular. Today, where the eye perceives shapeless shadows, the mind should paint in gilded heraldic beasts, initials entwined with lovers' knots, and armorial emblems. The ornamental and ornate ceilings were once alive with colour, and the papiermâché ribs and pendent balls of Tudor design were painted in gold and blue, the octagonal and lozenge-shaped depressions in the ceilings each enclosing a gaudy escutcheon. Where today stands the grey stone of a heraldic badge or the chipped terracotta of some long-forgotten motto, there were once rich and gilded forms, while whole palaces were ablaze with the vivid colours of Tudor heraldry. Rooms were hung with costly and marvellous tapestries of 'pure gold and fine silk' garnished with pearls and precious stones, and at Hampton Court there were entire suites done in blue and crimson cloth and lush velvets of green, and brown, and yellow.[40] It is hardly surprising that a papal legate remarked that, 'the wealth and civilization of the world are here.'[41] The image that comes to mind is that of the rich fantasy and sensuous extravagance of costume jewellery. Inside and out the aim was the same – exuberant display and primitive hues.

As if to rival the décor, polite society presented a merry dance of noblemen in velvets, prelates in silks, and courtiers in cloth of clashing colours. Slashed doublets with artfully padded shoulders, carefully tapered waists, and extravagant codpieces, were all contrived to enhance the personality, magnify the vanity, and display individuality. 'Whole estates' were worn on courtiers' backs; cloak, doublet, pleated shirt, and hose were cut from the most expensive materials, embroidered with gold, and studded with jewels. Sir Nicholas Vaux's garments were valued at £1,000, and the Duke of Buckingham dressed in a cloak wrought with gold and lined with satin that cost £1,500.[42] The 'excess of apparel' was such that Bishop Skip complained that 'a man cannot well discern a gentleman from a yeoman, a lord from a gentleman, a prince from a lord,' and he warned that more than one young gallant had ended his life in a debtor's prison or dangling from a gibbet for having squandered a fortune on the silly vanity of dress.[43]

In marked contrast to gilded ceilings, costly tapestries and princely attire were stark floors covered with rushes, trestle tables, and wooden benches in the great hall and draughty corners. Chairs were a rarity and reserved for women, who generally preferred to sit on pillows and cushions on the floor. Sanitation at court, in an age that could scarcely conceive of cleanliness rivalling godliness, was on a level with Horsham. The slush bucket continued to be the standard method of disposal, and people were not particular about throwing refuse on the floor. It is not surprising that Cardinal Wolsey, when he ventured either into the lower regions of his own residence or risked the pervasive odours of the streets of London, commonly carried a spice-ball to counteract the stench. In fact, the Cardinal's sense of smell need not have been very acute, since immediately outside the great door of St Paul's was an open urinal which induced one visitor to comment that it gave 'a pleasant odour to the passers-by'![44]

Catherine's world and the society of the court was a strange mixture of richness and squalor, of sumptuousness and primitiveness. Perhaps the final paradox is found in the description of the materials used in the construction of Henry VIII's close-stool. It cost £4, and was covered in black velvet, stuffed with 3 pounds of down for the seat, arms and side, and was held together with 2,000 gilt garnishing nails and 26 'bullion' nails, but no matter how it was decorated, it still remained a chamber-pot.[45]

In an atmosphere of prodigious confusion and magnificent filth, which neither gold nor precious jewels could entirely cloak, and in a society where passions were close to the surface, rigid discipline and brittle ceremony became essential to a well-ordered organization. Both Cardinal Wolsey and Thomas Cromwell endeavoured to introduce into the snarl of the royal household some slight notion of routine, so as to mitigate the laxity and dishonesty that flourished in the rich soil of confusion. They aimed at introducing at least a minimum of restraint that might bridle the violence, wantonness, and dangerous neglect for hygienic principles, within the court.

The officers of the household were strictly commanded to search for strangers at meal-times and for 'rascals and vagabonds' who were constantly creeping into the system and passing themselves off as servants of the Crown.[46] Efforts to achieve a certain degree of economy and system were not limited to denying food and board to those who had no right at court. Strenuous, if not always successful, attempts were made to curb the number of menials who surrounded every person of rank. Labour shortage was still a curse of the future, and every gentleman or nobleman was waited upon by a clamorous throng of hangers-on who endured a hungry existence on the periphery of a great man's following. The desire to keep servants had more to do with prestige than with service, and if the court regulations had not strictly limited the number, the household would have been hopelessly jammed. The allocation was carefully made according to status. The King's councillors, the lord chamberlain, the captain of the guard and the master of the horse, plus the six gentlemen of the privy chamber were each allowed to keep 'one page to attend upon the court so that always he be a gentleman born, well mannered and apparelled, and well conditioned'. Other more lowly-born servants were ordered 'to remain in town or elsewhere out of the court', and sergeants-at-arms, heralds, messengers, minstrels, falconers, and the like were commanded not to bring boys, rascals, or others of their servants into the court, on pain of severe fine and possible expulsion.[47] Likewise the number both of beds and of horses was limited according to title. A duke could claim twenty-four horses and nine beds for his retainers, and an earl could have eighteen horses and seven beds. The gradations were minutely worked out: a dowager duchess could command seven beds, the Queen's maids, three; the master of the jewels, one; the lord chamberlain, seven; and the grooms of the privy chamber were given two between the four of them.[48]

Laxity and simple laziness plagued every branch of the organization, and efforts were made to root out or at least to curb the natural lassitude of mankind. Strict orders were issued that those who had duties to perform should execute them promptly and not delegate them to their servants. The highborn grooms of the privy chamber were ordered to refrain from using their 'pages and servants and other mean persons' to 'make ready the fire, dress and straw the chamber, purging and making clean the same of all manner of filthiness', so that the King's Highness might find the 'chamber pure, clean, wholesome and meet without any displeasant air or thing'. All these tasks were assigned to the grooms of gentle and noble blood, and they were commanded to be in the King's chamber by six and seven in the morning so as to complete their menial duties.

At the same time that the grooms were sweeping and cleaning, the gentlemen of the chamber were to attend to the 'apparel and dress' of the monarch, 'putting on such garments in reverent, discreet, and sober fashion'[49] Fines were levied if the groom-porter failed to collect the remains 'of torches and other wax remaining overnight by nine of the clock in the morrow'. A signing in and out system was introduced for those who attended upon the King's person, so that there would always be the correct number of gentlemen and grooms to minister to Henry's desires. Even the members of the royal council had to be disciplined, and the lord steward, the lord treasurer, and the comptroller were evidently not above playing truant, since they were commanded to be daily 'in the Comptinghouse between the hours of eight and nine in the morning'. Finally the tendency for courtiers to shirk their ceremonial duties and to seek a certain degree of privacy had to be curtailed, for 'sundry noblemen, gentlemen, and others do much delight and use to dine in corners and secret places not repairing to the King's chamber nor hall', and consequently orders were given that all should eat at their allotted dining-places.[50]

Efforts were also made to discourage the chronic dishonesty and peculation which plagued the court. Decrees were issued that the clerks of the greencloth were to:

> View and see that the said meat be served forth wholly and entirely and in due proportion, to such places as it is provided for, without fraud, embezzling or diminution of any part thereof as they will answer to their uttermost perils.

The practice of petty stealing to supplement insufficient wages was almost universal. The yeomen of the pantry were sorely tempted to cut off pieces of bread and sell them back to those in charge of feeding the royal mastiffs, while the ordinances of the household noted that 'the relics and fragments of such meat and drink as daily hath been spent in the King and Queen's chamber and household, have not been duly distributed unto poor folks by way of alms.' Instead, they were 'embezzled and purloined' to the profit of dishonest servants.

In fact, commands had to be given that, when the King ventured forth on progress visiting the houses of his subjects, strict vigilance be observed that 'locks of doors, tables, forms, cupboards, trestles and other implements of household be [not] carried, purloined, and taken away by such servants and others as be lodged in the same houses and places.'[51]

Strict control, in theory at least, was maintained over infection and disease. Greyhounds, mastiffs and hounds were barred from the court, to keep the household 'sweet, wholesome, clean, and well furnished'. The only exception to this regulation was that ladies' spaniels and lap-dogs were sanctioned, since it was thought 'wholesome for a weak stomach to bear such a dog in the bosom'.[52] Likewise, the royal barber was commanded to take:

> Especial regard to the pure and clean keeping of his own person and apparel; using himself always honestly in his conversation, without resorting to the company of vile persons or of misguided women in avoiding such dangers and annoyance, as by that means he might do unto the King's most royal person.

These rudimentary hygienic measures were extended to the kitchen, where the three master-cooks received twenty marks a year to pay the scullery boys, so that they should 'not go naked or in garments of such vileness as they now do, and have been accustomed to do', and should have a place to sleep other than the kitchen hearth. Moreover, sanitary principles were recognized to the extent that the cooks were enjoined to have the kitchens scrubbed and swept twice daily to free them from 'noisome filth'.[53] To what extent these regulations were enforced or observed is difficult to say. Probably the rules remained nominal, considering the natural inertia of any large and tradition-ridden establishment. Brutality, violence, and slovenliness were far too prevalent at all levels of society to be checked merely by a written code of household etiquette. As with the law of the realm, the enforcing agencies were not very effective, and sloth as well as passion and brutality went unpunished.

For those who were inaccurately, if flatteringly, called polite society, there was a more subtle variety of restraint upon passion, viciousness and crudity. It has been said that 'nothing but ceremony, rigid and complicated, will be strong enough to prevent mere nastiness of behaviour.'[54] One might add to this formula that nothing but ceremony was able to curb a society which lacked most of our modern methods of social control, and in which animal instincts of survival were dangerously close to the surface. Rather like some monster lightly chained, cruelty and violence were checked by nothing except the slender constraint of ceremony.

Gentlemen were swift to anger and unrestrained in the use of the dagger. Justice Anthony Sonds on one occasion fell out with Mr Culpeper, while at supper, over the disposition of certain monastic estates. Strong words ensued: Culpeper accused the justice of lying 'like a fool', while Sonds rejoined that Culpeper 'lied like a knave'. Words spoken in anger led to drawn daggers and bloodshed until the two were forcibly separated by friends. The argument was prevented from being settled next morning on Fynnesbery Field only by Mr Anthony Sonds's timely recollection that he was a justice of the peace.[55] It was customary that both master and servant should go armed with dagger and rapier, and nothing was more common than the sight of fighting 'about taking the right or left hand, or the wall, or upon any unpleasing countenance'.[56] Clashing swords furnished daily music in the streets, and men were wont to act first and ask questions afterwards, as when the Duke of Norfolk with twenty retainers attacked and murdered a kinsman of the Duke of Suffolk, over a supposed slight to the Duke's honour.

The code of fair play had few if any rules that might curb a man in anger. Paid assassins were not uncommon, and John Stanhope did not hesitate to attempt the liquidation of his opponent, Sir Charles Cavendish, by overpowering him with twenty professional murderers.[57] The days of private feuds and clan wars had not completely vanished from England's broad and pleasant lands, and the ugly spectre of bloody encounters besmirched society with alarming regularity. One need only contemplate the fate of Marlowe in a Tavern brawl to sense the truth that violence in Renaissance England was regarded 'as a characteristic of greatness'.[58]

The men who strove to tear down whatever obstacles they encountered in the path of their ambitions were insistent upon the importance of conventional formalism and rigid etiquette. Ceremony did two things: it elevated many of the more servile and disagreeable services surrounding the royal person into cherished honours, and it tended to obscure and at times even restrain sordid brutality and offensiveness by encompassing both in a thick veil of pomp and circumstance. The sixteenth century was well aware that 'in pompous ceremonies a secret of government doth much consist.' It was the single check that strong and egotistical men would accept, and it was the one restraint that was capable of raising society out of its Hobbesian state of nasty brutishness.

The degree to which ceremony could mask even the most predatory actions is evidenced in the close encounter that Catherine Howard's cousin experienced with Tudor law. In 1541 Sir Edmund Knyvet had a row on the tennis court with Thomas Clere, a gentleman retainer of the Duke of Norfolk and an old crony of the Earl of Surrey. The quarrel may have had its origins in the mutual distaste existing between Sir Edmund and the Earl, but the immediate brawl probably had to do with sportsmanship, for Sir Edmund administered a resounding punch upon Thomas Clere's nose.[59] This kind of rowdiness was far too common at court, and Henry decreed by statute that offenders should lose their right hand as punishment – a typical example of Tudor belief that the punishment should fit the crime. Sir Edmund was duly tried and sentenced, and the arrangements for the execution fell to the royal surgeon, whose appointed duty it was to supervise the torturing and maiming of State prisoners. Besides the surgeon, other members of the household combined both private and public activities by participating in the proceedings. The sergeant chirurgeon officiated with his surgical equipment; the sergeant of the woodyard was on hand with his mallet and block on which Sir Edmund's hand was placed; the King's master-cook supplied the execution knife; the sergeant farrier, the searing iron; and the sergeant of the poultry, the cock which 'should have his head smitten off upon the same block, and with the same knife'. Finally, the yeoman of the scullery came with coal to heat the searing iron, and the sergeant of the cellar supplied wine, ale, and beer for the occasion. 'Thus every man in his office [was] ready to do the execution.'[60] Sir Edmund pleaded that his left hand be taken, so that his right might continue to do good service for the King. Actually, as the French Ambassador reported, the knight was 'more frightened than hurt' since, at the pleading of Catherine Howard, the sentence at the very moment of execution was stayed and the culprit reprieved.[61]

Eating as well as justice was surrounded by the most intricate and elaborate forms. Each person had his allotted and ceremonial task; the sewer supervised the building of the fire, the clerk of the ewery set the table and issued the towels with which the carver and the panter handled all the food and silver. The assay or tasting of the King's food involved numerous individuals, who handled and nibbled the royal menu with appropriate flourishes and ritual.[62]

The closer to the royal presence, the greater the degree of elaborate ceremony, until one reached the epitome of pompous regulation in the organization of the King's privy chamber. The number of individuals who could claim entrance into the inner sanctum of the royal presence was rigidly limited and defined. The monarch was to be waited upon by six gentlemen, two gentlemen ushers, four grooms, a barber, and a page, all of whom were appointed for 'their good behaviour and qualities', and who diligently attended upon the royal person, doing 'humble, reverent, secret, and lowly service'. The grooms of the chamber were not to 'lay hands upon the royal person or intermeddle with preparing or dressing' the King. This responsibility was the much sought-after task of the gentlemen of the bedchamber, who received the royal clothes at the door of the inner chamber, after they had been carefully warmed before the fire.[63] Later in the reign the size of the entourage about the King was more than doubled to allow these well-born servants a certain degree of relief from their constant vigilance and domestic cares.

Equally intricate was the process by which the royal bed was prepared each morning. Both the straw mattress and the box on the bedstead had to be rolled upon by one of the yeomen of the bedchamber to test it for hidden daggers. On top of the mattress was laid a canvas cover and feather bed, which again was tested for 'treacherous objects'. Finally came embroidered sheets and soft blankets until all was completed except the concluding ceremonial flourish of placing the King's sword at the head of the bed, while each of the four yeomen kissed the places where their hands had touched the royal couch.[64] Even the humble process of supplying the monarch with between-meal snacks was a matter of a complex chain of command, rather like A. A. Milne's monarch who desired a little bit of butter for his bread. It was ordered that:

> In case the King's grace will have bread or drink that one of the gentlemen ushers of the privy chamber shall command one of the grooms of the same to warn the officers of the buttery, pantry and cellar to bring the said bread and drink to the door of the said privy chamber, where one of the ushers taking the assay, shall receive the same bringing it to the cupboard.[65]

In the sixteenth century, kings had to be blessed with endless patience if they desired anything to eat.

Such elaborate routine kept a host of unnecessary hands industrious, but its essential function was to create a mysterious and splendid atmosphere of pomp and elegance about the sovereign, and to supply a degree of dignity and discipline to an otherwise uninhibited society. Those may have been 'but painted days, only for show',[66] but the paint was nevertheless necessary. As cosmetics and perfumes are not a substitute for cleanliness but make the consequence of foulness less noxious, so ceremony did not prevent disorder, filth and violence, but it did at least limit and restrain them. The intent was not unlike the objective of Tudor gardens – the imposing of human determination upon the wild vitality of nature. Here in the Tudor garden, medieval delight in the exotic, *nouveau riche* bad taste, and the Renaissance desire to make nature conform to the will of man, united to produce a riot of artfully contrived and 'marvellous beasts as lions, dragons' and other heraldic fantasies.

Human imagination and ingenuity knew no bounds, and the landscape was festooned with garlanded creations of Tudor whites, reds and greens.[67] The design had not yet attained the mathematical perfection of seventeenth-century clipped hedges and paths laid out with geometric precision, but the execution, though crude, was the same – the effort to impose humanity's will upon the confusion and violence of nature in the same way that the prodigious magnificence of flamboyant and elaborate ceremony imposed restraints upon the violence and bestiality of man's nature and instincts.

Life at court and in the city was harsh and dangerous, yet Catherine accepted the brutality of law, the callousness of ethics, and the extremism and violence of society for what they were part of the normal fabric of life. Catherine herself could be both cruel and generous, coarse and charming, meek and arrogant, with no thought of inconsistency. Reflecting every facet of society, her emotions were unbridled, and she moved easily from the frenzied bitterness of remorse and self-criticism into ecstasies of reckless love and heedless passion. If she was proud and indifferent to the suffering of others, if she frantically endeavoured to compress into a single moment the pleasures of an entire life, then she did no more than the rest of society that lived on the brink of destruction.

CHAPTER 5

RIVAL QUEENS

The moment Catherine Howard was rowed across the Thames to take up residence at the court at Westminster, she found herself in a hornet's nest of political, religious and personal intrigue. The activities of statesmen, the designs of sovereigns, and the fond fancies of preachers were all converging upon a crisis that marked the conclusion of the first stage of the English revolution in religion. Upon the broad chessboard of domestic and international events, bishops were donning mitre and cassock in readiness for a religious sweep, knights were preparing their nimble-footed political leaps, and kings were ponderously planning their devious designs. Only the red and black queens were missing from the board, and the two ladies put in their appearance in December of 1539, when the Lady Anne of Cleves stepped ashore at Deal Castle and Mistress Catherine Howard won her heart's desire by receiving an appointment at court.

Each side marshalled its forces; the black of instinctive conservatism in religion and feudal inclination in politics stood arrayed against the red of spiritual and political revolution. The most powerful man under the monarch, the King's Vicar-General in matters spiritual, Thomas Cromwell, faced that polished prelate and consummate manipulator of men and words, Stephen Gardiner, Bishop of Winchester, and his temporal, if less able, confrére, Thomas Howard, third Duke of Norfolk. The concluding months of 1539 found the two sides relatively balanced. The parry of reform and revolution rejoiced that the princess of Cleves was journeying to London to consummate the alliance of schismatic England with Protestant Germany and become Henry's fourth wife in six years. The conservatives, on the other hand, continued to control a majority of spiritual and temporal lords within the house of peers, and they had not entirely given up the hope of influencing their susceptible sovereign by means of feminine guile. The absence of a black queen, it was true, constituted a serious handicap, but as yet the red queen of Cleves was an untried quantity, known in England only by her highly flattering Holbein portrait. The precedent for replacing queens had already been established, and it was no idle dream that some Agile and comely pawn might be transformed overnight into royalty by the magic of the King's affection.

Just exactly when Catherine was selected by the conservative party for such a role is not known. It could not have been when she first arrived at court in late November or early December of 1539, for as yet no one suspected that Henry would evidence such a positive distaste for his new bride that he would risk political and international crisis to free himself. There is some indication that Catherine's fate was irrevocably written the instant Henry laid eyes upon her, for it was reported to the Dowager Duchess at Lambeth that the 'King's Highness did cast a fantasy to Catherine Howard the first time that ever his Grace saw her.'[1] If the Dowager was so apprised, one can feel assured that those two astute and well-informed gentlemen, the Duke of Norfolk and the Bishop of Winchester, also knew of this important and hopeful event and planned their strategy accordingly. The first positive indication that the King's conscience had again crept too near another lady of the court, appeared in April of 1540, when Mistress Catherine became the recipient of a steady flow of royal gifts and favours.

If the sequence of events leading to the political crisis of 1540 did not necessarily begin when the King's Highness first 'cast a fantasy to Catherine Howard', it might be said that it did so when he first beheld the other lady. The German princess of Cleves had landed at Deal Castle on Saturday, 27 December 1539, and her official welcome by the King was scheduled for 3 January at Greenwich. Henry, with his accustomed impatience and impetuousness, could not wait to judge the words of his Vicar-General, who had assured him that his future wife excelled the Duchess of Milan in beauty as 'the golden sun did the silver moon'.[2] Disguised and laden with gifts, he waylaid his bride at Rochester and dumbfounded the conventional-minded Flemish maiden by prancing unannounced into her tent. The meeting, even under the most auspicious circumstances, was likely to have been strained, for Anne knew no tongue but her own and Henry spoke no German. Linguistic difficulties only in part caused the King's tongue-tied silence, for it was reported that his grace was 'marvellously astonished and abashed' by the sight of his new bride; and later Henry growled that the lady was 'nothing so well as she was spoken of'.[3]

The thunderhead of the storm that cost Thomas Cromwell his head, lost Anne of Cleves her regal dignity, and swept Norfolk and Gardiner into political pre-eminence in the wake of the King's marriage to Catherine, had begun to form many months before the fateful meeting with Anne at Rochester. The twenty embarrassed and hurried words that the King managed to blurt out, and his hasty retreat in the face of the lady's phlegmatic and pockmarked features, were only the signal for the storm to break. The instant that Henry 'very sadly and pensively' fled back to Greenwich and complained that he was not well handled by his councillors,[4] the man who had been responsible for the fiasco walked in the shadow of the block. The cruel and reproachful eye of an unhappy and embarrassed sovereign was constantly upon the Vicar-General, and Cromwell's enemies took new hope that the King's emotional disappointment and brooding disposition would bring about the eventual destruction of the hated upstart. Their fondest hopes were realized in July of 1540 when Henry claimed his Vicar-General's head, but the political convulsions that led to Cromwell's death had their roots back in the reaches of Tudor history. The scheming and manoeuvring of the early summer of 1540 represented the culmination of three quite

Previous page and above: 1. and 2. Henry VIII and Catherine Howard as depicted in the Window of King Solomon and the Queen of Sheba, King's College Chapel. There is no authenticated likeness of Catherine. The only statement that can be made with any degree of certainty about Catherine's birth is that she was one of the youngest children of a family of ten, and that she was born before 1525, most probably in 1521.

Left and opposite page: 3. and 4. Portraits of Henry in later life, when he had become very overweight.

Sixteenth-century London as Catherine would have known it. The panoramas are from *Anthony Van den Wyngaerde's Panorama of London, Westminster and Southwark*, produced in 1544. Where Catherine was born and reared is still a total mystery. Some sources indicate London, others suggest the Howard residence at Lambeth, while still others favour Oxenheath in Kent, the home of Catherine's maternal uncle, William Cotton. The only really authenticated fact is that Catherine spent her childhood with her step-grandmother, the Dowager Duchess of Norfolk, who divided her time between her estates at Horsham in Sussex, and the Howard suburban residence at Lambeth.

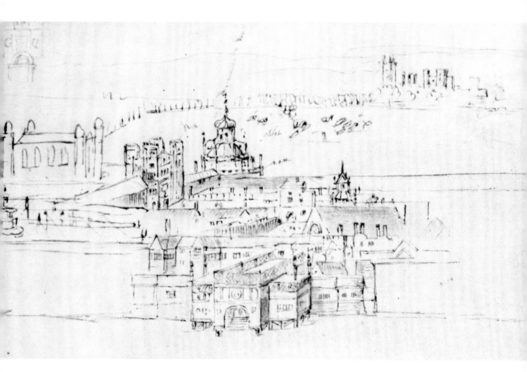

5. The Palace of Whitehall.

Opposite: 6. and 7. London Bridge where the heads of Catherine's lovers, Francis Dereham and Thomas Culpeper, were impaled on spikes following their execution.

8. and 9. Old St Paul's Cathedral.

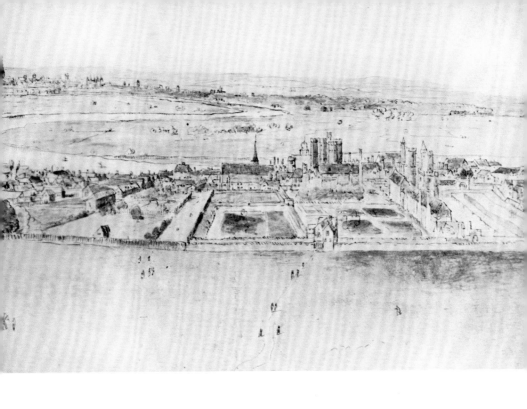

10. and 11. Greenwich Palace.

Above: 12. Westminster.

Below: 13. Richmond Palace.

Opposite page: 14. Henry VIII in Council.

King Henry the eyght.

ANA BOLINA   ANG · RECIN

16. Thomas Howard, the Third Duke of Norfolk, the ambitious uncle of both Anne Boleyn and Catherine. He encouraged Henry's courtship of his niece, Catherine, in spite of her unsuitability for the role of queen.

Opposite: 15. Anne Boleyn was Catherine's cousin.

17. The Red Queen, Anne of Cleves.

18. The most widely used portrait of Catherine but not an authenticated likeness of her.

19. It fell to Archbishop Thomas Cranmer to inform Henry of his young wife's adultery.

Below: 20. At Hampton Court there is what is described as the 'haunted gallery', which adjoins the Queen's chambers and Henry's chapel. It is there that Catherine is said to have eluded her guards, and sought out her husband, who was hearing Mass. Just as she reached the door, she was seized and forced back to her chambers, while her screams resounded up and down the gallery. This presumably is the explanation of the female form, dressed in traditional white, which drifts down the gallery to the door of the chapel, and then hurries back, 'a ghastly look of despair' upon its face and uttering 'the most unearthly shrieks', until the phantom disappears through the chamber door at the end of the gallery.

This page and following: 21., 22. and 23. Catherine passed through Traitors Gate on 10 February 1542 and on to her short stay at the Tower of London.

Above and following page: 24. and 25. The Chapel of St Peter ad Vincula and the site of the scaffold on Tower Green, where Catherine was beheaded by a single axe blow on Monday 13 February 1542. She was later buried in the Chapel.

separate but intimately related crises in religion, in foreign policy, and in personalities; and Catherine Howard found herself hopelessly enmeshed in all three.

The term Reformation is at best a deceptive word. In England it is a singularly inaccurate description for the religious upheaval that took place when Henry's tender conscience was strained beyond endurance by the fascination of Anne Boleyn and by his failure to beget a male heir by his first wife, Catherine of Aragon. Little was reformed by the English Reformation under Henry VIII, but much was transferred; the temporal authority of the Pope in Rome was assumed by the King in London; much of the spiritual power claimed by the vicar of Christ was shouldered by God's anointed lieutenant on earth; and the monastic lands were turned over to a national aristocracy. As one disillusioned and embittered Lutheran complained: 'Harry only wants to sit as anti-christ in the temple of God, and that Harry should be Pope. The rich treasures, the rich incomes of the Church, these are the Gospel According to Harry.'[5]

The Reformation in England was never the work of a single will. The seizure of the ecclesiastical machinery in England, the denial of papal supremacy, and the destruction of an independent clerical organization were in a sense the culmination of the main currents of English and Western European history. The eighth Henry achieved what the second had failed to do – the subjugation of an international priestly order that recognized an authority beyond and above that of the national monarch. The Pope was a foreigner living in dissolute luxury in Rome, and Englishmen had for centuries resented the jurisdiction and financial extractions of an alien potentate. The Tudor sovereigns were dedicated to the destruction of any supremacy outside their own, and as the feudal magnates of the northern shires ended their lives upon the scaffold, so did those abbots and bishops who acknowledged a law higher than that of the Crown. They died upon the altar of the sovereign national state that recognizes no power on earth except its own.

Whether or not momentous events are the result of inevitable forces that underlie the sweep of history, or simply further evidence of the infuriating perversity of human destiny that can transform the loss of a horseshoe into the loss of a kingdom, the indisputable fact remains that the English Reformation was an act of State. What began, however, simply as an extra-legal manipulation of the constitutional structure governing a cosmopolitan Church with its head in Rome, rapidly involved the entire fabric of Tudor society. The royal divorce quickly became a social, economic, and emotional revolution in which far more was at stake than mere political expediency. Henry VIII did not have to be told the truth of one confirmed Protestant's warning that 'if there be no better stay for the maintenance of these godly preachers, the King's authority concerning his supremacy shall lie post alone, hidden in the act of parliament, and not in the hearts of his subjects.'[6] It was far safer if political necessity could be linked with religious conviction, and consequently the State found and fostered the support of that militant minority, which was confident that Mistress Rose of Rome was in fact the 'stinking whore of Babylon' and looked upon the Reformation as not only politically wise but spiritually just and godly.

The English Reformation may have received its characteristic features from the fact that its driving force was political and governmental rather than religious and emotional, but it is a tragic misconception to view the events in England of the 1530s as separate from the spiritual crisis that was convulsing all Christendom. When in 1555 Hugh Latimer turned to Nicholas Ridley, as both stood chained to the stake, and said: 'Be of good comfort, Master Ridley, and play the man. We shall this day light such a candle, by God's grace, in England, as I trust shall never be put out,'[7] the defrocked Anglican bishop was speaking the simple truth. It was not Henry's 'great matter', not the need for a male heir, nor the fact that the Pope was un-English, that kept the candle burning and gave the Protestant martyrs the strength to 'play the man'; it was the conviction and discovery that in Protestantism they had something worth the torments of the Stake – a sense of spiritual satisfaction and personal salvation.

The faith that moved these Protestants was deep and esoteric; it glowed with the intense flame of inner conviction, which alone was sufficient to sustain them. They needed none of the props which the medieval Church had afforded the average man, and they were impervious to the beauty of religious ceremony or the magnificence of stained glass windows. There could be no mediator between the faithful and the Divinity other than Christ himself, for it was faith and faith alone that could open the gates to the kingdom of heaven. It was this profound belief – this passionate insistence that they alone in a depraved and sinful world were the elect of God – that gave to the reforming Protestant divines the determination not merely to deny papal authority, but to spiritualize the world and to create on earth the standards of heaven. It was not enough simply to denounce the Bishop of Rome and abhor idolatry and superstition; the man who sought the joys of the afterlife on the sands of such insincerity was told to 'depart in the devil's name, thou wicked person, to eternal pain'.[8] No excuses could be made for the busy citizen who complained that 'I am busied about matters of the common-wealth', or who argued that it was not for him to read and study the scriptures.[9]

Uncompromising in their morality, destructive in their determination to improve both men and society, and rigid in their idealism, the Protestant radicals became invaluable storm-troopers in the army of the Lord's anointed. For them, the divorce and constitutional break with Rome were merely first steps – a prelude to the future community of saints on earth. They saw the existing Church as deformed and debased, a harlot grovelling in the lust of the flesh and in the pride of life – a mockery saddled with sumptuous and unbelieving prelates, idolatrous ceremonies, fornicating clerics, and the Devil's disciple presiding in Rome. It was not enough that the strange voice of the Bishop of Rome be silenced in England; instead the Church of England had to be thoroughly revised and revitalized, and the cry went up to 'get rid of the poison with the author'. 'Our King,' lamented Bishop Hooper, 'has destroyed the Pope, but not popery.'[10] Henry's divorce had loosed upon the realm a force that would not be controlled, and the inner spiritual drive that belonged to Protestantism did not always sit easy with the cautious doctrines of political expediency and constitutional manipulation. Men who felt close upon them the fires of hell and the joys of salvation turned their eyes heavenward, not earthward; they felt obliged to control life, not countenance it. The militant soldiers of the Protestant ranks were the useful, if unruly, revolutionaries of their age and the godly, if dangerous, allies of the Crown.

Political advisability stood behind the original break with Rome and the advent of the Reformation in England, but by 1539 the forces of carefully controlled religious change were evincing an alarming tendency to deteriorate into unrestrained revolution. As one contemporary Catholic put it: Henry 'was like to one that would throw down a man headlong from the top of a high tower and bid him stay when he was half way down.'[11] The King remained the Defender of the Faith, and for him the faith continued to be the ancient creed – with the slight modification that it was Catholicism without the Pope. Unfortunately, by the late 1530s such a middle position was becoming increasingly difficult to maintain, for the monarch, in consolidating his constitutional revolution, had placed the safety of the new regime in the hands of individuals who had no intention of stopping half-way.

Religious discord was rife – all was either 'as black as pitch, vice, abomination, heresy, and folly' or 'all fair roses and sweet virtue'.[12] The King's 'simple loving subjects' were 'arrogantly and superstitiously' arguing and disputing 'in open places, taverns, and ale houses' upon spiritual topics and theological questions.[13] On all sides there were tactless, if sincere, ministers of God who were voicing new and disturbing notions; and it was noted in London that the city was teeming with preachers, 'but they come not from one Master, for, as it is reported, their messages be divers.'[14] When one impassioned reformer and idealist could suggest that the gospel be read and set forth in all places 'even in brothels', while an equally stern advocate of the old faith could preach that he 'would like to see the head of every maintainer of the New Learning upon a stake', there was little doubt that the time for a positive and official statement of religious faith had arrived.[15] The only question that remained was whether conformity of mind would be enforced upon the basis of a Catholic or a Protestant interpretation of the Christian faith.

Religious sentiment at court and in the King's own mind during 1539 was beginning to swing in the direction of retrenchment and orthodoxy, and the Norfolk-Gardiner faction was optimistic that uniformity of religious thought would be decided once and for all on the basis of Catholicism without the Pope. On 5 May, 1539, Henry's government served notice that dissension in religion had gone far enough! The Lord Chancellor warned the two houses of Parliament that His Majesty desired, 'above all things that diversities of religious opinions should be entirely rooted out and destroyed with all dispatch from his dominions'.[16] An ecclesiastical committee of the upper house was selected to inquire into the nature of religious discord, and to suggest some basis for banishing contention from the realm. If the royal council thought that such a committee would produce the desired unanimity of sentiment, it was sadly mistaken, because the members were evenly divided between the advocates of the new and old learning. Within eleven days they had battled to a hopeless deadlock, and so great was the tension that society was put in mind of Erasmus's words that, 'to all appearance the long war of words and writings will terminate in blows.'[17]

Then on 16 May, the secular authority stepped in to end the religious stalemate. Significantly, it was Thomas, Duke of Norfolk, who suggested that the issue be introduced for debate upon the floor of the House of Lords and the decision be enforced by parliamentary statute. In other words, for the first time the temporal authority was accepting responsibility for both enforcing and prescribing religious conformity. The King himself listened to the debate, and, finally, on 28 June, the Act for Abolishing Diversity of Opinion was passed by a unanimous vote representing little except that the monarch had thrown his influence behind the Bill. The Whip with the Six Strings, as the Bill was popularly termed, re-avowed basic Catholic doctrines such as transubstantiation, communion in one kind, celibacy of the clergy, private masses and auricular confession. All these points had been a source of endless controversy, and they were now decided in a markedly Catholic fashion. The nation was vastly impressed by the spectacle of its sovereign displaying his theological talents and assuming his responsibilities as Defender of the Faith, and most men agreed with John Hussey that the Bill was the 'wholesomest Act ever passed.'[18]

Though the conservatives had won a resounding victory, ultimate success in the form of the destruction of the Vicar-General and his disciples had to wait upon the coming of Catherine Howard to court and Cromwell's diplomatic blunder that saddled Henry with the German princess of Cleves.

During the summer and autumn of 1539, diplomatic considerations began to cloud the clarity of the theological atmosphere. Six powers faced one another; each claimed the special sanction of the deity in support of its cause, but none of the six ever allowed religion to stand in the way of political self-interest. The Sultan of Turkey was Caliph of the True Believers; Charles V was Emperor of the Holy Roman Empire and His Most Catholic Majesty of Spain; England's sovereign proudly displayed his theological title of Defender of the Faith; Francis I was the Most Christian King of France; and the Pope laid claim to the keys of the kingdom of heaven as Christ's vicar on earth. International relations in the sixteenth century have an Alice-in-Wonderland quality about them. Chivalric monarchs shed endless tears, but continued their predatory policies of national and political aggrandizement; France and Spain maintained a noisy but singularly inconsequential battle for the mastery of Italy; and the Poe, that elderly white knight, was constantly falling off one side or the other of his horse, and being stuck together with bits of wire so that he might continue at the doubtful game of the balance of power in Europe. The international kaleidoscope was constantly changing, but, as Alice discovered, the more things changed, the more they remained the same.

English diplomacy of the 1530s was based upon what were accepted as the three constants of European relations. Primary among the principles of Tudor diplomacy was the rivalry between the vast Habsburg possessions – united in the person of Emperor Charles V

– and Valois France – personified by Francis I, that elegant sovereign with the fine calf to his leg. An equally important consideration was the embarrassment caused by Henry's divorce from his first wife and his consequent break with the Apostolic See. Finally, no English foreign policy reckoned without the time-honoured conflict between England and France. The first consideration could be depended upon to keep France and the Emperor at odds, while England held the crucial balance; the second might be expected to guarantee the enmity of both the Emperor, who was Catherine of Aragon's nephew, and of the papacy, whose dearest desire was to lead a united Habsburg-Valois force against the English heretics. As for the English-French rivalry, this was a sacred axiom of international relations, treasured almost to the point of insanity, since no one could recall or even conceive of a time when the two nations had not been snarling at each other. Thus the international tangle was predicated upon the *sine qua non* that both Charles and Francis disliked their brother Henry, but detested each other even more.

In the spring and early summer of 1538 the impossible happned – Charles began to betray signs of ultimate lunacy by indicating a willingness to accept an invitation extended by his rival brother of France, to pay a State visit to Paris. More incredible still, the Emperor was planning to place the safety of his imperial person in the hands of his traditional enemy, with no greater warranty of protection than Francis's chivalric word of honour. For an instant it appeared as if the two states would submerge their own enmity in a holy alliance aimed at exterminating the heretical menace across the Channel. As a further blow to English safety, the sovereigns of France and Spain in January of 1539 agreed to make no new alliances with the anathematized English without each other's consent. Isolated and alarmed by the possibility of a Catholic crusade, Henry suddenly found himself anxious to win the friendship of the other Protestant princes of Europe, and in March of 1539 Cromwell commenced negotiations for the hand of the daughter of the Duke of Cleves.

The marriage treaty, which was eventually signed on 4 October 1539, was a disastrous blunder. From the start, Henry showed signs of being a reluctant groom; he disliked the thought of committing himself to a lady upon whom he had never set eyes; and he could not bring himself to believe that those two Christian monarchs of Spain and France would ever unite against either the heretic or the infidel. It soon became obvious that the King had allowed himself to be panicked into an alliance, which had no observable merits except to encumber him with an unattractive wife, whose sole accomplishment was to grunt in German. In fact, the entire marriage alliance retained the usual Alice-in-Wonderland atmosphere – it never made any sense. Had the papacy really been able to patch up the ancient feud between Habsburg and Valois and direct their united forces against England, Cromwell's alliance with the Protestant powers of Europe would have been almost worthless. As one astute observer of these times noted:

> These three, the bishop of Rome, the French King, and the Emperor, be all one, and the King of Scots is the French King's man; and so we be left alone, and nobody with us but these Germans, a sort of beggarly knaves, and they are able to do nothing.

Finally, to cap the diplomatic blunder, it quickly became manifest that the much-heralded meeting between Charles and Francis in Paris when it actually took place in January of 1540 was a brittle, if sumptuous, display of chivalric posing and lavish courtesy, and Henry was gratified to discover that each side continued the tricky and damnable game of negotiation with the English heretics.

Henry had good reason to be unhappy in the spring of 1540, and the ranks of the conservative opposition were confidently anticipating the fruits of the royal discomfort, for the King's matrimonial disappointments had a peculiar tendency to coincide with political, social and religious change. Thomas Cromwell had risen in the royal estimation because he alone had been able to offer a means of marrying Anne Boleyn and divorcing Catherine of Aragon. That method had been the daring and successful policy of a break with Rome and the settlement of the divorce in an English court in defiance of the Catholic world. It now remained to be seen whether the Vicar-General could ride out another matrimonial storm and offer his sovereign escape from the marital yoke imposed by the alliance with Protestant Germany. The moment the King's shocked sensibilities had recovered from the sight of his bride, violent and unpredictable change both in ministers and policy was almost inevitable. The only question now concerned the nature of that change, and whose head would fly – Cromwell's, or Norfolk and Gardiner's?

Francis Bacon once remarked that Elizabeth's guiding principle in government was that matters of conscience, 'when they exceed their bounds and grow to be matter of faction, lose their nature'.[20] Whether it is worse to murder and intrigue in the name of factional hatred or of idealistic principle, is a debatable point, but the situation in the winter of 1539-40 was following Bacon's prescription – personal rivalry and the strife of personalities were beginning to outweigh both religious and diplomatic considerations. The aim of each faction was not so much a godly policy in religion, but simply the destruction of certain key individuals.

First, there was 'busy Gardiner', the wily Bishop of Winchester, 'the wittiest, boldest, and best learned of his faculty'.[21] Choleric and touchy, so unmanageable that only Henry's iron will and strong hand could curb him, and possibly a better Englishman than a Christian, the Bishop was the brains of the conservative forces. Winchester's opposite number and persistent rival was Thomas Cromwell, Lord Privy Seal and Vicar-General in matters spiritual. Both men were lawyers by instinct and training, both had the saving grace of humour and both could be terrifyingly ruthless, but here the similarity ceases.

There is something almost satanic about the King's chief minister, whose origins and education included soldiering, the law, moneylending, trading and the civil service. While Stephen Gardiner often gibbered with rage and blundered simply through exasperation, Cromwell never seemed to do anything without a calculated reason. His anger may at times have been real, but more often it was feigned. His ruthlessness was strangely impartial – he destroyed, but rarely hated his victims. Possibly this was why he was feared and detested by his contemporaries, for somehow Thomas Cromwell never seemed to have expressed the proper human emotions. He was far too impervious; he was immune to insults because he never made a pretence at being a gentleman; he was coldly tolerant, if only because he felt no passion. Outwardly bland and imperturbable, he ruled by the sheer force of his intelligence. For his own society he remained an enigma, and one baffled critic shook his head and said that for himself he would not be in Cromwell's shoes, 'for all that ever he hath, for the King beknaveth him twice a week, and sometimes knocks him well about the pate; and yet when he hath been well pummelled about the head', the Vicar-General would enter the great chamber 'shaking off the bush with as merry a countenance as though he might rule all the roost.'[22] Looking more like a pub-keeper than a minister of state, the man harboured a massive pride, and the agility and brilliance of his mind made him more than a match for wily Winchester. When the great oak finally fell, it was almost as though it crashed before the gale of historic necessity rather than to the ineffectual chopping of the Bishop's axe.

Behind each individual, Tudor society aligned itself. Norfolk, cunning and mercurial, was Gardiner's ally in favouring conservatism in religion, a pro-French policy in diplomacy, and an intense distaste for the hated Cromwell. If Gardiner supplied the brains and the pen of the conservative position, Thomas Howard lent it his sword and his brawn. Unpopular but indispensable, the Duke was a necessary evil, since Norfolk alone was able to supply the means of crushing rebellious subjects and curbing the unpredictable Scots. Norfolk was neither intelligent nor strong enough to be a serious threat to the Vicar-General, who allowed him to retain his rather uncomfortable seat upon the King's Council. In the conservative fold was also Cuthbert Tunstal, the venerable and affable Bishop of Durham, whose 'stillness, soberness, and subtlety'[23] won him the respect of both sides, and earned him a permanent place among Henry's closest advisers.

Of the opposite opinion was Thomas Cranmer, Archbishop of Canterbury and spiritual foster-father of the Reformation in England.

Pliable and naive, one of the few men for whom Henry ever felt real affection, and imbued with a quiet common sense and a divine gift for translating enduring ideas into the magic and majesty of the English language, Cranmer was helpless without the political acumen of Thomas Cromwell. More Christian than Winchester – deep down perhaps stronger than any of his colleagues or rivals – the Archbishop is of more ultimate importance than any of them, but in the crisis of 1540 he played a minor role, viewing what happened with something of the shocked astonishment of the child.

The struggle between personalities had been going on for years, but the crisis was reached in the late autumn of 1539 when Cromwell achieved the dismissal from the privy council of his two old enemies, the Bishops of Winchester and Chichester.

Behind the scenes, idle tongues were gossiping, rumours of promised change were being whispered abroad, and Cromwell's position, though strong on the surface, was slowly but surely being weakened. During the same autumn there were persistent hints that Cromwell was out of favour, and that Tunstal, Bishop of Durham, might replace him as the King's chief minister. Moreover, there was mounting hatred of the Vicar-General himself. As the instrument of a sovereign who could commit no wrong, the Lord Privy Seal was the whipping-boy for everyone who disliked his prince's doings. He was detested as a social climber, as a Protestant, as the scourge of the great abbeys and monasteries, and, above all, as a successful politician who controlled the good things of political life. Though Cromwell more often than not spoke for his master and not himself, he alone won the hatred inspired by Henry's rough and tactless policies. The situation was summed up by the French Ambassador when he reported in April of 1540 that should the Vicar-General remain in power, it would only be because 'he does nothing without first consulting the King.'[24]

In the meantime, Stephen Gardiner was not inactive. He also was developing his openings, countering his opponents' moves, pushing forward his own pawns, and endeavouring to undermine the Vicar-General's grasp of the political situation. In this he was immeasurably helped by the fiasco surrounding the King's fourth marriage. From the start the nuptials were unsuccessful. When the German princess arrived at Greenwich, Cromwell inquired of his sovereign how he liked his new bride, and Henry answered sharply, saying that 'she is nothing fair.' The Lord Privy Seal desperately endeavoured to point out to the King the bright side of the predicament and optimistically said: 'By my faith, you say truth, but me thinketh she hath a queenly manner withal.'[25] To this, Henry magnanimously agreed, but it shortly became obvious that he wanted a pretty wife and not a regal queen. The King snatched like a drowning man at the hope that perhaps Anne was legally incapable of marriage since she had been precontracted to the son of the Duke of Lorraine; and, when he learned that this constituted no barrier to his wedding, he grimly told Cromwell that he was 'not well handled'.

Neither the Lord Privy Seal nor any other member of the council could think of a way by which the King might escape the consequences of Cromwell's foreign policy, and pathetically Henry pleaded: 'Is there none other remedy but that I must needs, against my will, put my neck in the yoke?'[26] He sighed over the sad lot of monarchs who must wed for duty and not for love, and announced that he would marry the lady only because honour and duty demanded it. Henry and Anne were wed on Monday 6 January, and the next morning Cromwell hopefully trotted round to find out the result of a night in the connubial bed. The experience was not to Henry's taste, and he growled that he liked her worse than ever, 'for by her breasts and belly she should be no maid; which, when I felt them, struck me so to the heart that I had neither will nor courage to prove the rest.'[27] This was to be the monarch's position ever afterwards – that 'if she brought maidenhead with her', he never 'took any from her by true carnal copulation. Whether the world believed it or not, this was Henry's 'true and perfect declaration'.[28]

Cromwell was sufficiently alarmed by the course of events to try to shift the blame to the Earl of Southampton. That nobleman had escorted the Lady of Cleves from her barbarian homeland to England, and presumably should have noted that Anne was plain and not to the King's fancy. Southampton, not unreasonably, argued that he had been commissioned to accompany the princess to London, not to pass judgment on her beauty or lack thereof. Nor were the Vicar-General's fears allayed with time, for the King's complaints increased as the winter wore on, and in April 'he lamented his fate that he should never have any more children if he continued, declaring that before God he thought she was not his lawful wife.'[29] The ghosts of Catherine of Aragon and Anne Boleyn must have smiled at such words, for here was history repeating itself with almost ludicrous exactness. Again Henry's tender conscience was doubting the legality of his marriage; again he was justifying his actions in terms of an heir to the throne; and again his conscience had 'crept too near another lady' of the court, for by April the King's interest in one of the Queen's maids of honour was public knowledge. There is little doubt that Norfolk and Gardiner assiduously fanned the flame of Henry's lust in the hope that Catherine Howard might not only replace the red queen of Cleves, but also encompass the destruction of the King's Vicar-General.

Suddenly Mistress Catherine began to appear in more sumptuous garments; the Dowager Duchess gave advice on 'how to behave' and 'in what sort to entertain the King's Highness and how often';[30] and the Duchess's house at Lambeth was thrown open to the King. The entire Howard clan was at pains to 'commend and praise Catherine for her pure and honest condition',[31] while Gardiner was no less busy making his sovereign welcome at Winchester House, where Catherine and her royal lover were feasted and entertained by the hospitable ecclesiastic. By June of 1540 the citizens of London were commenting upon the frequency of Henry's daytime and midnight visits to Lambeth. Observers, however, misinterpreted the facts and concluded that these excusions across the river augured adultery, not divorce.[32] The King's loyal and interested subjects had forgotten that 'when this King decides on anything he goes the whole length.'[33]

From every side evidence of the Vicar-General's insecurity was mounting. Norfolk returned in February from a brief mission to France with words from Francis that augured ill for Cromwell. The

French monarch had suggested to the Duke that the removal of that 'wicked and unhappy instrument' would 'tranquillize the kingdom' and solve most of Henry's international difficulties.[34] A month later, in March, Cromwell went so far as to conciliate his rival, and over dinner he and Gardiner 'opened their hearts' to each other and pledged that 'not only all displeasures' should be forgotten, but also that henceforth they would 'be perfect entire friends'.[35] In April it was murmured abroad that 'Cromwell is tottering' and that the Bishops of Winchester, Durham, and Bath were all back on the council despite the opposition of the Lord Privy Seal. In fact, the situation was so serious that some time during these crucial months, Cromwell began to think in terms of flight, for he asked the German traveller, Hubertus Leodius, whether his prince had 'any castles or offices to sell or lease'. The Vicar-General then presented Leodius with a silver cup for his wife, so that 'she might be able to recognize him if ever he came to Germany and he were to refer to the said cup'. The Lord Privy Seal at this time was the picture of a man living under an unbearable strain and the shadow of the block. The German observer noted that he, 'walked with me through the gardens or galleries, for the most part sunk in thought', and he would 'stand still from time to time, as if he were about to say something but did not quite dare to do so'.[36]

The end came in May and June when the Vicar-General wrote Richard Pate that, 'the whole of Christendom hangs in the balance.'[37] On 10 April the French Ambassador had confidently written that, 'there will be seen in the country a great change in many things; which this King begins to make in his ministers, recalling those he had rejected and degrading those he had raised.'[38] A week later Marillac was forced to reverse his opinion, for all expectations were confounded by the elevation of Cromwell to the earldom of Essex. Then in rapid succession followed a series of Cromwellian triumphs. On 19 May Lord Lisle, the King's deputy in Calais and the bastard son of Edward IV, was sent to the Tower post-haste, charged with treasonable designs to turn the city of Calais over to the papal forces. No one, concluded the French

Ambassador, expects him to escape, 'unless by a miracle.'[39] On all sides conservative pawns continued to be swept aside by the Vicar-General's offensive, and by 1 June, Marillac was reporting that 'things are brought to such a pass that either Cromwell's party or that of the bishop of Winchester must succumb', and he thought that 'things seem to incline to Cromwell's side.'[40]

The exasperated Frenchman, who concluded that English politics were beyond Gallic logic – 'so great is the inconstancy of the English' – was in for yet another surprise when Richard Sampson, Bishop of Chichester and Dean of St Paul's, 'with all solenmity' was elevated to the new bishopric of Westminster on 30 May, and then 'two hours later was led to the Tower as accused of treason'. The unfortunate clergyman remained, 'with life only, which he shall lose immediately according to the usual penalty decreed to high treason, as horrible to tell as frightful to see.'[41] Even Sampson's ecclesiastical mule was confiscated to the Duke of Suffolk. No one doubted that the Bishop of Chichester had become the hapless victim of the duel between Gardiner and Cromwell, and it was reliably reported that the Vicar-General had a little list of five other bishops deserving the same fate. Presumably Gardiner and Tunstal stood high on the roster, and the imprisonment of Sampson and the nomination of Thomas Thirlby as Cromwell's selection to the See of Westminster, were merely the Lord Privy Seal's preliminary attack upon wily Winchester.[42]

Marillac was in for still a final shock. Ten days after the successful attack on Sampson, Cromwell himself was carried off, a prisoner to the Tower; eighteen days later the Vicar-General was executed. Cromwell's successes had been only on the surface. On 6 May he confided to his friend and disciple, Thomas Wriothesley, that no matter what he did, one problem continued to plague him – 'The King liketh not the Queen.' Wriothesley was 'right sorry that his Majesty should be so troubled' and suggested that the Lord Privy Seal should 'devise how his Grace may be relieved by one way or another'. Cromwell simply murmured in reply: 'Yea [but] how?'[43] During all the moves and counter-moves, the checks and counter-checks, the desperate fact remained that the Vicar-General had been unable to strike at Gardiner's most dangerous and essential pawn – Catherine Howard, who had cast her charms about the royal person.

Once Cromwell was removed, events developed smoothly and rapidly. A statute governing the nature of divorce and the degree of consanguinity of the marriage partners was rushed through parliament, because Catherine, as first cousin to Anne Boleyn, was within the prohibited degree. Anne of Cleves was quietly removed from court and sent off to Richmond on the pretext that she was in danger of the plague. Henry, however, continued to brave the contaminated air of the city, and observers were quick to perceive that more was involved than met the casual eye. Then on 6 July, 1540, the first step in the carefully rehearsed drama of the divorce commenced.

A delegation of the Lords and Commons made humble suit to the King that they were in doubt as to the validity of his marriage to Anne, and they requested his grace to place the matter in the hands of Convocation. Very properly, Henry replied that canon law prescribed that this could only be done with the consent of the Queen herself. Instantly, Gardiner and the Duke of Suffolk were dispatched to Richmond to interview the Flemish lady, who proved herself both obliging and perceptive. The very next day, the Bishop assembled the clergy in convocation and presented them with the problem – again the monarch was worried about the legitimacy of his marriage; again his conscience pricked him; and again he feared that continued doubt might place the true succession in jeopardy. Almost two hundred ecclesiastics pondered the evidence, and discovered ample proof that the marriage was invalid. The precontract between the princess of Cleves and the Marquis of Lorraine was sufficient, if not to negate, at least to refuse a future marriage; Henry had entered matrimony in good faith that no such uncertainty existed; and he had been forced by diplomatic necessity to solemnize a marriage about which he had the gravest doubts. Finally, upon the evidence presented by the sovereign himself, and by a host of lesser but obliging figures, it was proved beyond dispute that the marriage had never been consummated. On these considerations it was discovered that Henry's marriage to Anne was null and void, and though society may have doubted whether Henry had in actuality been so continent as he claimed, two archbishops, sixteen bishops, and 139 learned doctors determined otherwise.[44]

What had taken six long years and a social, religious and political revolution to accomplish against Catherine of Aragon, had now, in the case of Anne of Cleves, been completed in six days. The way was cleared for the monarch's humble and devoted council, conveniently headed by the 'King's own Bishop' Stephen Gardiner, in alliance with the Duke of Norfolk, to beg Henry 'to frame his most noble heart to love' some noble personage by 'whom his Majesty might have some more store of fruit and succession to the comfort of his realm'. Henry was itching to oblige, for in Catherine Howard he had found what he fondly and blindly believed to be a veritable 'jewel of womanhood'.

CHAPTER 6

'HARRY WITH
THE CROWN'

Henry and Catherine were married on 28 July 1540. Heads had fallen, the international scene had been confounded, and the world cynically speculated upon the life expectancy of this fifth wife of the lusty Harry. The wedding itself was a hurried and unproclaimed affair, and Catherine plighted her troth to Henry on the same day that Thomas Cromwell lost his head. The words of the marriage ceremony, by which the royal spouse took this second Howard bride to be his lawful wedded wife, were those of the time-honoured formula. Catherine murmured in response to Henry's promises: 'I, Katherine, take thee, Henry, to my wedded husband, to have and to hold from this day forward, for better for worse, for richer for poorer, in sickness and in health, to be bonair and buxom in bed and at board, till death us depart.'[1]

The marriage of a king was customarily a matter of State and public rejoicing – a moment heavy with religious and political significance, in which the deity was called upon to bless with the fruits of matrimony the union of man and woman into 'one flesh and body'. The state of wedlock was 'a high and blessed order ordained of God in Paradise', and husband and wife were cautioned to use the nuptial bed 'more for the desire of children, than bodily lust'.[2]

Legends are born in the imaginations of men and mirror the reputation of heroes, and the story of Henry's marriage proposal to Catherine has most of the attributes of a first-class fairytale. King, so the poets inform us, 'went every day to see his son, and one day in the afternoon he entered the room when all the ladies were there', and called Catherine Howard to him. She knelt before her lord, 'waiting to see what the King could want with her'. Henry wanted a good deal, for he 'held out his hand to her and raised her up, saying, "Catherine, from now henceorward, I wish you never to do that again, but rather that all these ladies and my whole kingdom should bend the knee to you, for I wish to make you Queen".' Mistress Howard was too stunned to answer and merely made a low bow in reverence to this divine monarch who had asked to be her husband. Henry then hastened to inform the council of his will, and his advisers humbly assured him that 'if your Majesty so wills it we shall be content; what pleases your Majesty pleases us.' What pleased the sovereign was to be wedded the following day and he 'sent for the Bishop of London to come and marry him'.[3] The fact that there is hardly a grain of truth in this fable does not in the least detract from the account, but it should be noted for the records that Henry knew Catherine for at least three months before their marriage, while a week before the ceremony it was rumoured that the lady herself was *enceinte*.[4]

This time the King was taking no chances. With the princess of Cleves he had been tricked by a flattering portrait and lulled by the saccharine words of his ministers. His bitterness was aggravated by the fact that he should have known better. Only the previous year, Henry had voiced the innate caution of his sex when he maintained that 'marriage touches a man too nearly' to accept blindly the choice of his ministers. Henry was considering a French bride at the time, and he advised the French Ambassador that he would trust no one but himself, and suggested that the French send him several sample damsels to 'sing to me a few times before I settle'. With Gallic and caustic humour the Ambassador misrepresented the King's words and 'with a half smile' asked whether 'Your Majesty would perhaps like to try them all, one after the other, and keep the one that suits you best.' Then, to make the point quite clear, he added: 'It was not thus, Sire, that the Knights of the Round Table treated their ladies in old times in this country.'⁵ Legend reports that this produced the only recorded blush ever to colour the royal cheeks. In choosing Catherine, however, Henry was free from doubt, for he had made his own selection and found his 'rose without a thorn'.

The royal groom laid double claim to Catherine's affections – as king and husband. 'Harry with the crown' exercised sovereignty based upon the double pillars of the divine right of inheritance and the authority conferred upon him by a willing and obedient high court of parliament. His title was majestic: Henry was 'by the grace of God, King of England, France, and Ireland, Defender of the Faith, and in earth, under God, of the Church of England and Ireland the Supreme Head, and Sovereign of the most Noble Order of the Garter'. It was here in this magnificent 'mirror of wisdom' that the crown, the court, and the commonweal united into a single symbol of authority. That 'most serene and invincible prince' was a living and vital image of the august power of majesty. For better or worse, the structure of government gave full vent to the character and idiosyncrasies of the person who wore the crown. Henry not only reigned, but he ruled; his every taste, the most obscure and trifling facet of his personality, became essential matters of State. Tudor England had not so much to reckon with a sovereign as with a man, who stamped both court and crown with the indelible print of his temperament.

When Catherine first encountered her sovereign, Henry was forty-eight, and though the monarch could no longer wear his massive tilting armour as if it were a masquing attire and capsize his opponents 'horse and all', he was still a magnificent if portly giant of a man. The King was in the autumn of life, a fleeting Indian summer when the agility and vitality of youth still kept at bay the wolves of disease, senility and decay. Henry remained flushed and jovial, fair and graceful; the unwrinkled skin was pink and piggish, and the mammoth frame and bull-like stature continued hard and massive. Like the Colossus of Rhodes, he towered over his subjects, both as a man and as a king. The gargantuan frame, in an age which counted five feet as the average height, measured six feet and more, while the royal chest, garbed in doublet and puffy sleeves designed to accentuate the width of the shoulders, exceeded forty-five inches. The image of the future was only just beginning to emerge. The features had swollen and lost their girlish delicacy; the royal pate was thinning; the auburn beard was flecked with white; and the florid face gave hint of sagging jowls, coarsened nose, and hooded eyes made cruel by disease and suffering. The athlete's slim waist had crept to fifty inches in girth, while the muscles of his chest were layered with fat.

For the moment, however, Henry remained incredibly solid, still a magnificent man and a mighty monarch. The effect was increasingly that of a gigantic beer barrel, rotund but tightly corseted, astride shapely legs spread wide to bear the weight of a man who must have tipped the scales at close to two hundred and fifty pounds. It seemed as if both God and man had conjoined to emphasize the Tudor flair for the spectacular; the King's mantle was of 'purple velvet, lined with white satin' and embroidered with 'thick gold cord' hung with golden acorns, while the royal doublet was striped with white and crimson satin. Henry had an inexhaustible zeal for the ornate and the exorbitant; his 'fingers were one mass of jewelled rings', and around his bull neck he wore a gold collar from which hung a diamond the size of a walnut.[6] Part was the consequence of Tudor taste for the prodigious and part was political calculation, but the total effect was to give to Henry's mortal frame the appearance of a god.

For a sovereign who has made such a splendid and momentous splash in history, Henry's character is strangely and frustratingly elusive. To contemporaries and moderns alike, the man appears as a Janus in which the satanic and the angelic are inexplicably opposed. At one moment Henry emerges as a beast, lustful and brutal, grasping and vengeful, vain and obstinate beyond belief; at the next instant the image changes, and we perceive the superb athlete, the generous scholar, the accomplished diplomat and the idol of the realm.

The monarch's vanity was insatiable, and he was inordinately proud of his physical and athletic prowess. Almost the first question he put to the Venetian Ambassador, after the succession to the throne of the young King of France, was whether his rival brother was as tall as he, as stout, and what 'sort of legs' he had? When the Ambassador replied that Francis's legs were 'spare', Henry 'opened the front of his doublet and placing his hand on his thigh', said, ' "Look here! And I have also a good calf to my leg".'[7] In an age that judged men by the sumptuousness of their dress, Henry was considered the 'best dressed sovereign in the world; his robes are the richest and most superb that can be imagined.'[8] The man loved nothing better than to impress those about him by his every act – the lavish display of his attire, the inexhaustible energy that could tire eight horses in a single day, and the physical prowess that surpassed all at archery, tilting, hunting and hawking.

The legend of the King's cavalier handling of his wives, the picture of a monarch who went through spouses 'as some men go through socks', is standard historical lore, and his own generation went so far as to note that Henry was 'inclined to amours'.[9] His relations with the opposite sex were notorious even in a society that looked with tolerance upon the marital antics of sovereigns and accepted with amused cynicism the fate of disgraced and barren queens. More than once during the reign it was whispered abroad that Henry's sexual appetite explained his sterility, and it was reported by one of the King's more biased critics that the Duchess of Milan had dismissed Bluff King Hal as a possible mate, since she liked 'not to be wife to such a husband that either putteth away or killeth his wives'.[10]

Again on the less savoury side, England's monarch was a confirmed hypochondriac, combining the healthy man's distaste for sickness and disease in others with a profound interest in his own ailments. The faintest rumour of the plague was sufficient to send him scampering to the clean air of Windsor Castle, and not even Anne Boleyn's 'pretty duckys' that he hoped soon to fondle, and the memory of his 'sweetheart's arms' were sufficient to lure him back to London.[11] Henry evidently agreed with Doctor Boorde that the only sure antidote to the infection was to leave town, but he generously advised those less fortunate than himself to use a prescription consisting primarily of sage, rue, elder and bramble leaves liberally mixed with wine and ginger. 'Take a spoonful of the same,' the royal apothecary enjoined, 'and you shall be safe for twenty-four days.'[12] As he grew older and learned that not even his cast-iron constitution was immune to disease and suffering, Henry developed a discriminating medical knowledge. The royal cure for an ulcerated leg was an ointment comprised largely of ground pearls. Yet for all the care and worry about his physical well being, Henry continued to eat and drink prodigiously. In the end he grew so obese that the ground shook when he moved, and he had to be carried up and down the stairs in a sedan chair.

Both foreign and domestic observers of the English court were at constant pains to comment upon the King's obstinacy, cruelty and fickleness. Campeggio, the papal legate, reported that even 'an angel descending from Heaven would be unable to persuade him' once he had made up his mind, while Castillon, the French Ambassador, observed that he had 'to do with the most dangerous and cruel man in the world.'[13] Another Frenchman was even more critical and suggested that Henry was tainted with three vices 'which in a king may be called plagues'. These were insatiable covetousness, distrust and fear, and, finally, lightness and inconstancy.[14] There is endless evidence to make of Henry a brutal and consummate egotist, a monstrosity of a king, and a devil of a man, and history abounds with those who for both good and bad reasons see him in this light. But behind this ugly face appears another, with features angelic and divine.

The patriotic humanist, William, Lord Mountjoy, was boundless in his praise of the youthful Henry and he wrote to his good friend Erasmus, saying:

> If you could see how all the world here is rejoicing in the possession of so great a Prince, how his life is all their desire, you could not contain your tears for joy. The Heavens laugh, the earth exults, all things are full of milk, of honey, and of nectar![15]

Mountjoy was certainly not above a certain amount of calculated flattery and deliberate exaggeration, since he wished Erasmus to share in the milk and honey that were expected to flow from this princely paragon. His eulogy can be balanced by the more objective report of the Venetian Ambassador, who could scarcely contain his enthusiasm when he first encountered Henry early in the reign. The young King was, he said, 'the handsomest potentate I ever set eyes on'. He then noted a fact that would have flattered Henry immensely: he is 'above the usual height, with an extremely fine calf to his leg, his complexion very fair and bright, with auburn hair'. Not only was England's monarch fair to behold but he was also astute, prudent and sage; could speak French, Latin and some Italian; was master of the lute and harpsichord; could sing from a book at sight; and draw 'the bow with greater strength than any man in England'.[16] In the circumstances there is little wonder that the world viewed him as being 'in every respect a most accomplished Prince', and it was the considered opinion of still another visitor to the court that God had 'combined such corporal and mental beauty, as not merely to surprise but to astonish all men'.[17]

There is no gainsaying that Henry was both fearful of and fascinated by sickness and disease, but this does not mean that he was either a coward or a weakling. He was a notoriously difficult patient, rarely allowing ill health to keep him from the council chamber or the hunt, and in the end it was only the extraordinary vitality of the man that prevented the swollen and abused body from disintegrating into a helpless mass. Moreover, his personal courage and endurance were attested to, time and time again. The royal person may have been too precious to risk upon the battlefield, but the King's life was in constant jeopardy during the joust at which he so excelled. No one could stand against him as the royal giant, clad in ninety-four pounds of armour, thundered down the jousting course. For hours on end he would test strength and match spears against the bravest of the realm. Monarchs as well as subjects could be killed at this mock warfare, and the King of France lost his life in 1559 while practising the dangerous sport. Twice Harry of England was unhorsed, and once he lay unconscious for two hours. On still another occasion he escaped death by a fraction of an inch, when either by mistake or through sheer bravado he failed to lower the visor of his helmet. The Duke of Suffolk's lance struck the King scarcely an inch above the opened visor; the impact was so great that the spear shattered and the King's helmet was filled with bits of splintered wood. By the purest good fortune Henry was not seriously injured, and he announced that 'none was to blame but himself' and insisted that his armourer put his helmet back together again so that he could continue to joust, 'by the which all men might perceive that he had no hurt'.[18] Except for the silent and deadly action of the plague, which could destroy and mutilate the most splendid physique, Henry seems to have been beyond fear, and the Spanish Ambassador was probably correct when he noted that the sovereign was always desirous of convincing society that he had 'no respect or fear of anyone in the world'.[19]

Again, the picture of a gross and lustful monster is deceptive. There is no evidence that Henry over-indulged in wine to the point of intoxication, and, if anything, the vast quantities he consumed indicate a strong head and a sturdy constitution. Moreover, his faithfulness to his wives (while he had them) was conspicuous in a monarch who could gratify almost every whim. In contrast to the promiscuous capers of his royal brother across the Channel, Henry's two recorded mistresses seem the epitome of virtuous domesticity. What sets Bluff King Hal apart from other sovereigns is not the adultery but the legality of his promiscuity. Unlike most kings of his generation, he insisted upon marrying his concubines. Henry has a reputation as a Bluebeard because he had six wives, while Francis I of France has achieved but negligible distinction, despite an infidelity remarkable even in a society that abounded with Lotharios.

Hernry was also one of the most accomplished diplomats of Europe, and even his enemies conceded that he was a dangerous and cunning foe. Obstinate and ruthless he may have been, but as the Imperial Ambassador acknowledged, he was 'more accessible to persuasion than to threat'.[20] Educated in the Machiavellian atmosphere that knew the value of the adage 'three may keep counsel if two be away,' Henry could be both nefarious and merciless,[21] but he also had that rarest and most precious of gifts – the ability to inspire loyalty and devotion. For all his brutality, the man had magnificent animal magnetism, and even when old and fat and helpless he could hold men to him. In a strange fashion, all men respected and many loved this bulging bully who wept and blustered, pranced and preened. It may have been that such loyalty was wasted upon a man who would sacrifice both friend and foe, minister and subject, upon the altar of his egotism, and the insight of Sir Thomas More may approach the truth when he predicted that if Henry thought that 'my head could win him a castle in France it should not fail to go!'[22] Nevertheless, councillors were loyal both to the man and to the crown he wore.

For all his cruelty, vanity and egotism, Henry was immensely aproachable. He may have delighted in basking in the reputation of being 'kind and affable' and full of 'graciousness and courtesy', yet he was willing to pay the price for such renown. Sovereignty was constantly on display. The endless and peripatetic progresses about the realm, the ceaseless royal appearances, and the incessant ceremony that enveloped every action were all matters of calculated statecraft, and, like any illusion, the pomp and circumstance of sovereignty were achieved at the cost of personal exhaustion and tedium. Henry never seemed to mind the grimy, grasping hands of the frenzied citizens of London, or their badbreath, noxious clothes and boisterous manners. Once when a throng of ecstatic subjects stripped their sovereign to his hose in a delirium of devotion and souvenir-hunting, Henry passed the affair off as a delightful game.[23] If this was play-acting to feed his self-esteem, then at least it was done magnificently, for King Hal was a past master at catching and holding men's imagination. Whatever the ultimate verdict may be, the indisputable fact remains that the sixteenth century held him to be both a great king and a great man, 'undoubtedly the rarest man that lived in his time'.[24] Even Cardinal Pole, whom Henry had done his best to destroy and whose family he had systematically liquidated, wrote at the monarch's death that he 'was the greatest king who ever ruled that realm'.[25] Possibly the final and most balanced judgment comes from the observer who, years before, had maintained that Henry was the most dangerous and cruel man on earth. With grudging praise, Castillon wrote that 'he is a wonderful man and has wonderful people about him; but he is an old fox.'[26]

Ever since he died on 28 January 1547, apologists and critics have been struggling to penetrate the ambivalence of Henry's personality. Two images keep merging and reappearing: the angelic-faced athlete who inherited a brimming treasury, a stable throne and boundless good health, and the Henry of later years who, in the most extreme language, died 'a pustular, syphilitic mass', degenerate both in body and in soul. How was it that the pleasant portrait of a cherubic-faced youth who heard up to five masses a day and coveted not his neighbour's goods should slowly give way to the harsh profile of a self-willed, if still charming, egotist with a suspicious and scheming mind that harbours its own counsel? The answers are many and contradictory. Henry may have concealed timidity and insecurity behind the bully's defences; his prodigious vanity, his blustering gestures, and ostentatious desire to excel may have been the brittle veneer of over-compensation. Since the sixteenth century never experienced our modern pastime of psyscho-analysis and preferred to reveal the hidden reaches of the mind and soul to the priest and not to the psychiatrist, history has been spared the knowledge of whether the King did in fact suffer from a complex, Oedipus or otherwise. A more fruitful, if equally elusive, explanation is that he suffered from a disease of the mind – from megalomania brought on by a society that viewed its sovereign as the only possible bulwark against a renewal of civil war, and that was determined to worship him both as a paragon of a man, and as the symbol of public peace and security. Certainly 'the worship of man as a god is apt to make him a devil.'[27]

Sickness of mind and soul may have been accompanied by disease of the body, and the theory that Henry suffered from syphilis has never been totally dispelled. The evidence is entirely circumstantial, resting on what appears to be a marked deterioration in the King's character, his ulcerated leg, and the dreary list of miscarriages that plagued his first two wives.[28] Another equally circumstantial thesis is that the King suffered a serious brain injury when, in 1536, at the age of forty-four, he was thrown from his horse and lay unconscious for two hours. Possibly it is not coincidence that it was in the following years that the ulcer on the leg first began to give serious trouble, or that it is after 1536 that we begin to perceive the picture of a man who is suffering from chronic headaches, is reduced to a staff and felt slipper for his game leg, and is constrained to forsake the violent exercise of his youth. In the circumstances, it is not surprising if Catherine found her royal spouse overweight, irascible, melancholic, unpredictable and brutal.[29]

More than brain damage and a draining ulcer are involved in the transformation of the royal character: we must include the nature of kingship and the personality of the sovereign. For all the splendid display and costly glamour that surrounded the monarch, the position of kingship had marked drawbacks. Ultimate authority is a lonely station, and when Henry alluded to himself as 'King, Emperor and Pope in his dominions',[30] he had to pay a fearful price in terms of normal human relationships. As the 'father and nurse to his subjects', the King was the final arbiter of national policy. Henry might sanctimoniously announce that he contented himself with what was his own, and wished only 'to command my own subjects', but he also added the proviso that 'I do not choose any one to have it in his power to command me, nor will I ever suffer it.'[31]

The irony, of course, was that many men conspired to command the sovereign, and a few actually manipulated him, breathing self-interested advice into the royal ear. All roads converged upon the King's person, and the councillor who could plant the seeds of policy in Henry's impressionable mind might elevate his family, win title and estate, and determine the political and spiritual fate of the kingdom. Consequently, each facet of the King's personality, every aspect of his health and well being, was avidly observed, dissected and analysed. His every act, his every need, and his most trivial fancy, became matters of grave concern. Traitors dreamed that the King's ulcerated leg would kill him and 'then we shall have jolly stirring';[32] the state of Henry's intestinal tract was a topic worthy of constant conversation;[33] and the royal person was incapable of retiring into even the most 'secret place' without a cluster of ambitious courtiers, office-seekers and hopeful policy-makers crowding in upon him for fear lest some privileged and intimate friend whisper dangerous counsel to the King when he was at his most vulnerable.[34] Henry may have stamped his personality upon both his court and his kingdom, but he was also a helpless prisoner of his office, and constantly had to be protected from the swarming clutch of nagging petitioners, office-seekers and supplicants who pervaded every inch of the royal household. All men came to 'hammer at this anvil, some for money and some for favour', and those about the sovereign had to be warned against molesting the 'King's person with suits'. Such petitions were to be presented in writing and delivered to a special council appointed to review them.[35]

These precautions were rarely satisfactory or effective. They might guard the sovereign from the approach of the lesser sort, but they could not save him from the artful requests and pregnant hints of those who were in constant attendance about his person. Moreover, Henry's wandering and amorous eye was always a subject of intense speculation, for a royal mistress or spouse might influence the mind as well as the passions of the man who shared her bed. Later in the century, popular interest in the subject of a royal mate for Queen Elizabeth was so much a matter of national discussion that gambling odds were given on almost anyone who received even the slightest recognition at court. When, for instance, Sir William Pickering arrived in London and was accepted with manifest favour, the bets were running twenty-five to a hundred that he would be king.[36] Henry himself was constantly being 'solicited by his council and nobles of his realm to frame his heart to the love and favour of some noble personage to be joined with him in lawful matrimony', so that His Majesty 'might have some more store of fruit and succession to the comfort of the realm'.[37] Not only were the King's matrimonial inclinations a question of immense international and domestic importance, but so was Henry's virility, and when the Imperial Ambassador questioned the King as to whether he thought he would be able to produce more progeny, Henry's temper snapped and he demanded thrice over: 'Am I not a man like others?'[38] What Henry forgot was that he was something more than a man; he was not only a King to be obeyed, but an idol to be worshipped'.[39]

The sovereign was a victim of yet another weakness of his office, for he was constantly at the mercy of flatterers and fortune-seekers. The oily blandishments of professional panderers and flatterers were the most destructive and vicious elements within the monarchical system, for such men made it a policy to 'shamefully and flatteringly give assent to the fond and foolish sayings of certain great men'.[40] Yet for all the susceptibilities of both the man and his office, Henry had neither sycophants nor toadies as companions on the hunt or servants in the privy chamber, and generally he was told the truth no matter how unpleasant it might be. But even so, kings lived with the nagging doubt that the truth, both of a man's motives and his information, might not appear on the surface, and Henry was painfully aware that the reports of courtiers and bureaucrats could easily be cut to suit the royal temper. In a frenzy of frustration, he once upbraided and lectured his council as if they were a group of wilful and rebellious school boys, and he stormed that 'most of his privy council, under pretence of serving him, were only temporizing for their own profit, but he knew the good servants from the flatterers' and 'he would take care that their projects should not succeed.'[41] The safety of kings may be built upon the fears of their subjects, but as the French Ambassador pointed out, Henry would never 'cease to dip his hand in blood' so long as he continued to doubt his people.[42] For all his keen sense of character and the magnetism that held men to him, it is little wonder that the young prince learned to harbour doubt and suspicion, or that the ageing monarch grew to distrust most men. When Marillac wrote to his master that Henry's 'subjects take example from the Prince, and the ministers seek only to undo each other to gain credit, and under the colour of their master's good each attends to his own', it may have been that the Ambassador had the situation reversed.[43] The King may have taken example from his subjects.

That Bluff King Hal suffered from megalomania is beyond dispute; for lesser men had become puffed up with the satanic pride that they could do no wrong. Early in the reign, when the monarch was engrossed in the pleasures of the joust, the masque and the hunt, Cardinal Wolsey, the King's *alter ego*, had fallen prey to the same self-destroying egotism. He started out his career humbly saying that 'His Majesty will do so and so', but subsequently and by imperceptible degrees he developed the habit of announcing 'We shall do so and so.' Finally, he attained the ultimate conceit of claiming 'I shall do so and so.'[44] The Cardinal's disgrace and death were apparent and obvious evidence that power rested elsewhere. He was simply the King's creature, the bubble of whose egotism was pricked by the sharp reality that final authority rested with his master. Henry, on the other hand, was nobody's creature except his own. The monarch was responsible to God alone and the will of the deity tended to become the voice of Henry's conscience – something he showed remarkable ability at manipulating to fit almost any occasion.

Henry united the well-disciplined inner conviction of the consummate egotist with the conscience-stricken religious orthodoxy of his generation. No one was more solicitous of his soul's health; no one was more scrupulous in his conformity to the prescribed religious formula of the day. In the midst of the pleasures of youth and the excitement of the chase he found time for three masses each day, while on holy days he insisted on five masses.[45] Regularly he chastised and humbled the royal frame by crawling on his knees to the cross, and he was constantly testifying 'his zeal for the faith' with all the 'resources of his mind' and body.[46] Henry was fortunate in the simple nature of his faith, and he remained strong in the naive conviction that God was on his side. The relationship between Henry and his deity was elementary; in return for a punctilious fulfilment of his religious duties, God rewarded him with material success and eternal salvation. Very early in life the King confessed to the Venetian Ambassador that he could not see that there is 'any faith in the world, save in me, and therefore God Almighty, who knows this, prospers my affairs.'[47] Should God remove his blessings and plague the King with misfortune, then it was assumed that somewhere, somehow, Henry had failed to propitiate the divine wrath. When Catherine of Aragon failed to secure the succession by a male heir, Henry searched his conscience for the source of such obvious divine malediction, and discovered that he had been living in unconscious sin ever since his marriage to his brother's widow. The monarch's religious convictions were grounded upon the prevailing belief that every good and every evil stems from God, and as the burning of a candle before the image of the Virgin might be expected to cure foot and mouth disease, so the removal of sin would regain for the King his material well being.

Henry may have been many things but he was never a hypocrite, for righteousness was always on his side. He constantly lived up to his side of the bargain, defending the Church by both the sword and the pen. 'We have done what became us', he once wrote, 'for [the] better discharge of our conscience, and found the truth so manifest that it ought to be allowed on all hands.'[48] Knowing himself 'to be in the right', the King never for an instant doubted that he merited salvation and all the good things that God could bestow in this world, for 'where there is the Spirit of God, there is freedom.'[49] Others might suffer from a sense of their own inadequacies, and Luther might hurl inkpots at the devil of doubt and fear, but Henry remained serene in the citadel of his faith. As a man, as a Christian, and as a king, he claimed God as his ally, and though he denied it to his subjects, he asserted for himself the ultimate Protestant position that 'though the law of every man's conscience be but a private court, yet it is the highest and supreme court for judgment or justice.'[50] No Christian Church has ever denied that eventually each individual must make his peace with his own god, but the conviction that God stands always at one's elbow, ready and willing to confer his blessings, is a dangerous self-deception for any man, whether he be priest, puritan, or king. Any act of violence, any level of monstrosity is sanctioned when a sovereign believes as Henry did that 'God and his conscience were perfectly agreed.'[51]

Royal self-deception went further than the confusion between the still small voice of conscience and the mandates of the deity, for the very essence of sovereignty is the art of deception. Every action must be performed upon a public stage; every move must be attired with the pomp and circumstance that fashion the spell of majesty. The monarch must feign grief when he feels only chilly apathy, must fabricate enthusiasm when pressed down with the weight of exhaustion, must listen with sympathy and understanding to those who stimulate nothing but anger and boredom. Deception is the badge of royal office, and in the end one suspects that Henry lost the ability to distinguish between what was real and what was simulated so that eventually his conscience fell victim to the self-deception of his office. As a young man, Henry once wrote a tender and moving melody in which he concluded:

My mind shall be;
Virtue to use,
Vice to refuse,
Thus shall I use me.[52]

Harry lived and died in the happy conviction that he had fulfilled the very letter of that virtuous standard, and two years before his death he had found no cause to change his mind or to doubt his principles, for he wrote that he 'had been all his life a prince of honour and virtue, who never contravened his word, and was too old to begin now, as the white hairs in his beard testified'[53] Whatever later generations might think, Henry himself presented his soul to God in the firm faith that he had lived a good and godly life. In his own estimation he remained a man more sinned against than sinning. The decision is not ours to make, but into the scales must be thrown the activities of Catherine Howard, fifth in the sad sequence of Henry's wives.

In any circumstances, marriage to Henry was fraught with danger, but what in the end proved fatal was the fact that Catherine's husband was something more than a man or even a king. He was also a semi-divine monarch, upon whose altar Tudor England sacrificed both friend and foe. Harry was a 'god on earth', a 'king among the stars', and a 'lion among beasts'. In contrast with the majesty of the sovereign, the nobility were mere 'ants in little hills', for all subjects received 'their nourishment from the King', even as the light of small stars 'proceedeth from the sun alone'.[54] The king and his crown were inseparable in a society which still comprehended the functions of State in anthropomorphic terms. In the sixteenth century, political abstractions were animate, and as heroism is a vacant concept without a flesh and blood hero, so the crown without a regal wearer lost most of its dignity and became unthinkable. Power, majesty, and divinity remained human, anthropomorphic symbols harnessed to the chariot of State. For Catherine and her generation, government was simple and personal: it was 'Harry with the crown' who was the source of authority.[55]

The lavish ceremony of the royal household was contrived to elevate this demigod, the man who wore the crown, above the lesser sort. His every act, his most humble and biological needs had to be transformed into actions of dazzling dignity. Only by the most rigid and pompous ritual could society manufacture the illusion of a monarch who 'does not seem a person of this world but one descended from heaven'[56] Almost by definition, Tudor England had to destroy the dangerous and seditious opinion held by Edward Foster, gunner in His Majesty's navy, who impudently and impiously asked 'if the King's blood and his were both in a dish or a saucer, what difference were between them, or how should a man know the one from the other?'[57] Such queries were tantamount to the most transparent treason, for once the divinity that doth hedge a king was doubted, the very essence of government collapsed. Princes were 'not as common people be, who die and perish with a few men's tears', for when they fail, 'the state doth whole default, the realm is rent in twain in such a loss.'[58] To an age that was only dimly aware of the ubiquitous nature of Leviathan, and the distortion of justice that could be perpetrated in the name of State necessity, justification for governmental action continued to rest upon the difference between the sacred blood of kings and the pale equivalent that coursed through the veins of common men. The time was not far distant when Englishmen would view judicial murders as pragmatic necessity, but for the generation of Henry VIII most men preferred to dignify social expediency by calling it divine necessity and not *raison d'etat*. Catherine married not simply a mortal monarch, but also the Lord's anointed governor on earth.

The problem remained elementary: God 'hath not only lent the King his figure, his throne, and his sword, but given him his own name' and called him a 'god on earth'.[59] Not even the hidden places of one's heart were safe from the omnipresent scrutiny of the monarch. Catherine Howard and her society felt close upon them the inspection of the King's bright eye. When she became Queen and commenced her dangerous love-affair with Thomas Culpeper, she warned her paramour that Henry could reach into the inner recesses of a guilty conscience. Catherine implored him not to spread abroad the secret of their love, nor even whisper it in the privacy of the confessional. She bade him beware that whensoever he went to confession he, 'should never shrive him of any such things as should pass betwixt her and him, for if he did, surely the King, being supreme head of the church, should have knowledge of it.'[60] There is, of course, another interpretation that can be placed upon her words: that Catherine realized that within the structure of a State Church the confessional was no place to divulge a secret, especially one involving the royal person, for priests were as much ministers of the Crown as of God. The scepticism of the twentieth century should not, however, obscure the uncomplicated faith of the sixteenth; Catherine and her society were the victims of a deep-seated, almost atavistic, conviction that in some mysterious fashion there was a direct pipeline between God's lieutenant on earth and the hidden secrets of a subject's sinful soul.

Foreign observers were vastly impressed by the almost divine authority with which the average Englishman surrounded the personality and actions of the sovereign. Nicander Nucius commented that the English are:

Wonderfully well affected [towards their king]; nor would any one of them endure hearing any thing disrespectful of the King, through the honour they bear him; so that the most binding oath which is taken by them is that by which "the King's life" has been pledged.'[61]

There is a fearful ring of truth to the words of Martin Luther when he said, 'Junket Heintz will be God and does whatever he lusts' for his word has become an article of faith 'for life and death'.[62]

'Harry with the crown' was undoubtedly God's vicar on earth and the inscrutable source of justice, but he was also the living symbol of national unity and corporate entity. Englishmen might be endowed with rights and privileges, but they were also born with duties. The State had not yet become a mechanical contrivance dedicated to the furthering of man's material well being. For King Henry as for Catherine Howard, the realm was of divine inspiration, and every man, woman and child was bound by obligations which he owed society. 'No man', wrote Richard Compton, 'is born only for himself but for his country also',[63] and every honest man was expected to 'refuse no pain, no travail, no study; he ought to care for no reports, no slanders, no displeasure, no envy, no malice so that he might profit the commonwealth of his country, for whom next after God he is ordained.'[64] The doctrine of anarchistic individualism, of mighty magnates who drew strength from their own bottomless sink of egotism was anathema to God and State, and both conspired to assure the traitor a warm and welcome place in hell, for those who rebel 'against their prince get unto themselves damnation'.[65]

Allegiance to the Crown knew no bounds and transcended all other loyalties. Every man was urged 'to forsake father, mother, kindred, wife, and children, in respect of preserving the prince'[66] Family honour and even love of one's 'own flesh' were not enough to stand in the way of obedience to the Crown, for he who nameth treason, 'nameth the whole puddle and sink of all sins against God and man'.[67] It was in the name of this dogma that friend forsook friend and kin betrayed kin. When Catherine Howard's star plunged into eclipse, her uncle, the Duke, coldly disowned her, calling her his 'ungrateful niece' and suggesting that she be burnt alive for her sins.[68] Her first cousin and brother showed an equal lack of sympathy and, feigning bravado and merriment, publicly paraded themselves in the streets of London dressed in their most costly finery. 'It is the custom,' the French Ambassador laconically noted, 'and must be done to show that they did not share the crimes of their relatives.'[69] It was a Tudor axiom that, 'the court, like heaven, examines not the anger of princes [but] shines upon them on whom the king doth shine, smiles if he smile, declines if he decline'.[70]

Only positive action was proof of a true heart; the creed demanded that the man who harboured in the secret places of his soul the thought of treason should be purged and exterminated, lest sulky silence and cautious inaction be a sign of 'evil intention and sure proof of malice'.[71] Men might disagree with the monarch but 'if misliking', warned Sir Thomas Wyatt, 'includes disobeying, I think him no good subject.'[72] As the devout Catholic genuflects before the altar in recognition of the king of heaven, so loyal subjects of the Tudor throne dared not tarry, except bareheaded, while they were 'in the chamber of presence when the cloth of estate is set'.[73]

The devotion and absolute discipline demanded by the King was little more than a reflection of the despotism existing within society itself. When children were treated only slightly better than chattels, to be farmed out and married off for the sake of family welfare, there is nothing peculiar about Henry VIII, who quite literally regarded himself as 'a father and nurse to his subjects', expecting the same kind of self-abnegation on the part of Englishmen. If children were trained to bow and scrape before their elders and to wait upon their betters, it was reasonable that subjects should speak to princes 'in adoration and kneeling'.[74] Discipline was essential to good order, whether it was exercised in the family or in the State, and only in obedience and conformity could the individual claim status and dignity. As Shakespeare's Kate was 'a foul contending rebel and graceless traitor to her loving lord' when she refused his 'honest will', so subjects lost not only life but also their justification for existence when they denied their lord, their king, their governor. In doing wrong to her husband, Catherine committed treason against the State. She betrayed her duty as a wife and her loyalty as a subject, and perpetrated the one crime for which society could find no excuse or sympathy.

CHAPTER 7

INDIAN SUMMER

The effect of marriage upon the ageing sovereign was immediate and miraculous. Suddenly new life was breathed into the elderly limbs and bulging carcass. Henry's Indian Summer had begun. Only four years before, the King had begun to feel the weight of age close upon him, and sadly confessed that he knew himself to be growing old, 'and doubted whether he should have any child by the Queen'.[1] Forty-eight months later Henry was filled with fresh vitality and had 'adopted a new rule of life', rising between five and six of a morning and hunting until dinner at ten. 'He tells me,' the French Ambassador reported, 'that being so much in the country, and changing his place so often, he finds himself much better in health,' and the Frenchman confessed that he had 'never seen the King in such good spirits or in so good a humour'.[2] As Henry grew older he seemed for the moment to ripen and mellow, the love of youth balancing the decay of advancing years. During the summer and winter of 1540, he was the picture of vigorous health, brimming goodwill, and bubbling humour. The King was at peace with the world and with himself, and with almost pathetic fervour he lavished his affections upon his young bride, constantly fondling and caressing her, and so obsessed that he could not find words to express his love. If Henry lacked verbal means to voice his devotion, at least he could vent his ardour by a shower of costly gifts and magnificent spectacles. From the instant Catherine became queen, nothing was denied her, and it was reported that 'she reigns supreme.'[3]

For Catherine it was a dream come true. The old days at Lambeth and Horsham were stark and dull in contrast with the delights of the court; the memory of clandestine meetings and midnight suppers at the Dowager's residence were dim shadows that receded before the brilliance of Henry's affections. The Queen's confession had about it the ring of truth, when later she begged the King to recollect the frailties of a young girl, 'so desirous to be taken unto your grace's favour and so blinded with the desire of worldly glory' that she had failed to consider how grievous a sin it was to conceal from her lord and husband the truth of her 'former faults'.[4] Whether a young woman under twenty-one, educated to the standards of her society and caught in the amorous advances of a royal suitor, ever for an instant regarded the passing affairs of her youth as being serious sins is doubtful. Certainly she evidenced no sign of remorse until the King's majestic wrath, the cold and disagreeable interrogations of the Privy council, and the moral homilies of the Archbishop of Canterbury had all impressed Mistress Catherine with the full and abysmal nature of her misdemeanours.

Catherine had reason enough to wax proud and careless in the warmth of Henry's besotted attentions. As one not very reliable chronicler described the situation: 'the King had no wife who made him spend so much money in dresses and jewels as she did, who every day had some fresh caprice.'[5] Nothing was too good for the King's new bride, and Henry endeavoured with his usual literal turn of mind to fulfil his marriage vows when he said: 'with this ring I thee wed, and this gold and silver I thee give, and with my body I thee worship, and with all my worldly chattels I thee endow.'[6] The royal bounty knew no limits. Not only did the Queen receive as her marriage jointure the castles, lordships and manors that had once belonged to Jane Seymour, but she profited from the more recent political convulsions that had ended with the triumph of her party. Henry lavished upon his wife the lands of the late lamented Thomas Cromwell, Walter, Lord Hungerford, and Hugh, late Abbot of Reading, who with his colleague from Glastonbury had been, 'rotting on a gibbet near his abbey gate'. Of more apparent and immediate value were the jewels and rich apparel presented by a doting husband. At Christmas and again at New Year of 1540-41 Catherine was bedecked with the costly evidence of Henry's love. Among other extravagant gifts she received a 'square containing 27 table diamonds and 26 clusters of pearls'; a brooch constructed of 33 diamonds and 60 rubies with an edge of pearl; and a 'muffler of black velvet furred with sables containing 38 rubies and 572 pearls'.[7]

Not only was Catherine presented with the wealth and riches of the Tudor treasury, but every evening witnessed a radiant and giddy round of banqueting and dancing. Overnight the daughter of a Howard ne'er-do-well was elevated to the estate of royalty. When she travelled between Chelsea and Baynard's Castle, the Queen had her private barge with twenty-six bargemen and twenty other gentlemen 'serving the train', while fresh rushes and rosemary were spread on the deck.[8] In honour of her first State entrance into London, the lord mayor and aldermen, with all the guilds of the city, rowed out 'in barges goodly hanged and set with banners' to meet the royal couple as they passed down the river, and the great cannons of the Tower and the guns of the fleet shot salvoes as the royal barge passed by.[9]

Then there was the Queen's household, for Henry spared no expense in bestowing upon his bride an entire domestic organization including a lord chamberlain, a chancellor, a master of the horse, a secretary, a solicitor and an auditor. The new Queen also had her four gentlemen ushers, two gentlemen waiters, a cup-bearer, a clerk both of her council and of her wardrobe, two chaplains, six great ladies, four ladies of the privy chamber, nine attendants of exalted rank, five maids with a 'mother of maids', twelve yeomen of the chamber, four footmen, seven sumptermen, two litter men and seventeen grooms – all at the annual cost of slightly over £4,600.[10]

The dignity of a Queen was laden with responsibilities, for Catherine was expected to receive petitions, listen to requests to influence her husband, administer her household and estates, and, like any worthy wife, conduct herself in a discreet, chaste, good, meek, patient, and sober fashion. Unfortunately, Catherine did did not see fit to spend her days in the sober administration of her house and in duties becoming her wifely station. Instead, she was 'the most giddy' of the King's wives and spent her time dancing, rejoicing and enjoying the riches of the moment. The process by which a lady of fashion dressed and adorned herself was so tedious that a ship could sooner be 'rigged by far, than a gentlewoman made ready'.[11] It was no simple matter for ladies of the age to garb themselves in bodices, farthingale hoops, smocks, petticoats, kirtles, gowns and cloaks. Then there was the problem of cosmetics. Extensive use of face powders was just beginning to become fashionable in court circles, and society had not yet adopted the painted mask of the Elizabethan belle who could scarcely 'blush with [the] sense of her own shame'. Ladies of elegance in Henry's generation, however, adorned 'their face, neck, and pappis with ceruse' or white lead, and coloured their cheeks with red ochre, vermilion, and purple, achieving a rather garish and artificial effect of peaches and cream. Eyebrows were plucked, and court ladies tempered their 'eyes by art', brightening them with belladonna and endeavouring to make them appear wide apart.[12] The peaked and winged caps, rather like that of the Queen of Hearts, and the tightly-dressed hair, parted in the middle and combed close to the forehead, were designed to accentuate the eyes, which were regarded as the most exquisite feature of the feminine form.

When that worthy and dignified ecclesiastic, Bishop Stubbs, suggested that the homely features of Henry's wives were 'if not a justification, at least a colourable reason for understanding the readiness with which he put them away',[13] he was judging by relatively modern standards of beauty. Tudor England demanded striking effects wherever the hand of man could devise them, and society would have dismissed as dull and faded the unpainted faces of Victorian beauties, or even the more colourfully arrayed ladies of the twentieth century. Sparkling eyes set far apart, with whitened skin unmarred by freckles and tinted with a high and contrasting colouring, was regarded as the epitome of feminine loveliness. Both Catherine and her cousin, Anne Boleyn, had these characteristics, and although the Venetian Ambassador was not captivated by Anne's charms, he admitted that her eyes were 'black and beautiful' and that these more than anything else pleased the King.[14] Catherine Howard was not unlike her cousin, and legend has it that she was Henry's most beautiful queen. Whatever the truth, all her critics agree that she had auburn hair, was small, plump and vivacious – overflowing with so much vitality that Marillac could write that he had nothing to report except a continuous round of banqueting and dancing at court.[15]

Marriage to a monarch had its drawbacks, and wedlock to the Lord's anointed could be both disillusioning and difficult. Henry had a highly precise notion of the proper submission to be found in a wife, and he strenuously advocated the principle that 'all women in their degree should to their men subject be.' He must have felt it quite natural that Catherine selected as her device the words: 'No other wish save his.'[16] Spoiled, pampered and adored, it could not have been easy for the Queen to live up to her husband's high and demanding ideal.

Moreover, it soon became apparent that Henry's Indian summer had more than a touch of winter mixed with it, and he grew increasingly difficult to handle as the months slipped by. Slowly, reluctantly, but inevitably, Henry made concessions to man's mortality. The aching and ulcerated thigh forced the once indefatigable dancer, who could cut capers the whole night through, to hobble painfully on a staff. It was increasingly obvious that the sovereign's chronic headaches and attacks of gout 'sharpened the King's accustomed patience'.[17] Only two years before, Henry had rudely awakened to the fact that there were limits to even his Herculean frame, and that after all he was not immortal. In May of 1538, when he was forty-six, his draining ulcer suddenly clogged so that he was 'like to have stifled' and was 'without speaking, black in the face, and in great danger'.[18] Imperceptibly men grew accustomed to the thought that the King could die. By the time Catherine had become the centre of the monarch's middle-aged but still lusty affections, Henry had reluctantly given up the joust and contented himself with watching others accomplish the feats of arms to which he could no longer attain. Though he had to forgo the pleasures of the all-day hunt, the King still ignored physical suffering and the pleas of his physicians by persisting in several hours of hard riding between mass at seven and dinner at ten in the morning. Even so, the energy of the man was running down. The reserves of stubborn determination were tremendous, but in contrast to the early years of the reign, Henry was becoming more and more like his grandfather, Edward IV, 'in loving rest and fleeing trouble'.[19]

The unpredictable nature of his moods was such that it was remarked that the King was 'often of a different opinion in the morning than after dinner'.[20] He began to evidence signs of nervous restlessness and sought release in ceaseless perambulations between Windsor and Westminster, Greenwich and Richmond, in the hope that a change of air might arrest the steady advance of sickness, age and indisposition. Catherine may have married a semi-divine king, but as a man Henry was growing fretful and 'waxen fat'. Union with a god is at best a hazardous adventure. When that god is peevish and petulant, it becomes downright dangerous, and the Queen was soon to discover that not even her most winning smile provided immunity against her husband's fickle moods and violent passions.

In March of 1541 the chronic ulcer on his leg again suddenly closed and for almost a week it was thought that the King might die. Henry recovered, but the dream of renewed youth that had been symbolized by his marriage to Catherine had vanished, and it was reported that 'besides the bodily malady he had a *mal d'esprit*.' Nothing was able to please him; he complained that he 'had an unhappy people to govern whom he would shortly make so poor that they would not have the boldness nor the power to oppose him'; he lectured his privy council, accusing them of 'temporizing for their own profit'; and in a huff he spent the festival days before Lent without music, dancing, or company, so that 'his court resembled more a private family than a king's train.'[21] More and more Henry fluctuated between extremes of moody and introverted nagging about his ailments and encroaching age, and vigorous bouts of youthful vitality. In one breath he demanded as a wife a nursemaid and companion to his dotage, while the next instant he craved a symbol of his youth, a doll upon which to lavish all the luxury and display of Tudor imagination. At twenty-one Catherine Howard, temperamentally, was quite capable of acting the role of the pampered and irresponsible child bride, but she lacked the wit, patience and understanding to play the companion.

There is an old sixteenth-century adage that a woman is 'an angel at ten, a saint at fifteen, a devil at forty and a witch at eighty'.[22] Catherine was precocious; at twenty-one she was ambivalent – both saint and devil. Cheerful, plump, and eagerly indulging in each new caprice, but totally incapable of appreciating the consequences of her actions, the Queen had most of the characteristics of the pampered child. Sulking when crossed, constantly demanding assurance of her own importance, and hysterically gyrating between poles of tearful remorse and haughty indifference, she existed in a hot-house environment that tenderly fostered most of her worst traits of personality.

Just before the King's progress to the northern shires in the summer of 1541, Catherine was thrown into a fit of gloom. When her husband inquired after the reason for such sadness she answered that, 'it was owing to a rumour that he was going to take back Anne of Cleves' as his wife. The Queen only regained her usual high spirits after Henry had assured her of his undying love.[23] She was slighted by the fact that the ladies of the court paid homage to the King's eldest daughter, the Princess Mary, and Catherine complained that Mary had offended her by failing to treat 'her with the same respect as her two predecessors'. In a fit of spiteful revenge the Queen endeavoured to have two of the princess's maids removed from court.[24] It was almost inevitable that the two ladies should have clashed, for they were temperamentally the antithesis of each other. Mary was like her father – strong-willed, oddly masculine, with a deep, mannish voice and athletic frame. She had all the inherited 'pride of a Spaniard from Aragon', conjoined with a Tudor flair for learning. In contrast, Catherine was ignorant of all languages save her own, and even that she handled with the clumsy mentality of a juvenile. The mercurial and infantile temperament of the Queen could have found little to love or admire in the granite determination of a stepdaughter almost four years her senior.

On the other hand, Catherine discovered in her rival from Germany a more congenial companion. In a way they were kindred spirits, for it was noted that the phlegmatic Lady Anne, who had since the divorce become the King's 'beloved sister', did not seem in the least put out by the abrupt termination of her reign. In fact she was 'as joyous as ever', and happily amused herself by appearing every day 'in a new dress of some strange fashion or other'. Society was unable to decide whether the lady was 'preternaturally prudent in concealing her feelings' or 'utterly stupid and insensible'.[25] Whatever the truth, she endeared herself to Queen Catherine when, at their first meeting at Hampton Court, she insisted on kneeling to address the new Queen. The two ladies made much of each other, and danced together; then Henry joined them and all three dined together in an atmosphere of connubial bliss.

The happy meeting of Henry and his two wives may have been a ridiculous farce, but it concealed the very real dangers to which Catherine was constantly exposed. The gilded cage had many of the characteristics of a goldfish bowl, and Catherine was shortly to learn that activities that could be carried out in relative secrecy in the Duchess of Norfolk's residence at Lambeth, could not be concealed at court.

From the start the Queen's position of regal grandeur masked the existence of a fatal weakness, for Catherine proved herself unable to produce the single bond that might have withstood both the studied intrigues of political and personal enemies, and the cooling ardour of an ageing husband – a male child. The world watched, waited, and made periodic inquiries as to the state of the Queen's health, and it was whispered abroad that because Catherine was still unfruitful, Henry might seek yet another wife.[26] The rumours were vigorously denied, but they were not without an element of truth, for Henry had signally failed to bestow upon his bride the royal title. Though the King ordered that his subjects make room for her in their prayers, and she was 'proclaimed Queen of England' on the eighth day of August, Catherine was never crowned, and remained Queen consort only.[27] Coronation evidently was contingent upon fertility, and in

April of 1541 the French Ambassador noted that the Queen was 'thought to be with child, which would be a very great joy to this King, who, it seems, believes it and intends, if it be found true, to have her crowned at Whitsuntide.'[28] For Henry, as with most of his age, the burden of proof rested with the wife, who had promised at the wedding ceremony to 'be bonair and buxom in bed and at board', and at the time of Catherine's disgrace, one of the many crimes arrayed against her was that 'physicians say she cannot bear children.'[29]

Insecure as the position of the royal spouse was, the danger was immeasurably increased by the fact that a queen was something more than 'part of the state furniture' and a fruitful bedmate to the monarch. Catherine was also essential to the successful operation of party and family politics. For all the exorbitant and abundant favours lavished upon her by a doting husband, the Queen was never her own mistress. She remained a Howard, and now that that 'foul churl', Thomas Cromwell, was disposed of, the Howards and their allies fondly expected to reap the harvest of their sowing, for policy and patronage – those two words that held the secret of political success – were now finally theirs. The Bishop of Winchester had regained his seat on the council, and as 'the King's own bishop' set the course of conservative action. Norfolk remained Lord Treasurer and a year later was appointed Lord-Lieutenant of the North. Robert Rateliff, Earl of Sussex, Norfolk's old ally and relation, became the Great Chamberlain; and another conservative by blood, if not by politics, William Fitzwilliam, Earl of Southampton, assumed Cromwell's key post of Lord Privy Seal. Thomas Cranmer still retained his place upon the council, but the Archbishop was marked by his enemies for destruction. Finally Thomas Audley, Anthony Browne and Thomas Wriothesley all made their peace with the conservative faction, while Gardiner and Tunstal, Sussex and Norfolk, ruled the roost and controlled the approaches to the royal presence.

The Howards were quick to grasp the fruits of power, and dutifully Catherine filled her household with Howard friends and relations. Every claimant to the new Queen's affections, every acquaintance, kin and servant who could conjure up a right to Howard patronage, now hoped for preferment, and even the family tailor said that 'if she [Catherine] were advanced he expected a good living.'[30] Joan Bulmer, the Queen's old associate and confidante of those almost forgotten days in the Dowager's dormitory at Lambeth, immediately wrote wishing Catherine all honour, wealth and good fortune, and suggesting that she share some of that prosperity with her childhood friend. The lady in question begged that the Queen recall the 'unfeigned love that my heart hath always borne towards you', and she beseeched Catherine to save room for her at court, for the nearer she was to the Queen the happier she would be.[31] Catherine, unfortunately, did not ignore Mistress Bulmer, and a place was found for her as one of the Queen's chamberers.

Generosity and family patronage were carried to the point of dangerous idiocy when, in August of 1541, Catherine remembered Francis Dereham and made space for her former paramour as her private secretary.[32] On all sides, former friends, servants, and relations made good their claims, and the Queen's household rapidly became a Howard stronghold. Three out of the six 'great ladies' of her court were close family relations; Catherine's sister, Isabel Baynton, became one of the ladies of the privy chamber; and Sir Edward Baynton was made governor of her household. Those three old friends from Lambeth and Horsham days, Katherine Tylney, Alice Restwold and Margaret Morton, received favoured and intimate positions as chamberers, and so close was their association with the Queen that the other ladies of the chamber began to complain that they were being ignored and replaced in the Queen's affections. Finally Lady Margaret Arundel, the Queen's aunt, and Lady Dennys, cousin to Catherine, were added to the growing family control as gentlewomen attendants.[33]

The good things of political life were not limited simply to the Queen's household. Catherine's brother, George Howard, was named one of the gentlemen of the King's privy chamber, and her brother-in-law, Sir Edward Baynton, received possession of the manor of Semleigh. The grants and favours bestowed by the Crown upon the Queen's immediate family are almost endless; the Howard brothers, Charles and George, acquired licence to import 1,000 tuns of Gascon wine and Toulouse timber into England; uncle William Howard and cousin Henry, Earl of Surrey, received new gowns and jackets from the royal wardrobe; brother George was presented with lands formerly belonging to the monastery of Wilton; brother Charles was appointed to the exclusive and coveted position of one of the King's spears; and the Queen's sister, Lady Baynton, received a gift of 100 marks in fee simple.

Catherine's influence did have its limits, however, and she soon discovered that the clamour for patronage far exceeded her ability to oblige. When, for instance, she wrote to the Archbishop of York asking him to bestow the advowson of the archdeanery of York upon one of her chaplains, he firmly but politely refused. The Archbishop explained that he never granted an advowson, 'saving at the King's command', and complained that those who conspired for such positions were like vultures who espy aged ecclesiastics and then 'hearken and gape every day' waiting for them to die.[34] On the other hand, the Queen, at the Duke of Norfolk's request, succeeded in persuading Henry to send her uncle William Howard as ambassador to France. The Queen's influence was felt in yet other ways – she could play the lady merciful as well as the lady bountiful, and on occasion interceded with her lord and husband to pardon those who had fallen foul of the law. It was reported that it was Catherine's tender tears that saved the life of a spinster lady by the name of Helen Page; her intercession rescued her cousin John Legh from the Tower and the suspicion of treason; and her efforts preserved the family friend, Sir Thomas Wyatt, from the unpleasant consequences of his follies.[35]

The price that Catherine paid for power, success and proximity to the King was the envy and hatred of those less favourably stationed. A wiser and more imaginative woman might have observed the mounting enmity and tension that began to close in about the Queen. Catherine was now absolutely essential to the fortunes of her party and family. As a consequence, she was caught up in the vicious game of political intrigue and manoeuvring on the part of those who sought vengeance upon the conservative faction and upon the Howard tribe, by striking at the source and symbol of their authority – the Queen herself. The French Ambassador sagely put his finger on the truth about Henry's court and Catherine's environment when he wrote that ever since Thomas Cromwell had sought to liquidate the conservative forces of Norfolk and Winchester, 'others have arisen who will never rest till they have done as much to all Cromwell's adherents, and God knows whether after them others will not recommence the feast.' The jackal of politics constituted an omnipresent threat to any party in power, and ever since the forces of vehemence and change had been set loose by the King's Great Matter, bitterness, religious passion and personal hatred had risen to plague the English political scene. Marillac was absolutely correct when he concluded that 'as long as they are making war on each other they will innovate nothing against France.'[36]

The Queen not only had her political ill-wishers; she also had those who hated her for herself and who saw her as an instrument of Satan. Protestant malice was a constant menace, and the man who eventually betrayed the secret of the Queen's intimacies with Francis Dereham undoubtedly did so out of religious fervour. This was John Lassells, whose sister had been one of the Duchess's servants at Lambeth. At the time of the conservative triumph, Lassells left no doubt about his position when he asked two friends what news there was pertaining to 'God's holy word'. He was informed that the faith languished and the forces of the Devil triumphed. The worthy Lassells proved himself a zealous, if cautious, Protestant, for he urged his colleagues to have faith and 'not to be too rash or quick in maintaining the Scriptures', for the enemies of God would shortly destroy themselves.[37] He was quite right; within a year, his sister, Mary Hall, had placed in his hands information which, if it did not restore 'God's holy word', at least led to the disgrace and overthrow of the Howard Queen of England.

Added to Protestant hatred was personal animosity, for Catherine never seems to have inspired loyalty or devotion in others. From the beginning she was surrounded by enemies, and at Lambeth John Lassell's sister, Mary Hall, was heard to remark in reference to the Dereham affair: 'Let her alone, for if she holds on as she begins we shall hear she will be nought within a while.'[38] Later, the same Mrs Hall was delighted to gossip about the Queen's evil and unchaste youth, and her brother was quick to perceive that here was the means by which the enemies of God might be brought low. Both for the 'discharge of his duty' and the welfare of his soul, John Lassells hastened to communicate to the council in London the story of that 'puffing and blowing' that had gone on at Lambeth.[39]

Mary Hall was not alone in her distaste for Catherine. There were plenty of others among the Queen's immediate household who also cordially disliked their Howard mistress. On all sides were animosity, spite and intrigue, and Catherine, in life as well as in death, became the victim of that malice. Almost everything we know about the girl stems from the mouths of enemies or colleagues frantic to dissociate themselves from the Queen's disgrace and to oblige their interrogators by painting as vicious a picture of Catherine as possible. Everywhere the evidence is confusing, contradictory, and on occasion downright dishonest. If the testimony purporting to prove the Queen's carnal desires and activities demonstrates anything, it indicates that imagination largely supplemented memory, and that almost everyone concerned lied like a trooper.

On the other hand, it was almost inevitable that Catherine should have played into the hands of those who conspired against her. To a girl who had many of the characteristics of a juvenile delinquent, who was spoiled, fawned upon, and flattered, the role of a meek, patient, dutiful and efficient wife and queen was extremely unpalatable. Once the first flush of novelty had disappeared, there was little left to occupy her time except to gossip and intrigue. If Catherine played at the risky game of courtly love and romance, she had plenty of examples before her. While she was still a maid to Anne of Cleves, it was a notorious bit of gossip that Dorothy Bray, another of the Queen's maids, had an accepted lover over whom she exercised absolute rule.[40] At the same time, Catherine's brother, Charles, was carrying on his dangerous flirtation with Lady Margaret Douglas, the King's niece. In the circumstances, it was inevitable that Francis Dereham should reappear on the scene and that Catherine should lose her silly head over the dashing Mr Thomas Culpeper.

Francis Dereham had been left fretting in the Dowager's service at Lambeth, while Mistress Catherine – as one of the Queen's maids – had moved into the new and vivid world of the court. He had endeavoured to get a release from the Duchess, and finally took leave of her service without warning or permission. Rumour had it that he had fled to Ireland to nurture a broken heart, since Catherine had refused his pleas for marriage. This was the story that the elderly and romantic matriarch of Norfolk spread abroad.[41] Since Dereham left Catherine the custodian of £100 to be kept for him until his return, and took himself off to Ireland to win a fortune by activities that the government later chose to view as piracy, it would seem that the basis for the tale that he had run away to 'Ireland for the Queen's sake' originated in the Duchess's fanciful imagination. Moreover, Dereham seems to have been somewhat surprised at the notion. Whatever his true sentiments, Catherine herself certainly did not know where he had gone, and did not contact her former paramour until his return to England some time in the late spring of 1540.[42]

The young gentleman arrived in London to discover a markedly changed state of affairs. Catherine Howard was no longer one of the maidens of the Dowager's dormitory, a country girl with whom a young man of birth but of no particular prospects might safely dally. Instead, she was the centre of attraction and eagerly sought after by a swarm of eligible suitors. How many youthful gallants of the court were caught in the circle of her admirers is not known, but certainly two were noticeably smitten by her charms. These were two gentlemen of the King's privy chamber, Thomas Paston and Thomas Culpeper, junior; and Francis Dereham shortly learned that in his absence rumours had spread that the fashionable Mr Culpeper and Catherine Howard were shortly to be married.[43] Dereham may possibly have felt that his own prospects were not entirely blighted by this new development, but all calculations were promptly upset by the evidence of the King's obvious infatuation for the young lady. The lesser suitors inconspicuously and judiciously faded into the background, leaving the field to royalty. Dereham, on the other hand, refused to take warning. Despite Catherine's blunt order not to trouble her further, 'for you know I will not have you', he still persisted in publicly stating that 'I could be sure' of Mistress Catherine, 'if I would, but I dare not,' for a simple country squire could hardly hope to compete with his sovereign. Dereham was willing to bow out to Henry but not to Thomas Culpeper, and he very unwisely remarked to friends that, were the King dead, 'I am sure I might marry her.'[44]

During the early months of Catherine's marriage to the Lord's anointed, Dereham tactfully vanished from court circles, but like everyone else who had ever known the lady, he ended up angling for a fat sinecure and good living in the Queen's household. The machinery of patronage soon began to operate, and family pressure was exerted on Catherine by the Dowager Duchess to find the young man a position at court. Exactly why the old lady should have been so fond of Dereham is difficult to decide, but he had always been one of her favourites. By the winter of 1540 Catherine had been induced to oblige her grandmother, for she told her aunt that 'my lady of Norfolk hath desired me to be good unto him, and so I will.'[45] She requested the Duchess to bring Dereham to court; she presented him with gifts of money; and finally, in August of 1541, she found him a place in her household as private secretary and usher of the chamber.

The folly of an act whereby an ex-lover was appointed to a position where he might be intimately closeted with the Queen is mitigated by the fact that both Lady Bridgewater and the Dowager thought it quite reasonable and proper that Catherine should make room for and bestow favours upon her old friends and relations. The question remains whether either of the ladies realized the past familiarity that had existed between the two young people. Naturally, both the Duchess and her daughter denied knowledge of such intimacies, but even if they had known or suspected the truth, it is doubtful whether either would have been inordinately shocked or worried by Dereham's appointment as private secretary. Catherine, on the other hand, did express some slight awareness of the questionableness of the selection, for she warned Dereham to 'take heed what words you speak'.[46] The idiocy of the appointment was immeasurably increased by the unbelievable arrogance of Mr Francis Dereham himself. In fact, he seems to have been a perfect match for Catherine in that he was totally heedless of the cares and consequences of tomorrow, and incredibly boastful and insolent in the security of the moment. The instant he began to receive the Queen's attentions and favours, he acted in a fashion guaranteed to win enemies and antagonize people. He bragged to his friend, Robert Davenport, that:

> many men despised him by cause they perceived that the Queen favoured him insomuch that one Mr John, being gentleman usher with the Queen, fell out with him for sitting at dinner or supper with the Queen's council after all others were risen, and sent [some] one to him to know whether he were of the Queen's council, and the said Dereham answered the messenger – 'Go to Mr John and tell him I was of the Queen's council before he knew her and shall be there after she hath forgotten him.'[47]

When the crisis came, Dereham as well as the Queen had his ill-wishers, who were only too willing to remember or fabricate such conversations.

In the make-believe world of Catherine Howard, dark-haired beauties were by magic transformed into princesses; minstrels and troubadours sang songs of courtly love; and chivalry still retained its hold over the imagination. It is not surprising, then, that a young girl should have thought it romantic and exciting to accept a courtly gallant and play the lady bountiful. The gentleman selected for the role of devoted lover and prince charming, was a courtier eminently suited to the part. Thomas Culpeper appears to have been a young man in his late twenties and a person of considerable wealth and social position. He belonged to the King's privy chamber as one of the well-born servants, whose appointed task it was to care for the monarch's personal needs and to oversee the repairing and cleaning of the royal chambers. Culpeper was no stranger to the court; he had been a gentleman of the privy chamber for at least two years before Catherine met him; and there is some reason to suspect that he had been introduced into Henry's household as a child, working his way up from one of the pages who lit the fire and warmed the King's clothes, through the station of groom and finally to the cherished office of gentleman of the chamber.[48] Certainly he was a royal favourite and a person of sufficient importance for his favour and good-will to be worthy of cultivation. As early as 1537 there had been a discussion between Mr Hussey and Lady Lisle as to whether my lord of Sussex or Mr Culpeper was in a better position to be helpful at court, and which should receive the gift of a hawk. It was soon decided that 'there is no remedy; Culpeper must have a hawk.'[49]

There is a rather Gilbert-and-Sullivan tradition that Catherine and her gallant were first cousins and had loved each other with a pure and enduring passion ever since they had romped together as children in the nursery.'[50] The biological relationship, unfortunately, seems to have been slightly more distant: a conservative estimate makes them sixth cousins,[51] while the bit about a nursery romance is simply wishful thinking on the part of those who are determined to elevate their clandestine amour to the level of high romance.

The situation has always had a fatal fascination for maudlin authors who perceive in the relationship between Henry, Culpeper and Catherine the makings of an eternal triangle. Henry is obviously suited for the role of the villainous and bloated husband; Catherine is presented as the innocent and youthful wife who has been forced by her heartless family to marry a repulsive husband, and is led astray by a pure and sustaining love. Finally, the elegant Mr Culpeper is cast as the hero who sacrifices life and chattels for a few fleeting meetings with his true love. The 'romance' of Catherine Howard started within a generation of her death, when a Spanish chronicler, who may have been at Henry's court, wrote a delightful and sympathetic, if singularly inaccurate, account of her career.[52] According to this version, Culpeper was so infatuated with the fair Catherine that he went into a marked decline at the news that she was being forced to marry her sovereign lord. Our hero contained his true feelings for the Queen as long as flesh and good sense would endure, but finally risked all by writing her a letter 'and one day whilst he was dancing with her he was bold enough to slip' into her hand a note revealing his passion. Catherine answered by the same peculiar method, and 'Culpeper was overjoyed beyond measure.' When the terrible truth of their love was revealed to the King, and Culpeper had been cast into prison and threatened with the rack, he boldly dismissed his interrogators by saying:

> Gentlemen, do not seek to know more than that the King deprived me of the thing I loved best in the world, and, though you may hang me for it, I can assure you that she loves me as well as I love her, although up to this hour no wrong has ever passed between us. Before the King married her I thought to make her my wife, and when I saw her irremediably lost to me I was like to die.

The young and heroic gentleman then swore on his honour that he knew nothing more, to which the Duke of Somerset replied 'You have said quite enough, Culpeper, to lose your head.' This last was absolutely correct, and it is the only part of the legend that could possibly be true.

According to the story, Catherine behaved in the proper manner of all neglected and misunderstood heroines, for when Cromwell, who seems to have come back to life for the occasion, went to interview her, he found 'her nearly dead'. When she was accused of allowing the Devil to overcome her so soon, she said 'If I deserve to die for that you had better kill me, and you shall know no more.' At this point Henry is reported to have been so overcome by his former love for Catherine that he would have saved her, except that his council warned him that she deserved to die, 'as she betrayed you in thought, and if she had an opportunity would have betrayed you in deed.' Whether fictitious or not, this last statement is probably correct. Finally, Catherine mounted the scaffold to pay the ultimate price for her thwarted love and instantly became 'utterly memorable' by saying: 'I die a Queen; but I would rather die the wife of Culpeper. God have mercy on my soul. Good people, I beg you, pray for me.'

There is, alas, no evidence that any of this ever took place. In fact, there is considerable proof to the contrary. The Duke of Somerset, who is mentioned as Culpeper's inquisitor, would not become a duke for another six years; Cromwell, who interviewed the Queen, was peacefully in his grave at the time; Catherine vigorously denied that she had ever loved Culpeper, and at her death she did not say she would rather have died his wife;[53] and Culpeper, on careful scrutiny, turns out to be anything but the dashing and noble-minded hero of chivalric fiction.

It is somewhat difficult to unearth the truth about Thomas Culpeper because he had an elder brother of the same name. In an era of high child mortality it was not unusual for families to give to the first-born sons the same name, in the hope that one child at least might live to preserve the name and family. The situation is further complicated by the fact that both brothers were at court, and one is never quite sure which Thomas is doing what at any given moment. But it is fairly clear that Thomas junior was a gentleman of the privy chamber, while his elder brother – Thomas senior – was one of Cromwell's minions and servants. The Culpeper brothers were a passionate, swashbuckling, grasping pair, and the records are filled with their efforts to procure monastic lands, sinecures at court and pensions from the crown. The elder brother was on one occasion actually involved in a knife fight over a question of disputed land claims.[54]

As for Thomas Culpeper junior, he seems to have been an elegant young gentleman with a wayward air and considerable sex appeal. At the international joust held in May of 1540, in which the knighthood of England challenged all comers, he participated in the defence of national honour while Henry and Catherine looked on from the King's new gatehouse at York palace. The only drawback to the occasion was that Thomas had the misfortune to be defeated and overthrown by Sir Richard Cromwell. If, however, Culpeper fared poorly in mock war, he found easy victory with the ladies, for Lady Lisle sent him a coy and touching note, enclosing two bracelets of her colours and saying that, 'they are the first that ever I sent to any man.'[55] Moreover, the picture of Culpeper in the guise of an Arthurian hero who is willing to risk life and limb for the Queen's sake, is further marred by the report, which is in part substantiated by official evidence, of a particularly ugly scandal indicating that the gentleman was not quite as saintly as fiction requires. At the time of Culpeper's arrest and execution, a London merchant wrote to a friend in Germany mentioning that only two years previously Culpeper:

> had violated the wife of a certain park-keeper in a woody thicket, while, horrid to relate! three or four of his most profligate attendants were holding her at his bidding. For this act of wickedness he was, notwithstanding, pardoned by the King, after he had been delivered into custody by the villagers on account of this crime, and likewise a murder which he had committed in his resistance to them, when they first endeavoured to apprehend him.[56]

Royal favouritism could go far in protecting a man from the consequences of his violence. The law applied to all subjects, but the Crown could enforce it with rigid brutality or suspend its operation altogether.

History might have been able to overlook the questionable activities of youth and dismiss the ugly story of rape and violence as another example of the uninhibited vitality of the Tudor age, except for the fact that Mr Thomas Culpeper seems to have refrained from the proper heroic sentiments and actions during his interrogation and trial, for his role in the Queen's disgrace and treason. His evidence was totally contradictory, which is not surprising because torture was presumably used on him. But instead of steadfastly assuming the responsibility and defiantly telling his inquisitors not to investigate further into the ways of true love, he consistently endeavoured to shift the blame to Catherine, hinting that there were other gentlemen besides himself involved, and that he had met the Queen in secret only at her imperious demand. Worse still, instead of pining away as a result of unrequited passion for Catherine after her marriage to the King, he seems to have been happily sharing another lady's bed.'[57]

There is no evidence that Catherine and her distant cousin were brought up together, but they certainly met before she became Queen, for Culpepcr himself reported that Catherine said to him that, had she 'tarried still in the maidens' chamber', she 'would have tried' him.[58] Moreover, there were persistent rumours of a marriage between the two, reported not only by the lovelorn Francis Dereham but also by the Dowager Duchess. It is difficult to piece together the truth of their relationship. Culpeper in one breath said that the Queen, while still a maid at court, had been so desperately in love with him that, 'she could not but weep in the presence of her fellows', and in the next instant he reported that he had 'found so little favour at her hands' before her marriage to the Kung that 'he was then moved to set by others'.[59] Certainly Catherine vigorously denied ever being in love with him, and she claimed that she had awarded him those dangerous and secret midnight meetings simply to please him, since he had pleaded for these treasured moments. On the other hand, Culpeper later stated that he had come to the backstair conferences only at the bidding of the Queen herself, who was 'languishing and dying of love for him'.[60] Finally, to complicate the situation still further, we must reckon with that remarkable female, Lady Rochford, who functioned as agent provocateur and liaison officer between the young people. She was a Howard by marriage, having wedded George Boleyn, Lord Rochford, who was Anne Boleyn's brother and at the time of the Queen's death had been accused and executed for incest with his sister. Lady Rochford went into retirement after her husband's death but returned to court to serve in Catherine Howard's household as one of the ladies of the privy chamber. She seems to have won the new Queen's trust, which was unfortunate since the lady was a pathological meddler, with most of the instincts of a procuress who achieves a vicarious pleasure from arranging assignations.

Out of this tangle of fiction and falsehood two truths emerge: first, the Queen, her paramour, and Lady Rochford, all acted with unbelievable imbecility; second, neither Catherine nor Culpeper behaved in the high-minded and self-sacrificing fashion expected of heroes and heroines, but instead consistently lied and endeavoured to wriggle out of the consequences of their folly by blaming each other. The Queen accused Culpeper and Lady Rochford, claiming that the latter 'would at every lodging search the back doors' and secret meeting-places. Moreover, Catherine insisted that she had promised to speak to Culpeper only at the constant nagging of Lady Rochford, and had done so only after Lady Rochford had sworn 'upon a book' that Culpeper 'meant nothing but honesty'. Catherine was willing to oblige, but she warned: 'Alas, madam, will this never end? I pray you, bid him desire no more to trouble me or send to me.'[61] Jane Rochford naturally had an entirely different story to relate, claiming that she had acted at all times upon the Queen's explicit instructions.[62]

As far as the facts are concerned, we know that Catherine was showing Thomas Culpeper marked favours in March and April of 1541, some eight months after her marriage to Henry, and that she presented him with a velvet cap garnished with a jewelled brooch. That she realized this was an action capable of being misrepresented is evidenced by the warning which accompanied the gift – Culpeper should put it under his cloak, 'that nobody see it'.[63] Presumably it was during the same month that Catherine wrote her only extant letter; a note, as she confessed, written with considerable pain by an inexperienced hand, and, one is tempted to add, by a singularly naive young lady:

Master Culpeper, I heartily recommend me unto you, praying you to send me word how that you do. It was showed me that you was sick, the which thing troubled me very much till such time that I hear from you praying you to send me word how that you do, for I never longed so much for [a] thing as I do to see you and to speak with you, the which I trust shall be shortly now. The which doth comfortly me very much when I think of it, and when I think again that you shall depart from me again it makes my heart to die to think what fortune I have that I cannot be always in your company. It my trust is always in you that you will be as you have promised me, and in that hope I trust upon still, praying you then that you will come when my Lady Rochford is here, for then I shall be best at leisure to be at your commandment, thanking you for that you have promised me to be so good unto that poor fellow my man which is one of the griefs that I do feel to depart from him for then I do know no one that I dare trust to send to you, and therefore I pray you take him to be with you that I may sometime hear from you one thing. I pray you to give me a horse for my man for I have much ado to get one and therefore I pray send me one by him and in so doing I am as I said afor, and thus I take my leave of you trusting to see you shortly again and I would you was with me now that you might see what pain I take in writing to you.

Yours as long as life endures

KATHERYN

One thing I had forgotten and that is to instruct my man to tarry here with me still for he says whatsomever you bid him he will do it.[64]

The expression 'yours as long as life endures' was quite enough to cost the Queen her head, and does not sound like the words of a girl who is meeting a young man simply to be obliging. In fact, the evidence, such as it is, indicates that the initiative came from Catherine, and if we can believe the interrogations of the Queen's servants, it was Catherine herself who pestered Lady Rochford, asking her 'when she should have the thing she promised her'.[65] The Queen was not disappointed, for Lady Rochford successfully arranged a number of secret meetings between Catherine and Culpeper in which softly-spoken words were whispered in dark corners. Only Lady Rochford was present as chaperon, and on one occasion the lady claims to have been asleep during most of the meeting. Not even the King's long-delayed progress to the northern counties in the late summer and autumn of 1541 prevented the meetings, and along the route Catherine and the helpful Lady Rochford arranged means whereby Culpeper could be notified of the proposed hour and place.

All three seem to have recognized the risk involved. Culpeper reported that their meetings were skittish and jittery, and that the

Queen was 'as one in fear lest somebody should come in'.[66] Catherine confessed that if these conversations 'came not out she feared not for no thing', and she warned Lady Rochford to deny them 'utterly'. There is some confusion over who warned whom, since both ladies claimed that the other spoke the words of caution,[67] but the result is the same – they both appreciated the risk involved. Recognition of danger did not, unfortunately, engender caution, and all three seem to have been caught up in a mad circle of events from which there was no escape. Once they were almost detected by the night watch, while a growing circle of servants became aware that something was going on, if only because the Queen never seemed to go to bed and all but Lady Rochford and Katherine Tylney were barred from her privy chambers. In fact, it was the cuckold husband who was the one person totally ignorant of and unprepared for the disclosures of his wife's extra-marital activities.

What went on in the minds of those involved is beyond analysis. Lady Rochford went mad under the strain of disclosure and ceaseless interrogation, and perhaps it is charitable to believe that she was insane from the start. Possibly Catherine and her 'little sweet fool', as she not inaccurately dubbed Culpeper, were in love. At least it is best to hope so. But behind Thomas Culpeper's actions loom the system and ethics of politics and success. He may have loved his Catherine, but he may also have found the attention of a queen not only flattering but also profitable. He was undoubtedly a highly favoured and personable young man, who cultivated a reckless daring to the point of absurdity. Rash exploits and foolhardy dangers were the mark of gallantry, and success in the Tudor political world depended upon whom you knew and how well you knew them. As for Catherine, her charms proved her undoing. Abandoned if never daring, mercurial if not venial, incapable of sustained emotions, the Queen was caught up in a situation, which she had neither the strength nor the intelligence to control. The rather sordid backstairs flirtation and heedless cuckolding of an elderly and besotted husband became grand tragedy and high politics because of something that Catherine never seemed capable of comprehending – there was a difference between a Howard daughter in the girl's dormitory at Lambeth and a queen at Henry's court.

157

CHAPTER 8

ROAD TO TRAITORS' GATE

After eight months of marriage, Henry's honeymoon began to wear thin. The happy careless round of dancing and banqueting was over, and during Lent of 1541 the King was seized with a fit of melancholy. He was irked by his young wife, to whom he barred the door of his privy chamber for over a week; and he was cruelly hurt and physically weakened by a second flaring-up of his ulcerated leg that again blackened and distorted his face with pain. He growled at the thankless and pusillanimous nature of his subjects; and he shortly found reason other than perversity to complain about his people, for once again there were alarming reports from the northern counties.

Spring time in the distant shires was historically a time of stirring, when ancient wrongs and family feuds, nurtured during the long cold nights of the northern winters, burst forth into clan warfare and sedition. The people of Lincoln and York and further north along the Scottish border, had not forgotten the great uprising of five years before, that mass social movement that had called itself the Pilgrimage of Grace and had taken as its badge the five wounds of Christ. Northern families still recalled with loathing the sight of softly swaying figures dangling from makeshift gibbets, and the desecration of the sacred land of venerable abbeys and monastic foundations. They continued to dread the steady encroachment of bustling bureaucrats, who were usurping the ancient privileges and independence of the northern shires. In April 1541 political rancour and frustration again erupted.

Desperate men conspired to meet at the great spring fair at Pontefract, raise the standard of rebellion, denounce the King's tyranny, and strike down all who might oppose them. Fortunately for the Tudor government in London, the little band of traitors, who numbered less than three hundred, had within their midst an informer, and the conspiracy was quickly and efficiently nipped in the bud.[1] Futile and senseless as the revolt had been, it had one consequence other than the brutal fate in store for those who had dared treason against the Lord's lieutenant on earth: Henry remembered his promise made five years previously to exhibit his royal person to his none-too-loyal subjects in the northern parts. Physical, diplomatic and matrimonial difficulties had all contrived to weaken the original promise, and year after year the long-awaited progress had been postponed. Now, however, it was deemed politic to delay no longer.

The concentration of population in the southern shires, the disloyal sentiments of the northern counties, which still sheltered feudal and Yorkist sympathizers, and the general condition of the roads, had kept the Tudors close to the heart of their popularity and the centre of population around London. Henry VIII during a reign of thirty-two years had never before ventured further north than Boston. In an age that was happily ignorant of radio and television, and struggled along without the benefits of the press, the average citizen was dependent on gossip, rumour and personal experience for knowledge of the great affairs of State, and the men who ruled the realm. Consequently, it was essential that the monarch should perambulate about the kingdom, and expose himself to the sight of common folk, who tended to judge the weight of regal authority in terms of the personal stature of the sovereign. All the Tudors had a flair for exhibitionism. Both Henry and his daughter Elizabeth had been born with physical magnificence, and they were at pains to enhance by artistry and ceaseless effort what the deity had bestowed, for each perceived that personal popularity was the well-spring of Tudor absolutism.

The full weight of the Tudor personality, organization and treasury went into the royal progress north in the summer of 1541. Actually

159

it was more a theatrical invasion than a normal progress, for Henry was anxious not only to advertise his royal person, but also to intimidate the wicked and seditious, with a show of impressive military strength. No cost was spared and the full Tudor flair for exorbitant display was given free rein. Five thousand horses were commandeered to carry the army of men and supplies. Two hundred tents were required to house the court, which was ordered out in full strength and regalia; artillery pieces were sent ahead by sea to York; and a thousand armed soldiers accompanied the monarch. From London were transported the King's richest tapestries, his finest plate and his most sumptuous apparel. Every effort was made to achieve an extravaganza of pomp and circumstance, designed to stir the hearts of loyal subjects and strike fear into those who harboured seditious sentiments.[2]

Never before had the court migrated with such splendour or in such numbers. For Catherine, those summer months of 1541 must have embodied the fulfilment of every conceivable dream, for, next to Henry himself, she was the most lavishly dressed, the most flattered, and the most flooded with attention. Her dress was regularly of crimson velvet, and on ceremonial occasions she changed to gowns of silver. Everything was accomplished with showy opulence, and when, for instance, Henry and his Queen entered the city of Lincoln, they were preceded by eighty archers with drawn bows, and the greatest dignitaries of the realm rode in close attendance. Behind the royal pair was led the King's 'horse of state', while children of honour, all dressed in cloth of gold and crimson velvet, and ladies and gentlemen of the court in carefully ordered protocol, brought up the rear. At the gates to the city the procession was met by the citizenry, who had spent weeks decorating their town with pennants, badges and escutcheons, commemorating Tudor triumphs. Finally, as the church bells heralded the coming of the sovereign, the mayor presented Henry with the sword and mace of the city, as symbols of submission to the King.[3]

The pomp and formality were often so intricate and complex that specialists had to be sent ahead to instruct provincials unversed in the ways of court and royal etiquette, and an 'experienced man' was dispatched to help the sheriff of Northamptonshire, the alderman of Stamford, and the bailiff of Peterborough to decide whether a white rod or a mace should be carried in front of the sovereign upon his ceremonial entry into Stamford. Even the hunt was transformed into an extravagant and magnificent display. At Hatfield two hundred stags and does were slaughtered, while Henry himself officiated at the destruction of 'a great quantity of young swans, two boats' full of river birds, and as much of great pikes and other fish'.[4] In part, such carnage was necessary to the commissariat of the royal host, but in large measure it was done to satisfy the King's passion for hunting, which was so insatiable that the Duke of Suffolk's full-time task during the progress was 'to provide for the King's amusement'.[5]

Even the business aspects of the migration were conducted with careful ritual and protocol, and at York, those who had remained loyal to their sovereign were received into the royal presence in a separate body, graciously welcomed and loaded with favours. The other group, those who had been less than loyal during the Pilgrimage of Grace, were received on their knees and, prostrate, they confessed that, 'we wretches, for lack of grace and of sincere and pure knowledge of the verity of God's words, have most grievously, heinously, and wantonly offended your Majesty in the unnatural and most odious and detestable offences of outrageous disobedience and traitorous rebellion.' Henry was sufficiently charitable to accept their humble petition and acknowledgment of their faults, but the royal benevolence seems to have been contingent upon a sizeable monetary gift, which the ex-rebels added to their plea for clemency.[6]

Such an excursion into the northern parts was a matter of endless preparation, and although the decision to progress northward was made in April, the royal retinue did not get under way until the last day of June. Norfolk was sent ahead to prepare the road, organize the reception committees, and arrange for housing. The Tower of London was swept clean of prisoners; and just before the King set forth, London was favoured with a fine display of Tudor justice, when the Countess of Salisbury was finally executed for treason,

Lord Dacre of the South for murder, and two of the King's archers for robbery. Finally, after appointing Archbishop Cranmer, Chancellor Audley and the Earl of Hertford as deputies to rule in his absence, Henry was ready to move. Unfortunately the weather remained obdurate; the roads north became impassable and the progress was stalled for almost three weeks. Eventually the cavalcade was able to advance, reaching Lincoln by 9 August, Pontefract Castle on the 23rd, and York on September 16th.

Everywhere the sovereign was greeted with evidence of goodwill and handsome hospitality. He sent out before him the announcement that whosoever among his subjects, 'found himself grieved for lack of justice' should have free access to declare his complaints and, 'have right at the hand of his Majesty'.[7] Henry aimed at making his presence known and his authority felt. At Hull he inspected fortifications, and outside York he constructed a vast lodging, rebuilding an ancient abbey, adding tents and pavilions and furnishing them with all the grandeur at his disposal. Men wondered and speculated at the cause for such display, and some suggested that Catherine might finally have earned her coronation by showing signs of pregnancy. The rumour was unwarranted; instead, Henry was preparing to entice James of Scotland to a brotherly meeting at York.

Catherine's passion for courtly romance was in no way dampened by the difficulties of a migratory court. At each new town, Lady Rochford and the Queen took pains to investigate the architecture and location of the backstairs and privy entrances to the Queen's chamber. All along the route, private and hurried meetings with Culpeper were arranged – at Greenwich, Lincoln, Hatfield, Pontefract and York. The danger of disclosure was a constant menace, and the liaison was conducted under extraordinarily difficult conditions. On one occasion, Culpeper had to pick the lock of the Queen's suite, and at another time he lurked on the backstairs ready to slip away at the slightest noise.[8] The affair was carried on with unbelievable neglect of even the most elementary precautions. At Hatfield, Catherine was so transparent in her infatuation that her servants began to suspect the worst simply by the way she looked and spoke to Culpeper.

Throughout the progress, gossip was rampant as to what was occurring in the Queen's chamber late at night, when Catherine barred the doors to her ladies and allowed none to enter save her old friend Katherine Tylney, and the remarkable Lady Rochford.

No one bothered to inform the King, and Henry returned home to London in excellent spirits, reckoning that he had much for which to be thankful. His health was good, his subjects had expressed a touching and gratifying humility, devotion and repentance, and his Queen, though not yet pregnant, was young, vivacious and exciting. With a full heart and a sense of contentment Henry expressed his gratitude to his Maker, 'for the good life he led and trusted to lead' with Catherine, and he required that the Bishop of Lincoln publicly 'make like prayer and give like thanks with him'.[9] This was 1 November, All Hallows Day; twenty-four hours later the King was handed a letter by Archbishop Cranmer, which revealed the story of the Queen's past and accused her of having 'lived most corruptly and sensually'.

The timing is one of ironic coincidence, for shortly after the court began its slow return from York in early October, the council in London stumbled upon the dangerous news of Catherine's early relations with Francis Dereham. The three ministers left in charge of the King's government in the south were all envious of Howard influence about the King, and the news of the scandal was highly welcome to them. Here, in the information reported by John Lassells, the anti-Howard forces had the instrument by which the conservative faction might be overthrown. On the other hand, they recognized the extreme danger of the situation. Exactly when John Lassells presented the Archbishop with the information is not clear, but Cranmer immediately perceived that the, 'weight and importance of the matter' was so great that he felt obliged to consult his two colleagues, who, 'having weighed the matter and deeply pondered the gravity thereof', resolved to inform the King.[10] The day following Henry's return to Hampton Court they determined to act. One highly embarrassing problem arose when it became apparent that none of the three councillors cared to be the bearer of such tidings, for the

King's 'affection was so marvellously set upon' his young wife that, 'no man dared take in hand to open to him' the terrible truth.[11] In the end, Audley and Hertford persuaded the pliable Archbishop to accept the unpleasant task, but not even Cranmer had the courage, 'to express the same to the King's Majesty by word of mouth'.[12] Instead, he wrote a letter narrating the entire story of how Lassells's married sister, Mary Hall, who had once been a chamberer in the Dowager Duchess's household, had revealed to her brother the details of what presumably had transpired in the girls' dormitory at Lambeth. Armed with this explosive epistle, Cranmer hurried to Hampton Court, where he discovered the King at his devotions. 'With over much importunity' he handed him the note, bidding Henry read it in private.[13]

The King reacted in a most unexpected fashion. Instead of turning wroth and violent, he was 'much perplexed', and such was his love and 'constant opinion' of his young wife's character, that he dismissed the letter as a slanderous forgery. All the evidence points to the fact that Henry placed absolutely no faith in the report, for he continued in high spirits for the rest of the week, and simply ordered an investigation of the story so as to search out the source of the rumour, and protect the Queen from idle tongues and malicious gossip. Quietly he ordered William Fitzwilliam, Earl of Southampton and Lord Privy Seal, back to London to re-examine Lassells, who stuck to his story. Still unconvinced, the King sent Southampton down to Sussex to interview Mary Hall, while Sir Thomas Wriothesley rounded up Dereham and Manox. Not a breath of what was occurring was allowed to leak abroad. Southampton gave out that he was headed to Sussex for a hunting expedition; Wriothesley detained Francis Dereham on the pretext of his having committed piracy while in Ireland the previous year; and no one noticed the arrest of someone so insignificant as Catherine's former music teacher. Suddenly the figment of Henry's fantasy was shattered when Manox confessed that he, 'had commonly used to feel the secrets and other parts of the Queen's body', and Dereham blurted out the truth about his relations with Catherine, admitting he 'had known her carnally many times, both in his doublet and hose between the sheets and in naked bed'.[14]

On Saturday noon Fitzwilliam returned from his interview with Mary Hall, who confirmed all that her brother had said. The rump of the privy council was in session when the Lord Privy Seal arrived, and it continued to meet far into the afternoon, listening to the Earl's report and arranging for absent members of the council to return post-haste to London. In the face of the mounting evidence, Henry remained incredulous, the thick hide of his egotism acting as protection against the knowledge that his wife was not an innocent 'jewel of womanhood' who had loved him with 'perfect love'. As yet the only action that he was willing to take was to order the Queen to keep to her chambers and wait upon the King's pleasure.[15]

At this point legend takes over; if Mistress Catherine Howard lacks most of the essential and fitting characteristics of a romantic heroine, she at least has a ghost. At Hampton Court there is what is described as the 'haunted gallery', which adjoins the Queen's chambers and Henry's chapel. It was there that the Queen is said to have eluded her guards and sought out her husband, who was hearing Mass. Just as she reached the door, she was seized and forced back to her chambers, while her screams resounded up and down the gallery. This presumably is the explanation of the female form, dressed in traditional white, which drifts down the gallery to the door of the chapel, and then hurries back, 'a ghastly look of despair' upon its face and uttering 'the most unearthly shrieks', until the phantom disappears through the chamber door at the end of the gallery. Unfortunately, Catherine's ghost has found the atmosphere of the twentieth century uncongenial and has manifested a marked reluctance to present itself in modern times.[16] If the Queen ever did endeavour to reach her royal spouse it must have been the morning of Sunday 6 November, 1541, for that evening Henry slipped away to London, never to return until Catherine had been taken prisoner from Hampton Court. The King was still at great pains to conceal the scandal. On the pretext of a chase he ordered dinner in the open field outside the palace, and there secretly met the Lord Chancellor and the Duke of Norfolk, who had been ordered to return the previous evening. Then, without returning to the palace, Henry stepped aboard a small barge and was rowed downstream to London, where he met the Privy council in an all-night emergency session at the Bishop of Winchester's residence in Southwark. There the monarch was confronted with indisputable proof, wrung by Wriothesley from Manox and Dereham.

'No pain so fervent, hot or cold as is a man to be called cuckold.'[17] Henry was stunned by the revelation, and there is something pathetic in the picture of an elderly giant struck down by the knowledge of his wife's infidelities. It seems incredible that he had never guessed, or that he refused to believe until disbelief was no longer possible. Henry, in the autumn of his career, had been captivated by Catherine's vitality, gaiety and determination to enjoy every moment of life to the full. Her fascination had never included the attraction of wit or great beauty; instead, what King Hal prized most highly was the image of youth that he himself had lost. Suddenly the tough armour of self-esteem that wards off the small voice of doubt and fear, was ripped aside. As the King sat listening to the evidence during that extraordinary meeting at Winchester's house, the old Henry of consummate conceit and boundless energy died. For a moment he raged in black despair, and it seemed as if his love had turned to consuming hate, for he shouted for a sword with which to slay the girl who had betrayed him, and he swore aloud that she would never have 'such delight in her incontinency as she should have torture in her death'. Suddenly, the royal wrath turned to tears of self-pity, and the council was acutely embarrassed by the sight of the cuckold spouse weeping, 'which was strange in [one of] his courage.' Tearfully he regretted his 'ill-luck in meeting with such ill-conditioned wives', and true to form, he shifted the responsibility, blaming his council for 'this last mischief'.[18] The days of sustained indignation and righteous disavowal had vanished. Perhaps he was too old and too hurt to desire vengeance; perhaps even now he was unable to accept the terrible truth that his marvellous illusions had been shattered; perhaps, after all had been revealed, he could not stop loving his fifth wife. Whatever the cause, Catherine Howard fared better than her cousin, Anne Boleyn, who was dispatched with callous disregard, and it was reported that Henry 'would bear the blow more patiently and compassionately' than expected and 'a good deal more tenderly than the Queen's own relatives' desired.[19] Possibly Chapuys was correct when he wrote that the King's 'case resembles very much that of the woman who cried more bitterly at the loss of her tenth husband than she had on the death of the other nine put together, though all of them had been equally worthy people and good husbands to her: the reason being that she had never buried one of them without being sure of the next, but that after the tenth husband she had no other one in view, hence her sorrow and her lamentations.'[20]

For Henry the end of life, if not of the reign, had arrived. He stepped forth from the meeting of the council a grey and crippled old man. He sagged; the bluster of his youth evaporated; and more and more the satanic began to obliterate the remains of what had once been an angelic countenance. The King suddenly had to confront the awful truth that he was old, and never again could hold a young girl's fancy. There was nothing left except to seek solace in hunting – the one thing that the immense body could yet perform – and while his council struggled to discover the full depth of the Queen's follies, Henry took to the field for 'the purpose of diverting his ill humour'.

Distasteful as the situation was, the privy council had to act, and on the following day, 7 November, Cranmer and Norfolk were ordered to return to Hampton Court to interrogate Catherine and to arrange for her confinement to her chambers. It was carefully stipulated that they should not take 'from the Queen her privy keys', indicating that she was to have considerable freedom within the confines of her rooms. Though this was a sign of mercy, the effect was mitigated by the order to seize and inventory the Queen's jewels. In the face of such ominous activity, Catherine dissolved into tears, denying everything and continuing in such a frenzy of 'lamentation and heaviness' that the Archbishop and the Duke were totally helpless, and deemed it wisest to retreat in the face of feminine hysterics. The following day Cranmer returned to resume the inquisition. He had originally intended to use severity, exaggerating the 'grievousness of her demerits', threatening her with the terrible picture of the punishment that 'she ought to suffer', and finally softening the impact of his words by extending the hope of royal mercy. The ecclesiastic, however, was alarmed that a 'recital' of her manifest sins, might drive Catherine into 'some dangerous ecstasy' so that 'words of comfort coming last might peradventure have come too late.' In between floods of tears and bouts of hysterics, Cranmer finally heard the full story.

The Queen's confession and behaviour were regarded by the government as being far from satisfactory. She maintained that there had never been anything resembling a marriage contract between herself and Dereham, and, worse, she evidenced a disturbing tendency, the moment the Archbishop had left the room, 'to excuse and temper' her actions, and suggest that Dereham had forced his love upon her through, 'violence rather than of her free consent and will'.[21] in fact, Catherine betrayed most of the characteristics of an infantile mind – imperious and categorical denial, then wild hysterics followed by abject confession, and finally qualifications and temporizing once the immediate danger had passed.

Despite the unsatisfactory nature of the confession, it was sufficiently damning. Catherine admitted that she and Dereham had called each other husband and wife and that there had been talk at Lambeth of their marriage. She allowed that Dereham had divers times:

> lain with me, sometimes in his doublet and hose, and two or three times naked; but not so naked that he had nothing upon him, for he had always at the least his doublet and as I do think, his hose also, but I mean naked when his hose were put down.[22]

Catherine also wrote a much more general statement of her faults, addressed to the King, in which she confessed her sins, acknowledged herself worthy of death, and referred judgment of her offences unto the King's mercy. As a statement of guilt it leaves little to the imagination, and by itself was sufficient to warrant the death penalty:

I your grace's most sorrowful subject and most vile wretch in the world, not worthy to make any recommendations unto your most excellent majesty, do only make my most humble submission and confession of my faults. And where no cause of mercy is given upon my part, yet of your most accustomed mercy extended unto all other men undeserved, most humbly on my hands and knees, [I] do desire one particle thereof to be extended unto me, although of all other creatures [I am] most unworthy either to be called your wife or subject. My sorrow I can by no writing express, nevertheless I trust your most benign nature will have some respect unto my youth, my ignorance, my frailness, my humble confession of my faults, and plain declaration of the same referring me wholly unto your grace's pity and mercy. First at the flattering and fair persuasions of Manox, being but a young girl, [I] suffered him at sundry times to handle and touch the secret parts of my body which neither became me with honesty to permit nor him to require. Also Francis Dereham by many persuasions procured me to his vicious purpose and obtained first to he upon my bed with his doublet and hose and after within the bed and finally he lay with me naked, and used me in such sort as a man doth his wife many and sundry times, but how often I know not, and our company ended almost a year before the Kings Majesty was married to my lady Anne of Cleves and continued not past one quarter of a year or little above. Now the whole truth being declared unto your majesty, I most humbly beseech the same to consider the subtle persuasions of young men, and the ignorance and frailness of young women. I was so desirous to be taken unto your grace's favour and so blinded with the desire of worldly glory that I could not, nor had grace, to consider how great a fault it was to conceal my former faults from your majesty, considering that I intended ever during my life to be faithful and true unto your majesty after, and nevertheless the sorrow of my offences was ever before mine eyes, considering the infinite goodness of your majesty towards me from time to time, ever increasing and not diminishing. Now I refer the judgment of all mine offences with my life and death wholly unto your most benign and merciful grace, to be considered by no justice of your majesty's laws but only by your infinite goodness, pity, compassion, and mercy, without the which I knowledge myself worthy of most extreme punishment.[23]

So far everything was running according to the prescribed formula, for Catherine had produced a most abject and convincing, if not entirely accurate, confession. But one nagging problem remained – the Queen's absolute refusal to acknowledge any form of marriage contract between herself and Dereham. For a moment it appeared as if the council and the King were working for a divorce based on the claim that a pre-contract between Dereham and Catherine invalidated the marriage with Henry. If this could have been established as a justification for divorce, the Queen's life might have been spared, and the council was not altogether pleased by the thought that such an argument might, 'serve for her defence'. Certainly Dereham pleaded innocent on the grounds that there had been such a promise of marriage. Even the Dowager Duchess was not particularly alarmed about the fate of her granddaughter, and argued that Catherine could not be executed for what had taken place at her house before the marriage with the King. She rather expected that the Queen would be sent back to her after the divorce; a possibility that the Duchess was anything but enthusiastic about. On 10 November current rumour reported that Henry was pretending 'that Dereham had been actually betrothed to the Queen before her marriage, which is therefore invalid.'[24]

Three problems complicated such a solution. First, the Queen herself, either through insatiable Howard pride, which refused to acknowledge the possibility that she had never been Queen of England even for eighteen months, or possibly through an almost pathological need to cling to the one exceptional aspect of an otherwise ordinary life, refused to allow the pre-contract.[25] Second, the question whether Catherine's relations with Dereham actually constituted a sufficiently legal marriage to invalidate the union with the King, was in considerable doubt. By customary and ecclesiastical law it was possible to argue that the two young people were in fact married. In the sixteenth century the Church always claimed that a couple were wedded in the eyes of God and the law, even without a public engagement or a religious ceremony, if they had agreed between themselves and that agreement was accompanied by carnal knowledge.²⁶ The issue was debated by the doctors of theology, but before any final decision could be reached a third and far more dangerous factor suddenly entered the picture. It soon became apparent that the complete story of the Queen's activities had yet to be revealed, for, as Wriothesley remarked, 'an appearance of greater abomination' was now suspectcd.²⁷

So far the worst that could be directed against Catherine was that she had committed bigamy. This was bad enough, since the crime united both felony and perjury, and was punishable by death. Evidence was now beginning to appear that the Queen had not, as she hopefully confessed, 'intended ever during my life to be faithful and true unto your majesty'; nor had she kept the sorrow of her early offences 'ever before her eyes'. Instead, she had taken into her service Katherine Tylney, who had known and connived at her early amours with Dereham, and she had actually introduced her former lover into her regal household as an usher and secretary within the privy chamber. These were difficult actions to rationalize, and the government immediately placed a dangerous and fatal interpretation upon them. The council wrote on 12 November that what this portended was easy to conjecture, and that further scandal would shortly be revealed.²⁸ Though Dereham frantically denied adulterous activities with the Queen, it was simply a matter of time and probably of torture, before further evidence was disclosed.

In the meantime, orders were sent to prepare the Queen for removal to the suppressed monastry of Syon. There she was to be 'furnished moderately, as her life and conditions hath deserved; that is to say, with the furniture of three chambers, hanged with mean stuff without any cloth of estate.' Again the Crown was being strangely lenient; even though Catherine was deprived of the glittering jewels and sumptuous gowns that she loved so dearly, yet she was allowed to retain her privy keys, was attended by four ladies-in-waiting and twelve servants, and was presented with a wardrobe consisting of six French hoods edged with gold, six pair of sleeves, as many gowns, and 'six kirtles of satin damask and velvet'.²⁹ While Cranmer was arranging for the closing of the Queen's household at

Hampton Court, orders were also issued that on the 13th the Lord Chancellor should call the great council together and 'declare to them the abominable demeanour of the Queen', but not mention any possibility of a pre-contract.[30] This was the first public announcement of the scandal, but why it was decided to pass over the pre-contract question is not known. Possibly it was feared that not only Catherine but also Dereham might use it as a justification for their actions. A more likely explanation is that evidence of further scandal had already been detected.

The council had finally fastened on to the scent of Mr Thomas Culpeper. The secret of the King's matrimonial difficulties had been well kept; not even the foreign ambassadors, who made it their profession to ferret out court secrets, knew until 11 November what was brewing, and even then the French Ambassador was not sure why Henry had left Hampton Court for London so hurriedly. Bad news from Ireland, possible war with Scotland, and the rumoured disclosure of financial peculation among high government officials, were all voiced as possible explanations. As for the unfortunate Thomas Culpeper, he appears to have been totally unaware of the danger that surrounded him, or the fatal words that were being wrung from prisoners in London, and he spent his days 'merry a hawking'.[31] His name had been linked with that of the Queen certainly as early as 11 November, and probably even earlier, for Catherine herself mentioned the rumour of an engagement to him while she was maid of honour to Queen Anne of Cleves. This was an innocent enough association until Francis Dereham, 'to show his innocence since the marriage, said that Culpeper had succeeded him in the Queen's affections'.[32] This was a clue worth chasing, and on the 11th, Wriothesley first questioned Catherine upon 'the matter now come forth concerning Culpeper'. Evidently the interview was not satisfactory, for the council ordered further queries, saying, 'she hath not, as appeareth by her confession, so fully declared the circumstances of such communications as were betwixt her and Culpeper', as the evidence seemed to indicate. The interrogators were informed that Henry was anxious that they endeavour once more 'to get of her more information'.[33] Consequently Cranmer and Wriothesley tried again, but how successful they were is not certain, for if they wrung a second confession from the Queen it has not been preserved.

The first confession was quite sufficient to cost Culpeper his head. Catherine admitted the meetings on back stairs, she even confessed to calling him her 'little sweet fool', and she admitted presenting him with a cap and a ring. On the other hand, she denied 'upon her oath' any carnal relationship. Moreover, she claimed that she had begged Lady Rochford not to bother her further 'with such light matters', and warned her that 'alas madame this will be spied one day, and then we be all undone.' She not only placed the blame squarely on Culpeper, but painted Lady Rochford as the agent provocateur, who had engineered the whole affair for mysterious reasons of her own. According to Catherine, Jane Rochford had said that not even the threat of being 'torn with wild horses' could induce her to mention the meetings with Culpeper, and she had warned the Queen that if she, Catherine, disclosed the truth, she would 'undo herself and others'.[34]

Though the council might have wished for more, Catherine's words were enough to send them in search of Lady Rochford, Katherine Tylney, Margaret Morton and others of the Queen's household and chambers. Mistress Tylney had already been interrogated about life at Lambeth, but now, on 13 November, she went through a second ordeal about the Queen's behaviour at court. Had the Queen gone out at night while at Lincoln? What messages had she taken between the Queen and Jane Rochford? How late had the Queen stayed up, and with whom had she been? The answers were disappointing and vague, for Katherine Tylney had never been allowed a chance to see who it was that Catherine met in the early hours of the morning. Lady Rochford was more accommodating. In an effort to disentangle herself from any responsibility, she accused the Queen and Culpeper of contriving the whole thing while she herself was forced to play the role of an unwilling and unhappy minion who did as she was told. Jane Rochford's evidence does not make much sense. She denied ever overhearing what Culpeper and Catherine murmured together, and she insisted that she had slept through at least one whole interview. On the other hand, she thought 'that Culpeper hath known the Queen carnally considering all things that she hath heard and seen between them'.[35]

So far the evidence was inconclusive, dependent upon idle gossip and the chattering of Lady Rochford, but Catherine's fate was sealed beyond reprieve when Culpeper himself confirmed Lady Rochford's estimation by confessing that 'he intended and meant to do ill with the Queen and that in like wise the Queen so minded to do with him.'[36] Right or wrong, true or false, here was a confession of treason that was more than sufficient to cost the Queen her silly head, and Henry's mercy, on which Catherine had so abjectly called, could not now be expected to save her.

At this stage in the narrative of these unhappy days, the reader is usually appalled by what appears to be the total and blatant disregard for the most basic and fundamental principles of justice. On what possible legal grounds could Thomas Culpeper, Francis Dereham, and Catherine Howard have been found guilty of treason? There is not a scrap of evidence to indicate an overt act of adultery; at worst, Dereham might conceivably have been guilty of misprision for having failed to disclose the existence of a pre-contract, and might have been said to have caused injury both to the State and the monarch, for having allowed Henry to marry under false pretences. Catherine could have been tried and condemned for bigamy, but not even the best efforts of the council could unearth positive proof that Culpeper had ever been the Queen's lover. His only crime seems to have been the normal and masculine tendency of allowing his imagination too great a scope. The victims appear to have been falsely accused of crimes they never committed, and condemned on the most tenuous, distorted and vicious evidence possible – testimony which today would be thrown out of court as totally false and unacceptable. The credibility of the evidence and the nature of their crimes, however, must be viewed in terms of the social and ethical assumptions existing in the sixteenth century.

The law determining the character of treason under Henry VIII had been enacted in 1534. It extended the punishment for the most heinous act a subject of the Crown could commit to all who 'do maliciously wish, will or desire by words or writing, or by craft imagine' the King's death or harm.[37] Stated in this fashion, almost any word, expression, wish or deed could be construed as high treason. All that was necessary was to prove the malicious nature of the act or desire. In other words, the key to Tudor trials and to the reaction of the juries was simply the question of intent; no overt act was required. Condemnation upon the basis of presumptive treason was in no way regarded as being a miscarriage of justice, for thought must precede action; the imagined attempt implies the treasonous deed; and the execution of the criminal on the grounds of treasonous intent was simply the judicious nipping of treason in the bud.[38] At the trial of Sir Thomas More in 1535, the King's attorney-general argued quite logically that, 'even though we should have no word or deed to charge upon you, yet we have your silence, and that is a sign of your evil intention and a sure proof of malice.'[39]

Culpeper, Dereham and the Queen were all caught on the basis of intent, on the secret malice that lay concealed within their evil hearts and the presumptive carnal desires that lay hidden in their imagination. In the case of Culpeper, the French Ambassador reported that he was condemned to death for having carnally known the Queen, 'although he had not passed beyond words; for he confessed his intention to do so, and his confessed conversations, being held by a subject to a Queen, deserved death.'[40] Dereham was executed upon a similar basis: 'that his coming again to the Queen's service was to an ill intent' and that he and Catherine had 'traitorously imagined and procured that he, Dereham, should be retained in the service of the Queen, to the intent that they might continue their wicked courses.' To this the government added the further crime that Dereham had concealed the pre-contract, 'to the intent of preferring the Queen to her royal marriage by which they deceived the King'.[41] Catherine herself was executed for like causes, for the appointment of Dereham as her secretary and Katherine

175

Tylney as her chamberer was construed as 'proof of her will to return to her abominable life'.[42] For a time even the Dowager Duchess was accused of presumptive treason, when she foolishly opened one of Dereham's chests left in her keeping, and destroyed a number of the documents. Henry argued that the breaking of the coffers imported, 'a marvellous presumption' that the writings contained matters of treason and that the Duchess's 'intent' had been to conceal such 'letters of treason'.[43] In the end the old lady of Norfolk escaped the charge of treason with its terrifying consequences. Instead, she was accused, along with other members of her clan, of misprision for having failed to divulge the truth about her granddaughter's early activities, and for having deliberately contrived to deceive the King, by her assurances that Catherine was of pure and chaste living.

The ease with which the government could 'construct' treason is obvious, but there was also an added advantage to the system – that the victims almost invariably had to acknowledge the justice of their accusations. Although Catherine and her two admirers vehemently denied adultery, in the end all confessed their faults. It was not torture that extorted the plea of guilty, for it was extremely difficult not to admit that somewhere in their relations they had harboured secret carnal thoughts. Nor did society and public opinion have any doubt that they were indeed guilty of presumptive treason. One chronicler recorded that Catherine was, 'found an harlot' before the King married her, and 'an adultress after he married her', while a servant of the Dowager Duchess declared that 'they were worthy to be hanged one against another.'[44] Even the French Ambassador, who viewed English politics with a critical eye and the King's matrimonial difficulties with Gallic cynicism, described Culpeper as a gentleman of the King's privy chamber who had shared the royal couch and, 'apparently wished to share the Queen's too'.[45]

A sceptical mind might remark at this juncture that, even allowing the legal basis of presumptive treason, it is still impossible to accept the evidence offered by the government to prove the Queen a harlot. Torture we know was used against Robert Davenport, a gentleman who must have keenly regretted his friendship with Francis Dereham.

The threat of physical coercion was directed against Culpeper, and in all likelihood both he and Francis Dereham were exposed to the more unpleasant niceties of sixteenth-century interrogation. Certainly the documents are filled with suggestive and pregnant phrases that support such a conclusion: the council in London reported early in the proceedings against Dereham that, 'this much we know for the beginning'; the Duchess of Norfolk was questioned 'both to make her confess' and 'also to cough out the rest not yet discovered, if any such dregs remain amongst them'; and with Davenport and others, the lords of the council endeavoured to 'travail and labour to find out the bottom of the pot if it may be gotten out'.[46]

Not only is there 'vehement presumption' that torture was used, but the methods by which the witnesses were questioned are reminiscent of the artful procedures practised in certain countries today. 'Everyone's faults' were 'toted on their heads',[47] and treason was constructed by the most devious means. All the individuals concerned were exposed to exhausting and excruciating hours of endless interrogation, and the Dowager Duchess found herself, 'so meshed and tangled' in her evidence that her inquisitors naturally concluded that 'it will be hard for her to wind out again.'[48] Words, sentences, passing remarks, all were seized upon and torn out of context; and Thomas Wriothesley asked the council to send him a complete set of examinations dealing with the Duchess, Dereham, and Catherine's life, both at Horsham and Lambeth, 'that we may peruse them and pick all such things out of them as may serve to the purpose of our business'.[49] Thus it was that Dereham was suddenly confronted with the damning statement of Robert Davenport, who unhappily recalled that Dereham had once told him he was sure of his influence over Catherine, and that if the King 'were dead I am sure I might marry her'.[50] Here was clear evidence of maliciously wishing, willing and desiring the King's death, and the punishment was execution by hanging, disembowelling and quartering.

Moreover, much of the testimony was founded on little more than idle, if imaginative, gossip, malicious and faulty memory, and a general desire to oblige the powers-that-be. It was, for instance, suddenly recollected that Katherine Tylney had said to Margaret Morton, 'Jesus, is not the Queen abed yet?',[51] while Mistress Morton herself helpfully remembered in detail how she had first begun to believe that the Queen had evil intentions concerning Culpeper. She 'never mistrusted the Queen', she said, 'till she was at Hatfield, where she saw the Queen look out of her privy chamber window on Mr Culpeper after such sort that she thought in her conscience that there was love between them.'[52] More than one lady's imaginative talents were exercised, as when a Mistress Anne Fox remarked that she had known for 'a year past that the Queen was of ill disposition.'[53]

Considerably more than the condemned man's life was at stake in treason trials. The government was not simply interested in what the Dowager Duchess harboured by way of seditious knowledge; it was also immensely curious about what she concealed in the form of cash deposits, and her interrogators were delighted when the old lady 'fell on her knees', and weeping 'most abundantly, besought God to save His Majesty and to preserve him in long and prosperous life', and then enhanced that prosperity by revealing where she had hidden some £800 in her mansion.[54] In the same fashion, Lord William Howard, Catherine's uncle, when imprisoned for his failure to divulge the truth about his niece's character, added to his sins by claiming that most of his silver and plate had been lost at sea en route home from France. The King's council was darkly suspicious of this explanation, and while the lord sojourned in the Tower, they gave orders to investigate whether this was true or some 'crafty means to conceal and embezzle the same'.[55]

Political struggle for power as well as money lay behind much of the interrogation, for Catherine's disgrace involved considerably more than a homily in Tudor morality. Enemies were quick to perceive in the scandal a means of implicating the entire Howard clan in a plot, which, if it had been credible, would have destroyed the whole conservative party. Efforts were made to dredge from the witnesses proof that the Howards had deliberately and maliciously misled the King into his fifth marriage, as a means of furthering their family political designs. Consequently the Duchess was tormented with such questions as:

178

in what sort she did educate and bring up Mistress Catherine, and what change of apparel she was wont yearly and ordinarily to give her? [When had she] first knowledge that the King's Highness favoured Mistress Catherine'? [And after the King's love became apparent] What apparel did she give her? What communication she hath had with Mistress Catherine of the King's favour and what counsel and advice she gave her how to behave herself, and in what sort to entertain the King's Highness and how often?[56]

There is little doubt that Audley, Seymour, Cranmer and others on the privy council opposed to the Howards, had high hopes of bringing down far more important game than Culpeper, Dereham or even the Queen. In fact, more than once it was suggested that the Duke of Norfolk's ruin was imminent, and Marfllac reported that 'of his future many presume ill and none good.'[57]

In the midst of such distortion, falsehood, and political malice, all the testimony is suspect from the start, and the only uncontroversial fact established was that Catherine was not a virgin at the moment of her marriage with the King, and that she might well have been the common-law wife of Francis Dereham. Unfortunately for the Queen and her associates, the truth of the testimony and the credibility of the witnesses were never paramount factors in determining the final outcome of their trials. Tudor England took pride in the fact that the common law forbade the use of torture, yet no one thought it a distortion of justice or of law that Davenport and the others involved with Catherine should have suffered upon the rack. The rights, liberties and privileges of the individual as embedded in the historic and common law of the realm had to be turned aside when appeal was made to the highest rule of the land – the welfare of the realm. The will of the State stood above the individual liberties of subjects; it even stood higher than justice itself. At stake was the most sacrosanct element of monarchy – the unquestioned succession. Every precaution had to be taken against doubt as to the purity of royal blood. Catherine and her lovers had committed the worst crime that could be committed, for they had confounded the succession 'to the most fearful peril and danger of the destruction of your most royal person, and to the utter loss, disherison and desolation of this your Realm of England'.[58] Kings might breed bastards with impunity, but Queens could not allow the breath of scandal to approach their lives. They could not even in the secret recesses of their hearts confess to adulterous desires, for in so doing they endangered the reputation of the royal offspring and the inheritance of the crown. In the eyes of the sixteenth century, it was obviously the benevolence of the deity that had prevented Catherine from giving birth to a royal heir, whose legitimacy would thereafter be in constant doubt. Catherine and her friends deserved death simply on the grounds that they had by their actions allowed adulterous rumour to touch the person of the Queen, and it made no difference whether those rumours were true or not. They still existed. Consequently, it made but little difference if the evidence on which the Queen was condemned was extorted by torture, or even if it was, strictly speaking, not true at all.

The veracity or falsehood of the testimony was the least important aspect of any trial for high treason, for the jury rarely if ever decided on the guilt or innocence of the prisoners. The question of guilt had already been settled by royal will, and the prisoners were considered guilty until proved otherwise. In the laconic words of Thomas Cromwell, the Abbot of Glastonbury was sent down to Glastonbury 'to be tried and executed'.[59] The outcome of the trial was never in doubt because the government always brought guilty men to court. Thus it was no great injustice to divide up and distribute Culpeper's property before his trial and not after it. The role of a jury in treason cases was primarily declaratory, not to sit in judgment on matters of fact. The twelve good men and true rarely did what a modern jury does – listen to both sides of the case, evaluate the evidence, and then determine guilt or innocence. Instead, guilt was in most cases presumed from the start, and the jury simply publicized and revealed the truth. Trials in which a jury failed to find a traitor guilty on the basis of the government's testimony were rare indeed in the sixteenth century, and the Tudors were justifiably wrathful when a jury failed in its manifest duty. One such case occurred in the house of peers in 1535, when the lords found William, Lord Dacres of the North innocent of the charges brought against him. Henry found it expedient to overlook this arrogant defiance of the royal pleasure, but when a London jury found Nicholas Throckmorton innocent of treason in April, 1554, Henry's daughter Mary had the jury fined and imprisoned for 'collusion and wickedness'.[60]

It was in no way regarded as being peculiar that foreign ambassadors and the entire privy council should have been present at the trial of Messrs Culpeper and Dereham. The lords of the council were not there to intimidate, but to lend dignity to the proceedings, which aimed at making public the awful truth of the culprits' guilt. 'Many people,' said the French Ambassador, 'thought the publication of these foul details strange, but the intention is to prevent it being said afterwards that they were unjustly condemned.'[61] The more elevated the individuals involved, the more essential it was to achieve complete publicity. The government took the same attitude at the trial of Robert Davenport, who was 'not only condemned by the order of the law, but [also] with such declaration of his offences as we think all the standers by did wonderfully both detest the man and the matter'.[62]

Once Thomas Culpeper had confessed his evil and seditious designs against the Queen's virtue, events moved forward with grim determination. Over the weekend the unfortunate gentleman had been interrupted in his hawking and conducted to the Tower, a prisoner suspected of high treason. On Monday 4 November, Catherine was transported under armed guard to Syon. Not even imprisonment could impress upon her the full magnitude of her sins, and she spent her time, 'making good cheer, fatter and handsomer than ever', and 'taking great care of her person, well dressed, and much adorned; more imperious and commanding, and more difficult to please than she ever was when living with the King, her husband'.[63] The council had not yet done with the Queen, and Cranmer and Wriothesley made periodic visits to inquire further into the details of midnight sessions with Culpeper. By the 22nd most of the evidence was in, and 'proclamation was made at Hampton Court that she had forfeited her honour, and should be proceeded against by law, and was henceforth to be named no longer Queen, but only Catherine Howard.'[64]

By the first day of December the government was ready to strike at the Queen's associates, and Culpeper and Dereham were arraigned at Guildhall, London, for their crimes of detestable and vile treason. Both men received the full and terrible penalty allotted by the law, and they humbly petitioned the King in his mercy to commute their punishment to the more humane death by decapitation. Though the council advised that the offence of Culpeper was so 'very heinous' that it warranted a 'notable' execution, Henry did extend his clemency to his late gentleman of the privy chamber, but Francis Dereham, whose claim upon the King's indulgence was less, and who lacked influential friends, suffered the excruciating death reserved for traitors.[65] True to the ethics of the age, both men died well. There were no last-minute pleas for mercy, no clarion cries for justice or statements of innocence. Instead, in the words of an eyewitness, on 10 December:

> Culpeper and Dereham were drawn from the Tower of London to Tyburn, and there Culpeper, after an exhortation made to the people to pray for him, he standing on the ground by the gallows, kneeled down and had his head stricken off; and then Dereham was hanged, membered, bowelled, headed, and quartered [and both] their heads set on London Bridge.[66]

Meanwhile the entire Howard dynasty had been shaken to its core, and all who had in any way been associated with Catherine either at Lambeth or at court were imprisoned. In fact, so many members, servants and retainers of the clan were involved that the Tower failed to house them all, and makeshift prisons had to be found elsewhere. The council had been on the trail of various of the Queen's relatives for well over a week, but now that Culpeper and Dereham were dead, room was made in the Tower for new suspects. Lord William was incarcerated on the 9th, the Dowager Duchess was seized on the 10th, and the Queen's aunt, Lady Bridgewater, was removed to the Tower on the 13th. While the less fortunate were gloomily meditating upon their sins in a stone cell in the Tower, other members of the Howard tribe were frantically endeavouring to dissociate themselves from the Queen's disgrace. Norfolk was shocked into horrified and transparent activity, and he exclaimed with tears in his eyes that his own anguish and horror were caused by the thought of the King's grief at this his second betrayal. Actually it was the fear of the King's wrath directed at the uncle of two adulterous wives that spurred the Duke into frenzied action. He sat with the rest of the council at the trial of Culpeper and Dereham and was remarked to have laughed loudly during the examination of the prisoners, 'as if he had cause to rejoice'.[67] He took excellent care to avoid his stepmother, the Dowager Duchess, and later boasted that it was he who had first revealed her treason when she broke open Dereham's chests and burned some of the contents. In a final effort to escape the consequences of his niece's dishonour and to ward off the political debacle that threatened, Norfolk tactfully retired to his country estate and wrote Henry a letter in which he hysterically denied any knowledge of the crimes committed by his 'ungracious' stepmother, his 'unhappy' brother, and his 'lewd' sister. Norfolk was terrified that the King would 'conceive a displeasure' against him, and he besought his sovereign, 'prostrate at your royal feet', to forgive him the sins of his seditious family and to 'continue my good and gracious Lord'.[68] The Duke was not alone in his efforts to disown his niece; Catherine's brothers and cousins, along with the relatives of the unfortunate Culpeper, were all in a frenzy to extricate themselves from the web of scandal. Catherine and her suitors stood alone, for they had placed themselves outside the limits of blood and family; they faced alone and unloved the truth that the King's wrath is death.

For a moment it appeared as if the Queen's disgrace would result in the family and political catastrophe for which the Protestant elements of the realm piously hoped. On 22 December the Howard tribe, with the exception of the Duke, were tried and found guilty of misprision and forfeited all their goods and possessions to the Crown and their bodies to perpetual imprisonment. Henry's vengeance, however, was short-lived. The Duke of Norfolk escaped completely and returned to London with only slightly tarnished authority; Margaret, the wife of Lord William Howard, and Anne, the wife of Catherine's brother Henry, were released from the Tower and pardoned of the crime of misprision within two months; the testy old Duchess was let out in May; and Lord William was pardoned in August of 1542.

Charles Howard, the Queen's brother, found it politic to remove himself from court and seek fame and fortune in the defence of Christendom against the infidel. Within a year he was back again, the government having decided to overlook his family misfortunes and his own dangerous flirtation with the King's niece. The sovereign's clemency and charity even included another brother, Henry Howard, who received within a month of his sister's execution a gift from the Crown of £10 given '*intuitu charitatis*'.[69] Only Lady Rochford, who had been the messenger and *agent provocateur* of Catherine's presumptive adultery with Culpeper, suffered the full penalty of the law.

December was a bleak and dreary month for the King. There was neither music nor festivities during the Christmas season, and Henry entertained himself with hunting and restless perambulation on the outskirts of the city. Old, weary and disillusioned, he waited for the new year and the new parliament. The assembly of lords and commons met on 16 January. The King himself was present and listened while Thomas Audley, the Lord Chancellor, gave the speech from the throne. The royal heart, so buffeted by his wife's betrayal, may have found solace in the words of his chancellor and the reaction of his devoted servants in parliament. Thomas Audley congratulated the assembled throng upon the good fortune that permitted so fine and wise a sovereign to rule over them; then, as the King's name was spoken, every member rose and bowed. Everyone must have recognized the nature of the monarch's sorrow and the unsavoury task that confronted the High Court of Parliament in regard to the Queen's fate. The Lord Chancellor, however, was at considerable pains to impress his audience with the notion that they had been called together to produce sound law, firm justice and good authority, and not for the sake of a single individual. When Audley had concluded, the lords and commons rose again, 'as if to acknowledge the truth of his words', and to give 'thanks to Almighty God who had preserved for so long a time such an exceptional prince over this kingdom'.[70]

Five days later, on the 21st, the Bill of Attainder against the Queen was introduced into the upper house. Evidently the peers were not altogether happy with the procedure against the Queen, for an act of attainder could condemn a person to death without a hearing or defence, and the Lord Chancellor suggested that they should not proceed too hastily for the 'queen was in no sense a mean and private person but an illustrious and public one. Therefore her cause had to be judged with such integrity' that no whisper of injustice might spread abroad. Consequently he proposed that a deputation be sent to Syon to calm Catherine's 'womanish fears', and allow her to speak in her own defence, for it was 'but just that a princess should be tried by equal laws' with peers of the realm.[71] Though a committee of the lords did visit the Queen, she was not given a chance to defend herself at law. Suddenly it was decided to go through with the act of attainder, with the important proviso that Henry himself would not be present at the passing of the Bill. Instead, the monarch would give his assent *in absentia*, 'by letters-patent under the great seal of England' so as to spare himself the grief and pain of hearing once again the 'wicked facts of the case'.[72] A week later, the Bill received a second reading; on 8 February it was read for a third time; and on 11 February the Queen's death warrant became law.

The statute under which Catherine and Lady Rochford suffered was unique. It set forth the high treason committed by the Queen, and then went on to reaffirm and give parliamentary sanction to the trial and condemnation of Culpeper and Dereham, and the sentence of misprision received by the various members of the Howard family. The royal assent by letters-patent was asserted to be 'as good strength and force as though the King's person had been there personally present, and had assented openly and publicly to the same'. Finally, the act locked the stable door after the horse had been stolen: it declared that should the King again 'take a fancy to any woman', esteeming her 'a pure and clean maid when indeed the proof may or shall after appear contrary', and should such a lady 'couple herself with her Sovereign Lord' without declaring to him the existence of 'her unchaste life', then 'every such offence shall be deemed and adjudged High Treason.'[73]

Throughout the long dreary weeks of tension and despair Catherine had been running true to form – alternating wild hysteria and agonizing self-appraisals with haughty disdain and senseless cheerfulness. Catherine is not easy to judge or to analyse. It may not be accident that no one seems to have been surprised by the revelation of her past life except the King, and it may be significant that no one came to her defence or appears to have pitied her fate. This was in part a matter of social ethics and political expediency, for she had placed herself outside the pale of sympathy. Others of the King's wives, however, had won passionate avowals of innocence, and even in the face of the monarch's wrath, men had risked much to express their trust and love. Catherine of Aragon, Anne Boleyn and Anne of Cleves all had their champions, but Catherine Howard had none. It may have been because she was shallow and brittle, arrogant in success and servile in distress.

Her actions can be excused on the grounds that she was an ignorant child of nature, but the evidence does not point that way. Catherine was just as well-educated as most of her contemporaries of an equivalent social position; she certainly had enough sense to conceal as long as possible the affair with Culpeper; and she appears to have had something resembling a guilty conscience since she warned Culpeper not to mention their meetings, even in the confessional, for fear that the King, being head of the Church, would in some mysterious and mystical fashion come to hear of it. The only deed that Catherine accomplished with splendid deliberation and studied magnificence was to die as befitted a queen and a Howard, for she shared in the universal conviction of her age that the 'chief care [of life] was to leave a good opinion in the people's minds now at parting'.[74] There was a peculiar pride in dying well. Not only was it necessary to the soul's salvation to die humble and repentant, confessing one's faults, but there was also a perverse pride in not wishing to manifest fear in the face of the inevitable. Breeding and training determined that on the eve of her death, Catherine should request that the block be brought to her cell so she might learn, 'how she was to place her head on it'.[75]

Just before the Queen was taken to the Tower she received a deputation of lords who were anxious to hear her cause before the act of attainder was passed. She 'openly confessed and acknowledged to them the great crime of which she had been guilty against the most high God and a kind prince'. Then, recalling that she was still a Howard, she 'begged them all to implore his majesty not to impute her crime to her whole kindred and family'. Lastly, she besought:

> his majesty that it would please him to bestow some of her clothes on those maid-servants, who had been with her from the time of her marriage, since she had nothing now [with which] to recompense them as they deserved.[76]

No words could have been more appropriate to the occasion, and the peers left Syon feeling deeply gratified that Catherine should not only acknowledge the justice of her death, but also act the role of a queen even on the threshold of death.

On 10 February 1542, she was escorted by water to the Tower. There was one anguished moment when the full impact of what was in store suddenly broke upon her and she had to be conducted forcibly into her barge. The small flotilla was led by a galley containing the Lord Privy Seal and other members of the council, plus a number of guards and servants. The Queen's vessel then followed, which was closed to inquisitive eyes; and finally the Duke of Suffolk in a barge crowded with soldiers, brought up the rear. As the procession drifted downstream it passed under London Bridge, with its impaled remains of Messrs Culpeper and Dereham, and finally came to rest at Traitors' Gate. There Catherine was accorded the full honours due to a queen, and, dressed in black velvet, she mounted the stairs to her prison chamber.

The time of the execution had not yet been determined, and it was not until the evening of the 12th that Catherine was commanded to 'dispose her soul and prepare for death', for she was to die on the following Monday morning. At seven the next morning the entire council, the foreign ambassadors, and a handful of curious Londoners gathered at the Tower – all, that is, except Norfolk who wisely remained in self-imposed exile, and Suffolk who had been taken suddenly ill.[77] At nine the executions commenced; Catherine suffered first. She was so weak that she had to be helped up the scaffold and could scarcely speak the customary words of edification and confession. Everything indicates that she made the 'most godly and Christian end that ever was heard tell of since the world's creation'. Both Catherine and Lady Rochford:

> desired all Christian people to take regard unto their worthy and just punishment with death for their offences [for they had sinned] against God heinously from their youth upward, in breaking all his commandments, and also against the King's royal Majesty very dangerously.

They had been, they confessed, 'justly condemned by the laws of the realm and parliament to die', and they begged 'the people to take example of them', to amend 'their ungodly lives, and gladly to obey the King in all things, for whose preservation they did heartily pray'.[78] After the severed body of Catherine Howard had been covered with a cloth, Lady Rochford took her place on the platform. She was still suffering from nervous shock, but she also died well except that one observer felt that she took too long in enumerating the 'several faults which she had committed in her life'.[79]

After all is said and done, one is tempted to ponder the whys and wherefores of Catherine's life. The brilliant spectacle of her career soon faded, leaving nothing but a King grown suddenly grey and aged, and a law declaring it to be treason for a lady to marry the King unless she were a virgin, which, it was noted, rather limited the number of candidates. When Henry stood before his council listening to the story of his wife's infidelities, the tears trickled down his cheeks as the illusions and obsessions of his life shattered around him. The King could never forgive Catherine for what she had taken from him – the image of his youth. But even in doing her royal husband wrong, Catherine is strangely inconsequential; Henry would surely have grown old and senile, even without the knowledge that he had been cuckolded and cheated. There is a certain inevitability in the tragedy that occurred, but somehow one feels that the shallow motives, the juvenile desires, and petty and vain considerations of the Queen had little to do with the final calamity – the end would have been the same, history would have been unchanged, had she never lived or died. Possibly no worse verdict can be passed upon a human life. Here in a twisted, obscure sort of way lies the essential failure of Catherine Howard's life: although she was caught up in the game of politics and was never a free agent, the Queen never brought happiness or love, security or respect, into the world in which she lived. She enacted a light-hearted dream in which juvenile delinquency, wanton selfishness, and ephemeral hedonism, were the abiding themes. Who is to say whose fault it was – Catherine's or that of her age?

ABBREVIATIONS USED IN NOTES AND BIBLIOGRAPHY

Manuscripts are cited and their location given under their usual abbreviations, which are as follows:

P.R.O. – Public Record Office, London
S.P. 1 – State Papers, Henry VIII
S.P. 6 – Theological Tracts, Henry VIII
Star Chamber 2
Inquisitions Post Mortem C 142

In the citation of printed books, the following abbreviations have been used:

Antiq. Rep. – *Antiquarian Repertory*
B.M. – British Museum
Cal. S.P. Spanish – *Calendar of State Papers, Spanish*
Cal. S.P. Venetian – *Calendar of State Papers, Venetian*
Cam. Soc. – Camden Society
Essex Arch. Soc. Trans. – *Essex Archaeological Society Transactions*
D.N.B. – *Dictionary of National Biography*
E.E.T.S. – Early English Text Society
H.O. – *Ordinances of the Household*
H.M.C. – Historical Manuscript Commission
H.S. – Harleian Society
J.H.I. – *Journal of the History of Ideas*
L.P. – *Letters and Papers of Henry VIII*
P.P.C. – *Proceedings of the Privy Council*
P.C.C. – Prerogatove Court at Cantebury (Somerset House)
Surrey Arch. Col. – *Surrey Archaeological Collections*
Surrey Arch. Soc. Trans. – *Surrey Archaeological Society Transactions*
Sussex Arch. Col. – *Sussex Archaeological Collections*
St. Papers – *State Papers during the Reign of Henry VIII*
V.C.H. – *Victoria County History*

Fuller titles, names of editors, and dates of editions are given in the bibliography of printed books. Spelling and punctuation of manuscript quotations have been modernized.

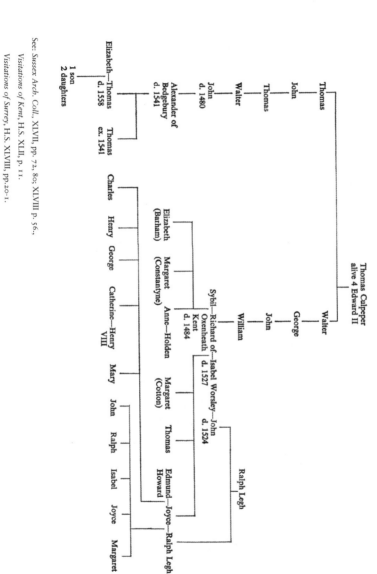

CATHERINE HOWARD'S BIRTH

There are several ways of computing Catherine's age. None of them is very conclusive and all are highly controversial. The only statement that can be made with any degree of reliability is that there are at least three contemporary reports that suggest that Catherine was unusually young at the time of her marriage to the King in July of 1540 (Hume, *Chronicle of Henry VIII*, p. 75; *Original Letters*, I, p. 201; *L.P.*, XVI, 1426). What this signifies is difficult to say. Catherine's mother was twelve when she married Ralph Legh, her first husband. Girls tended to be 'forward virgins' at fourteen, and childbearing began between sixteen and eighteen. On the other hand, in comparison with Henry's other wives, Catherine need not have been a child bride of fifteen to warrant the description of a young woman. Catherine of Aragon was twenty-five at her marriage; Catherine Parr was at least thirty; Anne of Cleves, Anne Boleyn and Jane Seymour ranged between twenty-five and twenty-six, which represented by sixteenth-century standards the age of discretion and experience.

There are, however, certain outside limits that can be set with reasonable accuracy as the extremes within which Catherine's birth must have fallen. She could not have been born after 1527, since Dame Isabel Legh, Catherine's maternal grandmother, mentions her in her will of that year (18 Porch). Four years earlier, in 1524, John Legh, husband to Isabel and Catherine's step-grandfather, failed to notice in his will the existence of any of the Howard girls. Instead he listed Catherine's three brothers – Charles, Henry, and George (15 Bodfield). This may have been because Catherine and her sister Mary were not yet born, or it may have been a reflection of the masculine standards of the age – infant girls did not warrant mention as beneficiaries in a will.

The earliest limit is harder to determine, since the marriage date of Edmund Howard to Jocasta Culpeper is far from certain. If Edmund and Jocasta were wedded sometime around 1514-15 (*D.N.B.*, article: 'Catherine Howard'; *L.P.*, 2nd edn., I, ii, 3325; Strickland, *Queens of England*, III, p. 101), and if her three brothers were her elders, as the genealogical tables suggest (*Visitations of Kent*, H.S., LXXIV, p. 81) then Catherine could not have been born before 1517-18.

There is considerable evidence for the belief that she was, in fact, born some time between 1518 and 1524. The French Ambassador reported that she was eighteen when she was sharing her bed with Francis Dereham (*L.P.*, XVI, 1426). The date of this affair, by Catherine's own confession, was in 1538-9 (H.M.C., *Marquis of Bath*, II, pp. 8-9). On the other hand, the Ambassador weakens the credence of his statement by adding that Dereham had been systematically corrupting Catherine ever since she was thirteen. If we accept her age as being eighteen in 1539, then she must have been born about 1521. The unknown author of the *Chronicle of Henry VIII* (p. 75), whose imagination is considerably better than his facts, says that the Queen was fifteen when she first encountered the King. This would push her birth forward to 1524.

There is one final clue: Catherine's portrait (Toledo Museum, Toledo, Ohio), about which there is considerable uncertainty, gives her age as twenty-one. Presumably it was painted in 1540 or 1541, and this would establish her birth in 1519 or 1520. The year 1521 seems as good as any, since we know that Henry Manox was first smitten by Catherine's charms in 1536 when she would have been a precocious thirteen or fourteen. This in turn fits with the report of the French Ambassador, who claimed her age as eighteen in 1539, and with the general suggestion that Catherine was relatively young to have been a queen.

All of this is of course pure speculation, since, among other things, her father's marriage in 1514-15 is conjectural, the statement that Catherine was the fifth child of the marriage is probably a guess on the part of Miss Strickland, since she does not bother to authenticate the statement (*Queens of England*, III, p. 101; see also *Visitation of Kent*, H.S., LXXIV, p. 81). Finally there is hopeless confusion over how many full and half brothers and sisters Catherine actually had. This last complication arises out of the fact that Jocasta Culpeper was married twice – first to Ralph Legh (by whom she certainly had two sons, John and Ralph, and very probably three daughters, Isabel (who married Sir Edward Baynton), Joyce (who wedded John Stanney), and Margaret (who married first Thomas Arundel and possibly at a later date a gentleman named Rice). Her second marriage was to Edmund Howard (who sired Charles, Henry, George, and Catherine). Mary Howard, who married Sir Edmund Trafford, was probably a Howard child also, but she is claimed by both families, and there is some evidence that there was still a fourth Howard daughter named Margaret, but this may simply be a confusion with Margaret Legh. All we know for certain is that Edmund Howard was claiming ten children in 1527 (Ellis, *Letters*, I, 3rd series, 160). For those who wish to try their hand at this muddle over Catherine's vital statistics, a start can be made by consulting the following: P.C.C., 15 Bodfield, 24 Bennet, 3 Crymes, 18 Porch, all of which are printed in the *Surrey Archaeological Collections*, LI, pp. 85-90; *Visitations of Cornwall* (edit. J. L. Vivian), pp. 4-5; *Inquisitions Post Mortem, Henry VIII*, I. 820; *Archaeologia Cantiana*, IV, p. 264; *Visitations of Surrey*, H.S., XLIII, pp. 20-1; *Visitation of Kent*, H.S., LXXIV: pp. 41-2 and 81 ; *V.C.H., History of Hampshire*, IV, pp. 185, 295-6; *Remains, Historical and Literary of Lancaster and Chester*, Chetham Society, LI, p. 72; LXXXI, p. 3 ; Strickland, *Queens of England*, III, p. 101; D.N.B., art. 'Catherine Howard'; H. Howard, *Memorials of the Howard Family*, pp. 1-26.

NOTES

CHAPTER 2:

1 Cornwallis, *Essayes*, No. 20, fol. M2.
2 Wagner, *Heralds and Heraldry*, pp. 79-80, 90; L.P., V, App. 38 (2).
3 *Paston Letters*, 1, 250, p. 341.
4 Round. *Studies in Peerage*, pp. 73-82, 435-57: Howard, *Memorials of the Howard Family*, pp. 1-26; Cokayne, *Complete Peerage*, IX, pp. 601 ff.
5 Campbell, *Material for the Reign of Henry VII*, 1, p. 208.
6 Camden, *Remains*, p. 354.
7 Weever, *Ancient Funeral Monuments*, p. 835.
8 *Cal. SP. Spanish*, IV, i, 460, p. 762.
9 L.P., IV, 6248, g. 21.
10 Stow, *Survey*, p. 81-2, Machyo, *Diary*, p. 294; *Cal. S.P. Venetian*, IV, 694.
11 Lodge, *Illustrations*, 1, pp. 12, 19, 23-4.
12 L.P., XI, 636.
13 P.R.O., Star Chamber 2, vol. 2, f. 178.
14 Holmes, *The Estates of the Higher Nobility*, pp. 4-5.
15 *Cal. S.P. Venetian*, II, 1287, p. 560; IV, 694, pp. 294-5.
16 Holmes, *The Estates of the Higher Nobility*, p. 58.
17 Stow, *Survey*, p. 81; *Bulletin of Historical Research*, XXVII, p. 103; Raines, *The Derby Household Books*, p. Ii.

18 *L.P.*, X, 816; *Paston Letters*, I, 244, p. 337.

19 *L.P.*, II, ii, 3446. pp. 1465, 1481; XIII, i, 1519, g. I; *P.R.O.*, Exchequer 405, 'List of Miscellaneous names given in the Teller of the Treasury Report for 1539-41', Rolls 109-10.

20 *Cal. S.P. Spanish*, IV, i, 232, pp. 367-8.

21 V.C.H., *History of Hampshire and the Isle of Wight*, IV, pp. 185, 295, 296.

22 D.N.B., Art. 'Francis Bryan'; *Essex Arch. Soc. Trans.*, XV, p. 52.

23 *Visitations of Norfolk*, H.S. XXXII, p. 289; *D.N.B.*, Art. 'Francis Knollys'; *Visitations of Cornwall*, pp. 4-7.

24 *Visitations of Kent* H.S. XLII, p. 11; *Archeologia Cantiana*, IV, p. 264; *Sussex Arch. Col.*, XLVII, p. 56; XLVIII, pp. 72, 80.

25 See Appendix.

26 Quoted in Einstein, *Tudor Ideals*, p. 161.

27 *L.P.*, VI, 1546; Cal. *S.P. Spanish*, IV, i, 232, pp. 367-8; 481, p. 790; V, ii, 77, p. 214

28 Quoted in Einstein, *Tudor Ideals*, pp. 115-116.

29 *Cal. S.P. Spanish*, V, ii, 77, p. 214; *Statutes of the Realm*, III, 28 Henry VIII, cap. 24, p. 680.

30 *L.P.*, XVI, 1333.

31 *LP.*, XXI, ii, 697.

32 Mattingly, *Catherine of Aragon*, p. 265.

33 *L.P.*. XII. ii. 1029.

34 *Cal. S.P. Spanish*, IV, i, 257, p. 450.

35 *Cal, S.P. Venetian*, IV, 694, p, 295.

36 Hall, *Henry VIII*, I, p. 162.

37 L.P., XII, i, 479.

38 Ibid., ii, 422 (2).

39 *Cal. S.P. Spanish*, IV, ii, 1097, p. 735.

40 Ibid., V, ii, 104, p. 269.

41 *St. Papers*, I, ii, 70, p. 518.

42 L.P., XXI, ii, 554.

43 *Cal. S.P. Spanish*, IV, i, 228, p. 360; 250, p. 422

44 Cavendish, *Life of Wolsey*, p. 116.

45 L.P., XVI, 101.

46 B.M., Harleian MSS, 422, No. 68, f. 87.

47 *Cal. S.P. Spanish*, IV, i, 429, p. 719.

48 Roper, *Life of More*, 71.

49 L.P., XII, i, 594, 636, 667.

50 *St. Papers*, I, ii, 98, p. 568.

51 Cal. S.P. *Spanish*, IV, ii, 934, p. 429; V, i, 122, p. 355.

CHAPTER 3:

1 *Archaeologia*, XLVII, p. 326.

2 *L.P.*, 1 (2nd edition), ii, 2246; II, ii, 'The King's Book of Payments', p. 1463.

3 *L.P.*, XII, ii, 463, 466.

4 *Register of Admissions to the Middle Temple*, I, p. 7.

5 P.R.O., Star Chamber 2, vol. 2, f. 178.

6 *Arehaeologia*, XXV, p. 376.

7 *L.P.*, XIII, i, 295.

8 *L.P.*, I (2nd edition), ii, 3325.

9 *L.P.*, II, ii, 'The King's Book of Payments', p. 1473.

10 *L.P.*, V, 220, g. 14; VIII, 1103

11 Wilson, *State of England*, p. 24.

12 Ellis, *Letters*, I (3rd series), 160.

13 *Archaeolagia Cantiana*, XXXII, p. 319.

14 *L.P.*, IV, it, 3732.

15 *L.P.*, V, 1757.

16 P.C.C., 15 Bodfield and 18 Porch (published in the *Surrey Arch. Col*, LI pp. 87-9).

17 *L.P.*, V, 1042.

18 *Surrey Arch. Col.*, LI, pp. 85-8; *Visitations, of Surrey*, H.S., XLIII, p. 21; *Inquisitions Post Mortem* – Henry VII, I, 820.

19 See Appendix.

20 *Surrey Arch. Soc.*, III, p. 174; *Notes and Queries*, CLIX, pp. 419-210. For further evidence of a third wife see, *L.P.*, XI, 1098.

21 Fuller, *Worthies*, p. 361; Strickland, *Queens of England*, III, p. 101 Brenan and Statham, *House of Howard*, I, pp. 268-9.

22 Strickland, *Queens of England*, III, p. 105.

23 Ibid.

24 Camden, *Elizabethan Woman*, p. 42; Hole, *English Home-life*, pp. 18-19.

25 *St. Papers*, I, ii, 174, p. 711

26 *Visitations of Suffolk*, p. 151; *Notes and Queries*, CLXVII, pp. 334-5; P.R.O., S.P. I, vol. 167, f. 136 (*L.P.*, XVI, 1321); P.R.O., Inquisitions Post Mortem, G 142, vol. 51, No.36; *Visitations of Norfolk* (Norfolk Arch. Soc), 1, pp. 227-31.

27 Brenan and Statham, *House of Howard*, I, p. 158, n. 1.

28 Quoted in Einstein, *Tudor Ideals*, p. 245.

29 *Paston Letters*, I, 72, pp. 91-2.

30 Osbourne, *Letters*, p. 135.

31 Sneyd, *A Relation of the Island of England*, p. 27; Hole, *English Home-life*, p. 56.

32 *Inquisitions Post Mortem* – Henry VII, I, 820.

33 Casady, *Henry Howard*, pp. 35-6.

34 Camden, *Elizabethan Woman*, p. 93.

35 Latimer, *Sermons*, pp. 81, 146.

36 *L.P.*, III, I, 1172.

37 Lyly, *Works*, II, p. 17.

38 *L.P.*, II, ii 3765.

39 Cleaver, *A Godlie Forme of Household Government*, p. 246.

40 Ascham, *The Scholemaster*, p. 50.

41 Mulcaster, *Positions*, p. 178.

42 *L.P.*, XV, 229; XVI, 1134; P.R.O., S.P. 1, vol. 167, f. 153 (*L.P.*, XVI, 1338).

43 P.R.O., S.P. 1, vol. 167, f. 159., (*L.P.*, XVI, 1339); *L.P.*, V, 1449.

44 P.R.O., *Inquisitions Post Mortem*, C. 142, vol. 69, No. 192.

45 P.R.O., S.P. 1, vol. 168, f. 10 (*L.P.*, XVI, 1385).

46 Ibid, ff. 97-8 (*L.P.*, XVI, 1416 ii).

47 *St Papers*, I, ii, 180, 722; *L.P.*, XI, 636, XVI, 1445.

48 *L.P.*, IV, ii, 4710.

49 J.R. Daniel-Tyssen, 'Parliamentary Surveys of the County of Sussex, 1649-1652,' *Sussex Arch. Col.*, XXIII, pp. 280-7, Elwes and Robinson, *History of the Castles and And Manors Western Sussex*, pp. 119-20.

50 Markham, *The English House-wife*, p. 4.

51 Harrison, *Elizabethan England*, p. 119.

52 P.R.O., S.P. I, vol. 167, ff 135-6 (*L.P.*, XVI, 1321).

53 Ibid., f. 139.

54 Ibid., f. 138.

55 Ibid., f. 130 (*L.P.*, XVI, 1320); f. 136 (*L.P.*, XVI, 1321).

56 Ibid., ff. 128-9 (*L.P.*, XVI, 1320).

57 Roberts and Godfrey, *Survey of London*, XXIII, *Southbank and Vauxhall, the Parish of St. Mary Lambeth*. i, p. 138.

58 P.R.O., S.P. 1, vol. 167, f. 129 (*L.P.*, XVI, 1320).

59 Ibid.

60 Ibid., f. 130.

61 Ibid., f. 138 (*L.P.*, XVI, 1321).

62 Burnet, *Reformation*, IV, 71, p. 505.

63 P.R.O., S.P. I, vol. 167, f. 136 (*L.P.*, XVI, 1321).

64 Burnet, *Reformation*, IV, 71, p. 505.

65 H.M.C., *Marquis of Bath*, II, p. 9; *L.P.*, XVI, 1426.

66 Burnet, *Reformation*, IV, 71, p. 504.

67 P.R.O., S.P. 1, vol. 167, f. 130 (*L.P.*, XVI, 1320).

68 H.M.C., *Marquis of Bath*, II, p. 9; P.R.O., S.P. 1, vol. 167, f. 130 (*L.P.*, XVI, 1320).

69 Ibid., f. 131 (*L.P.*, XVI, 1320).

70 Ibid., f. 155 (*L.P.*, XVI, 1339).

71 Nucius, *Second Book of Travels*, p. 10.

72 Rye, *England as Seen by Foreigners*, p. 14.

73 *L.P.*, XII, ii, 35.

74 Ibid., 143; XIV, i, 160.

75 *Gentleman's Magazine*, XXIII, i (new series, March 1845). pp. 265-6.

76 *L.P.*, XIV, i, 160.

77 *L.P.*, XXI, ii, 555, item 5.

78 Quoted in Friedman, *Anne Boleyn*, II, p. 200, from the Vienna Archives; P.C. 230, ii, fol. 20.
79 *Cal. S.P. Spanish*, V, i, 118, p. 344.
80 P.R.O., S.P. 1, vol. 167, f. 137 (L.P., XVI, 1321).
81 Ibid., *L.P.*, XVI, 1400.
82 *L.P.*,XVI, 1469.
83 Ibid., P.R.O., S.P. 1, vol. 168, f. 158 (*L.P., XVI, 1461*).
84 Burnet, *Reformation*, IV, 71, p. 505.
85 Ibid.
86 Ibid., p. 504.
87 Ibid.
88 Hall, *Henry VIII*, II, pp. 300-1; *L.P.*, XV, 22, 776.
89 *L.P.*, XIV, ii, 572 (4).
90 Ellis, *Letters*, 2nd series, II, p. 41.
91 Strickland, *Queens of England*, III, p. 62 (*L.P.*, XV, 216).
92 Ibid., p. 63 (*L.P.*, XV, 229).
93 Ibid., pp. 63-4.
94 Burnet, *Reformation*, IV, 71, p. 505.
95 Ibid.

CHAPTER 4:

1 Dekker, *The Seven Deadly Sinnes*, p. 38.
2 Lyly, *Euphues nnd His England*, pp. 434-5.
3 Moryson, *An Itinerary*, III, 496.
4 Stow, *Survey*, p. 76; Pendrill, *London Life in the 14th Century*, p. 12.
5 Stow, *Survey*, pp. 93-4.
6 Quoted in Salzman, *England in Tudor Times*, pp. 66-7.
7 Stow, *Survey*, pp. 360-1.
8 Quoted in Lees-Milne, *Tudor Renaissance*, p. 12.
9 Wilson, *Shakespeare's England*, p. 93.
10 Starkey, *Dialogue*, p. 88.
11 Rye, *England as Seen by Foreigners*, p. 7.

12 Perlin, *Description d'Angleterce* printed in *Antiq. Rep.*, IV, p. 505.

13 Harrison, *Elizabethan England*, pp. 227-8, 245, 247; Bullein, *Dialogue*, p. 93.

14 Perlin, *Description d'Angleteve* printed in *Antiq. Rep.*, IV, p. 513.

15 Hall, *Henry VIII*, I, p. 225.

16 Baildon, *Les Reportes del Cases in Camera Stellata*, pp. 37-8.

17 Platter, *Travels in England*, pp. 187-8.

18 Stow, *Survey*, pp. 171-2.

19 Bullein, *Dialogue*, p. 93.

20 Ibid., p. 94.

21 Fisher, *English Works*, p. 140.

22 Platter, *Travels in England*, p. 174.

23 Fisher, *English Works*, p. 240.

24 *L.P.*, XVI, 578.

25 Allen, *Opus Epislolarum Erasmi*, III, 623, p. 47.

26 *L.P.*, XVI, 223.

27 Longland, *A sermon spoken before the Kinge*, f. Eii-Eiii.

28 *L.P., Addenda*, I, ii, 1880; Nashe, *Works*, II, pp. 143-4.

29 Ibid., p. 139.

30 More, *English Works*, I, pp. 468-70.

31 Nicholas, *Literary Remains*, p. 60; Bullein, *Dialogue*, p. 9.

32 Prescott, *Mary Tudor*, p. 6.

33 H.O., p. 201.

34 Ibid., pp. 150, 164.

35 Salzman, *England in Tudor Times*, pp. 85-6.

36 Nott, *Works of Henry Howard*, I, App. II, pp. v-vi.

37 Machyn, *Diary*, pp. 143-4.

38 *H.O.*, pp. 174-5.

39 *Cal. S.P. Venetian*, II, 918, p. 398.

40 Rye, *England as Seen by Foreigners*, p. 18.

41 *Cal. S.P. Venetian*, II, 918, p. 400.

42 Sneyd, *A Relation of the Island of England*, p. 73.

43 P.R.O., S.P. 6, vol. 2, p. 41.

44 Platter, *Travels in England*, p. 176.

45 *L.P.* XXI, ii, 642.

46 H.O., pp. 229, 235.

47 Ibid., pp. 147-8.

48 Ibid., pp. 198-9.

49 Ibid., pp. 155-6.

50 Ibid., pp, 139, 144, 153, 228.

51 Ibid., pp. 139, 145, 154.

52 Harrison, *Elizabethan England*, p. 181; H.O., p. 150.

53 H.O., pp. 148, 157-8.

54 Prescott, *Mary Tudor*, p. 7.

55 *L.P.*, XIII, ii, 578.

56 Moryson, *An Itinerary*, III, p. 407.

57 Chamberlain, *Letters*, pp. 54-5.

58 Einstein, *Tudor Ideals*, p. 122.

59 *L.P.*, XVI, 760.

60 Stow, *Annales*, pp. 581-2.

61 *L.P.*, XVI, 903.

62 Leland, *Collectanea*, VI, pp. 7-11.

63 H.O., pp. 154-6.

64 Ibid., p. 121; *The Booke af Henrie Erle of Arundell*, printed in *Antiq. Rep.*, II, pp. 206-7.

65 H.O., p. 157.

66 *Sir Thomas More*, p. 84.

67 'The note and trewth of the moost goodly behavior ... of the Ladie Kateryne ... in marriage ... to Prince Arthur', printed in *Antiq. Rep.*, II, p. 316; Crisp, *Mediaeval Gardens*, I, p. 61.

CHAPTER 5:

1 P.R.O., S.P. 1, vol. 168, f. 60 (*L.P.*, XVI, 1409 (i), sec. 4).

2 *L.P.*, XIV, i, 552.

3 *L.P.*, XV, 823, 850 (6).

4 Ibid., 823.

5 Quoted in Rupp, *English Protestant Tradition*, p. 117.

6 Foxe, *Acts and Monuments*, VIII, p. 33.

7 Ibid., VII, p. 550.

8 Hooper, *Early Writings*, p. 247.

9 Cranmer, *Writings*, p. 119.

10 *Original Letters*, I, No. 21, p. 36.

11 Harpsfield, *Pretended Divorce*, p. 297.

12 Foxe, *Acts and Monuments*, IV, p. 688.

13 Wilkins, *Concilia*, III, p. 776.

14 *L.P.*, IX, 583.

15 Ibid., 611, 846.

16 *Lords' Journal*, I, p. 105.

17 *L.P.*, IV, iii, 6179.

18 *L.P.*, XIV, i, 1004.

19 Ibid., ii, 750 (2). pp. 281-2.

20 Quoted in Neale, *Elizabeth I*, p. 316.

21 *Arrhaeologia*, XXIII, p. 62-3.

22 *St. Papers*, II, No. 208, pp. 551-2, n. 1.

23 *Archaeologia*, XXIII, p. 63.

24 *L.P.*, XV, 486.

25 Ibid., 822.

26 Ibid., 823.

27 Ibid., 822.

28 Ibid., 825.

29 Ibid., 823.

30 P.R.O., S.P. 1, vol. 168, ff. 64-5 (*L.P.*, XVI, 1409, pt iii, questions 1, 8, 10).

31 *Third Report of the Deputy Keeper*, App. II, pp. 264-5.

32 *Original Letters*, I; No. 105, p. 202.

33 *L.P.*, XVII, 441, p. 252.

34 *L.P.*, XV, 785.

35 Ibid., 429.

36 Quoted in Robson-Scott, *German Travellers in England*, pp. 22-3.

37 *L.P.*, XV, 662.

38 Ibid., 486.

39 Ibid., 697.

40 Ibid., 737.

41 Ibid.

42 Ibid., 737. 758; *L.P. Addenda*, I, ii, 1457.

43 Strype, *Ecc Mem.*, I, ii, p. 460.

44 Froude, *History of England*, III, pp. 320-3.

CHAPTER 6:

1 *L.P.*, XVIII, i, 873 (these are the words of Katherine Parr, Henry's sixth wife, spoken at her wedding).

2 Herman V, *A brefe dedaratyon of the dewty of maried folkes*, A 2v; Vives, *Office and duetie of an husband*, R v2.

3 Hume, *Chronicle of Henry VIII*, pp. 75-6.

4 *L.P.*, XV, 902.

5 Thomas, *The Pilgrim*, note E, p. 119.

6 Giustinian, *The Court of Henry VIII*, I, pp. 85-6.

7 Ibid., pp. 90-1.

8 Ibid., II, p. 313.

9 Pollard, *Henry VIII*, p. 185.

10 *L.P.*, VI, app. 7; XII, i, 126; Harpsfield, *Pretended Divorce*, p. 278.

11 *L.P.*, XV, 848; Byrne, *The Letters of Henry VIII*, p. 82.

12 Quoted in Hole, English Home-life, p. 71.

13 *L.P.*. IV, ii, 4858: XIV, i. 144.

14 *L.P.*. XV, 954.

15 Nichols, *Epistles of Erasmus*, I, p. 457.

16 Giustinian, *The Court of Henry VIII*, I, pp. 86-7.

17 *Cal. S.P. Venetian*, IV, 694, p. 293.

18 Hall, *Henry VIII*, I, p. 320.

19 *L.P.*, X. 307.

20 *Cal. S.P. Spanish*, IV, i, 160, p. 221.

21 Cavendish, *Life of Wolsey*, p. 184.

22 Roper, *Life of More*, p. 21.

23 Hall, *Henry VIII*, I, p. 27.
24 Thomas, *The Pilgrim*, p. 79.
25 Quoted in Chamberlin, *Private Character of Henry the Eighth*, p. 380.
26 *L.P.*, XIII, i, 56.
27 Garvin, *The Great Tudors*, p. 31.
28 Chamberlin, *Private Character of Henry the Eighth*, pp. 268-82.
29 McNalty, *Henry VIII, a Difficult Patient*, pp. 95, 159-61, 198.
30 *Cal. S.P. Spanish*, IV, ii, 775, p. 225.
31 Giustinian, *The Court of Henry VIII*, I, p. 237.
32 *Third Report of the Deputy Keeper*, p. 255.
33 *L.P.*, XIV, ii, 153.
34 *H.O.*, p. 156, cap. 62.
35 *L.P.*, II, i, 1495; XVI, 127.
36 *Cal. S.P. Spanish* (Elizabeth), I, 31, p. 67.
37 *P.P.C.*, VII, p. 352.
38 *Cal. S.P. Spanish*, IV, ii, 1061, p. 638.
39 *L.P.*, XV, 954.
40 More, *Utopia*, p. 35.
41 *L.P.*, XVI, 589.
42 *L,P.*, XV, 954.
43 Ibid.
44 Giustinian, *The Court of Henry VIII*, II, p. 314.
45 Ibid., p. 312.
46 *L.P.*, III, i, 1297.
47 *L.P.*, II, ii, 3163.
48 *L.P.*, VI, 775.
49 *L.P.*, IV, iii, 6111, p. 2729.
50 Byrne, *Letters of Henry VIII*, p. 86.
51 *Cal. S.P. Spanish*, IV, ii, 1061, p. 636.
52 McNamara, *Miscellaneous Writing of Henry the Eighth*, p. 173.
53 *L.P.*, XIX, ii, 21.
54 Holinshead, *Chronicles*, IV, p. 910; *L.P.*, XIII, ii, 1140.
55 *L.P.*, III, ii, 3082.
56 *Cal. S.P. Venetian*, II, p. 151.

57 *L.P.*, XIV, ii, 165.

58 Greene, *James the Fourth*, act IV, scene 5, p. 211.

59 *Sir Thomas More*, p. 28.

60 P.R.O., S.P. 1, vol. 167, f. 159 (*L.P.*, XVI, 1339).

61 Nucius, *Second Book of Travels*, p. 16.

62 *L.P.*, XVI, 106.

63 Quoted in Einstein, *Tudor Ideals*, p. 190, from Richard Compton, *The Mansion of Magnanimity*, Sig. E.

64 B.M., Lansdowne MSS, 238, fol. 294.

65 P.R.O., S.P. 10, vol. 8, No. 37. p. 66.

66 Cobbett, *State Trials*, I, p. 1045.

67 Quoted in Allen, *Political Thought*, p. 132, from *The Homily of 1571*.

68 *L.P.* XVI, 1359.

69 Ibid., 1426.

70 *Sir Thomas More*. p. 82.

71 Stapleton, *Life of More*, p. 192.

72 *L.P.*, XVI, 641.

73 Smith, *De Republica Anglorum*, p. 63.

74 Ibid., p. 62.

CHAPTER 7:

1 *L.P.*, XI, 285.

2 Thomas, *The Pilgrim*, note F, p. 157.

3 Ibid., p. 155.

4 H.M.C., *Marquis of Bath*, II, p. 9.

5 Hume, *Chronicle of Henry VIII*, p. 77.

6 Quoted in Camden, *Elizabethan Woman*, p. 100.

7 *L.P.*, XVI, 1389.

8 Ibid., 804.

9 Wriothesley, *Chronicle*, I, p. 124.

10 *L.P.*, XV, 21 (The *L.P.* gives this incorrectly as the household of Anne of Cleves).

11 Quoted in Salzman, *England in Tudor Times*, p. 92.

12 Camden, *Elizabethan Woman*, pp. 178-80, 188-9.

13 Stubbs, *Seventeen Lectures*, p. 284.

14 *Cal. S.P. Venetian*, IV, 824.

15 Thomas, *The Pilgrim*, note F, pp. 154-5: Nucius, *Second Book of Travels*, p. 48; *L.P.*, XVI, 60.

16 *L.P., XVI*, 12.

17 Foxe, *Arts and Monuments*, V, p. 555.

18 *L.P.*, XIII, i, 995.

19 *L.P.*, XVII, 178.

20 *L.P.*, XVI, 590.

21 Ibid., 589.

22 Camden, *Elizabethan Woman*, p. 24.

23 *L.P.*, XVI, 864.

24 Ibid., 314.

25 Thomas, *The Pilgrim*, note F, p. 154-5.

26 *L.P.*, XVI, 240, 421.

27 L.P., XV, 976; Harpsfield, *The Pretended Divorce*, p. 260.

28 *L.P.*, XVI, 712.

29 Ibid., 1332.

30 Ibid., 1317.

31 P.R.O., S.P. 1, vol. 161, ff. 101-2 (*L.P.*, XV, 875).

32 *Third Report of the Deputy Keeper*, App. II, p. 261.

33 *L.P.*, XV, 21.

34 *L.P.*, XVI, 316.

35 Ibid., 449; 660: 678 g. 41; 878 g. 28; 1391 g. 18.

36 Ibid., 467.

37 Ibid., 101.

38 P.R.O., S.P. 1, vol. 167, f. 131 (*L.P.*, XVI, 1320).

39 *P.P.C.*, VII, pp. 352-4.

40 P.R.O., S.P. I, vol. 167, ff 158-9 (*L.P.*, XVI, 1339, Culpeper's confession).

41 *L.P.*, XVl, 1469.

42 *L.P.*, XVI, 1385, 1416.

43 H.M.C., *Marquis of Bath*, II, p. 10; Burnet, *Reformation*, IV, 71, p. 505: *L.P.*, XVI, 1416 (I).
44 Burnet, *Reformation*, IV, 71, p. 505; *L.P.*, XVI, 1414.
45 *L.P.*, XVI, 1416 (2).
46 P.R.O., S.P. I, vol. 167, f. 157 (*L.P.*, XVI, 1339, Dereham's confession).
47 Ibid., f. 161 (Davenport's confession).
48 *L.P.*, XII, ii, 1150 g. 31: XVI, 1366.
49 *L.P.*, XII, 711, 808.
50 Strickland, *Queens of England*, III, p. 115.
51 See Genealogy of the Culpeper family, pp. 212-3.
52 Hume, *Chronicle of Henry VIII*, pp. 82-7.
53 H.M.C., *Marquis of Bath*, II, pp. 9-10.
54 *L.P.*, XIII, ii, 578; XVI, 779 g. 14.
55 *L.P.*, IX, 612.
56 *Original Letters*, I, 108, pp. 226-7.
57 P.R.O., S.P. I, vol. 167, ff 157-9 (*L.P.*, XVI, 1339, Culpeper's confession).
58 Ibid., f. 159.
59 Ibid., ff: 158-9.
60 Ibid.; H.M.C., *Marquis of Bath*, II, pp. 9-10.
61 H.M.C., *Marquis of Bath*, II, pp. 9-10.
62 P.R.O., S.P. x, vol. 167, ff. 159-60 (*L.P.*, XVI, 1339, Lady Rochford's confession).
63 Ibid., f. 157 (Culpeper's confession).
64 P.R.O., S.P. I, vol. 167, f. 14 (*L.P.*, XVI, 1134).
65 *L.P.*, XVI, 1337 (I).
66 P.R.O., S.P. I, vol. 167, f. 158 (*L.P.*, XVI, 1339, Culpeper's confession).
67 H.M.C., *Marquis of Bath*, II, p. 10; P.R.O., S.P. I, vol. 167, f. 160 (*L.P.*, XVI, 1339, Lady Rochford's confession).

CHAPTER 8:

1 *L.P.*, XVI, 733. 763, 785.

2 Ibid., 868, 941, 1130, 1183.

3 Ibid., 1088-9.

4 Ibid., 1130.

5 Ibid., 1126.

6 Ibid., 1131; Hall, *Henry VIII*, II, p. 313.

7 *P.P.C.*, VII, p. 245.

8 *L.P.*, XVI, 1139 (Culpeper's and Lady Rochford's confession).

9 *P.P.C.*, VII, pp. 352-3.

10 Ibid., p. 353

11 Nichols, *Narratives of the Reformation*, pp. 259-60.

12 *P.P.C.*, VII, p. 354.

13 Nicholas, *Narratives of the Reformation*, pp. 259-60.

14 *P.P.C.*, VII, pp. 354-5.

15 *L.P.*, XVI, 1328, 1332; *P.P.C.*, VII. p. 352.

16 Law, *Short History of Hampton Court*, p. 142.

17 Gosynhyll, *Scholehouse of Women*, B iii

18 *L.P.*, XVI, 1426; *P.P.C.*, VII, p. 335.

19 *Cal. S P. Spanish*, VI, i, 207 p. 396.

20 Ibid., 211, 411.

21 Cranmer, *Writings*, 273, pp. 408-9.

22 Burnet, *Reformation*, IV, 71, p. 505.

23 H.M.C., *Marquis of Bath*, II, pp. 8-9.

24 L.P., XVI, 1328, 1331, 1401; XVII, Appendix B 4.

25 Cranmer, *Writings*, 273, pp. 408-9.

26 Camden, *Elizabethan Woman*, pp, 87-8.

27 *St. Papers*, I, ii, 164. p. 694.

28 *P.P.C.*, VII, p. 355.

29 *St. Papers*, I, ii, 163, p. 691; 164, p. 695.

30 *L.P.*, XVI 1331.

31 H.M.C., *Marquis of Bath*, II, p. 10.

32 *L.P.*, XVI. 1366.

33 *St. Papers*, I, ii, 164, p. 694.

34 H.M.C., *Marquis of Bath*, II, pp. 9-10.

35 P.R.O., S.P. I, vol. 167, f. 160 (*L.P.*, XVI, 1339, Lady Rochford's confession).

36 Ibid., f. 159 (Culpeper's confession).

37 *Statutes of the Realm*, III 26 Henry VIII cap. 13, p. 508.

38 Smith, 'English Treason Trials and Confessions in the Sixteenth Century', *J.H.I.*, XV, No. 4 (October 1954), pp. 472-5.

39 Stapleton, *Life of More*, p. 192.

40 *L.P.*, XVI, 1426.

41 *St. Papers*, I, ii, 167, p. 700; *Third Report of the Deputy Keeper*, App. II, p. 261.

42 *L.P.*, XVII, 28 II c. 21.

43 *St. Papers*, I, ii, 167, p. 700.

44 Harpsfield, *Pretended Divorce*, p. 278; *L.P.*, XVI, 1415.

45 *L.P.*, XVI, 1366.

46 *L.P.*, XVI, 1414; *P.P.C.*, VII, p. 355: *St. Papers*, I, ii, 168, p. 703; 174, pp. 710-11.

47 *St. Papers*, I, ii, 173, p709.

48 *L.P.*, XVI, 1411.

49 *St. Papers*, I, ii, 165, p. 696.

50 Ibid., 166, p. 698.

51 P.R.O., S.P. I, vol. 167, f. 149 (*L.P.*, XVI, 1337 (i), Katherine Tylney's confession).

52 Ibid., f. 153 (*L.P.*, XVI, 1338, Margyt Morton's confession).

53 *L.P.*. XVI, 1442.

54 *St. Papers*, I, ii, 180, pp. 722-3.

55 Ibid., 172, p. 709.

56 P.R.O., S.P I, vol. 168, f. 64, Nos. 1, 7, 8, 10 (*L.P.*, XVI, 1409).

57 *L.P.*, XVI, 1457.

58 *Statutes of the Realm*, III, 33 Henry VIII, cap. 21, p. 857.

59 *L.P.*, XIV, ii, 399.

60 Cobbett, *State Trials*, I, pp. 407-8, 869 ff.

61 *L.P.*, XVI, 1426.

62 *St. Papers*, I, ii, 183, p. 727 (*L.P*, XV, 1471).

63 *Cal. S.P. Spanish*, VI, i, 228, p. 465.

64 *L.P.*, XVi, 1366.
65 *St. Papers*, I, ii, 171, p. 707.
66 Wriothesley, *Chronicle*, I, p. 131.
67 *L.P.*, XVI, 1426.
68 *St. Papers*, I, ii, 179, p. 721.
69 *L.P.*, XVII, 415; 568; 1258, p. 693: XVIII, i, 415.
70 *Lord's Journal*, I, p. 165.
71 Ibid., p. 171.
72 Ibid.
73 *Statutes of the Realm*, III, 33 Henry VIII, cap. 21, p. 859.
74 Quoted in Einstein, *Tudor Ideals*, p. 263.
75 *Cal. S.P., Spanish*, VI, i, 232, p. 472.
76 *Lord's journal*, I, p. 171.
77 *Cal. S.P. Spanish*, VI, i, 232, p. 472.
78 Ellis, *Letters* (1st series), II, 147, pp. 128-9.
79 *L.P.*, XVII, 100.

LIST OF ILLUSTRATIONS

1. and 2. Henry VIII and Catherine Howard as depicted in the Window of King Solomon and the Queen of Sheba, King's College Chapel. There is no authenticated likeness of Catherine. The only statement that can be made with any degree of certainty about Catherine's birth is that she was one of the youngest children of a family of ten, and that she was born before 1525, most probably in 1521. Courtesy of Elizabeth Norton and the Amberley Archive.

3. and 4. Portraits of Henry in later life, when he had become very overweight. Courtesy of Jonathan Reeve. JR950b2p337 15001550 and JR951b53p505 15001550.

5. The Palace of Whitehall. Courtesy of Jonathan Reeve JR779b46fp192 14501500.

6. and 7. London Bridge where the heads of Catherine's lovers, Francis Dereham and Thomas Culpeper were impaled on spikes following their execution. Courtesy of Jonathan Reeve JR734b46fp34 14501500 and JR952b55p254 14501500.

8. and 9. Old St Paul's Cathedral. Courtesy of Jonathan Reeve JR715b46fp28 13001350 and JR947b15p421 15001550.

10. and 11. Greenwich Palace. Courtesy of Jonathan Reeve JR735b46fp186 14501500 and JR944b46fp180 14501500.

12. Westminster. Courtesy of Jonathan Reeve JR729b46pfp16 13001350.

13. Richmond Palace. Courtesy of Jonathan Reeve JR945b20p788 15001550.

14. Henry VIII in Council. Courtesy of Jonathan Reeve JR946b20p913 15001550.

15. Anne Boleyn was Catherine's cousin. Courtesy of Hever Castle Ltd.

16. Thomas Howard, the Third Duke of Norfolk, the ambitious uncle of both Anne Boleyn and Catherine. He encouraged Henry's courtship of his niece, Catherine, in spite of her unsuitability for the role of queen. Courtesy of Jonathan Reeve JR949b2p110 15001550.

17. The Red Queen, Anne of Cleves. Courtesy of Jonathan Reeve JR822b53p415 15001550.

18. The most widely used portrait of Catherine but not an authenticated likeness of her. Courtesy of Jonathan Reeve JR821b53p457 15001550.

19. It fell to Archbishop Thomas Cranmer to inform Henry of his young wife's adultery. Courtesy of Elizabeth Norton and the Amberley Archive.

20. At Hampton Court there is what is described as the 'haunted gallery', which adjoins the Queen's chambers and Henry's chapel. It was there that Catherine is said to have eluded her guards and sought out her husband, who was hearing Mass. Just as she reached the door, she was seized and forced back to her chambers, while her screams resounded up and down the gallery. This presumably is the explanation of the female form, dressed in traditional white, which drifts down the gallery to the door of the chapel, and then hurries back, 'a ghastly look of despair' upon its face and uttering 'the most unearthly shrieks', until the phantom disappears through the chamber doorat the end of the gallery. Courtesy of Elizabeth Norton and the Amberley Archive.

21., 22. and 23. Catherine passed through Traitors Gate on 10 February 1542 and on to her short stay at the Tower of London. Courtesy of Elizabeth Norton and the Amberley Archive and Courtesy of Jonathan Reeve JR948b4p688 15001550.

24. and 25. The Chapel of St Peter ad Vincula and the site of the scaffold on Tower Green, where Catherine was beheaded by a single axe blow on Monday 13 February 1542. She was later buried in the Chapel. Courtesy of Elizabeth Norton and the Amberley Archive.

BIBLIOGRAPHY OF
PRINTED BOOKS REFERRED
TO IN THE NOTES

Allen, J. W., *A History of Political Thought in the Sixteenth Century*, London, 1951.

Allen, P. S. and H. M., *Opus Epistolarum Des. Erasmi Roterdami*, 11 vols., Oxford, 1906-47.

Antiquarian Repertory, a Miscellany ... , edit. F. Grose and T. Astle in 4 vols., London, 1807-9 (cited as *Antiq. Rep.*).

Archaeologia: or, Miscellaneous Tracts relating to Antiquity, vols. XXIII, XXV, XLVII, London, 1831, 1834, 1883.

Archaeologia Cantiana; being the Transactions of the Kent Archaeological Society, vols. IV, XXXII, London, 1861, 1917.

Ascham, R., *The Scholemaster*, Arber's English Reprints, London, 1869.

Baildon, W. P., *Les reportes del cases in Camera Stellata, 1593 to 1609, From the original ms. of John Hawarde*, privately printed, 1894.

Brenan, G. and Statham, E. P., *The House of Howard*, 2 vols., London, 1907.

Bullein, W., *A Dialogue against the Feuer Pestilence*, E.E.T.S., extra ser. vol. LII, London, 1888.

Bulletin of Historical Research, vol. XXVII, London, May 1954.

Burnet, G., *The History of the Reformation of the Church of England*, edit. E. Nares, 4 vols., London, 1839.

Byrnes, M. St Clare, *The Letters of Henry VIII*, London, 1936.

Calendar of Inquisitions Post Mortem and other Analogous Documents preserved in the Public Record Office – Henry VII, 3 vols., London, 1898, 1915, 1955.

Calendar of Letters and State Papers relating to English Affairs preserved principally in the Archives of Simancas, edit. M. A. S. Hume, 4 vols., London, 1892-9, vol., 1, *Elizabeth,* 1558-1567.

Calendar of Letters, Despatches, and State Papers relating to Negotiations between England and Spain preserved in the Archives at Simancas and elsewhere, edit. G. A. Bergenroth, *et al.,* 13 vols., London, 1862-1954 (cited as *Cal. S.P. Spanish*).

Calendar of State Papers and Manuscripts relating to English Affairs, Preserved in the Archives of Venice and in other Libraries of Northern Italy, edit. R. Brown, *et al.,* 9 vols., London, 1864-98 (cited as *Cal. S.P. Venetian*).

Calendar of the Manuscripts of the Marquis of Bath preserved at Longleat, Wiltshire, 3 vols., Historical Manuscript Commission, London, 1904-8.

Camden, C., *The Elizabethan Woman,* London, 1952.

Camden, W., *Remains concerning Britain,* edit. John Philipot, London, 1674.

Campbell, W., *Material for a History of the Reign of Henry VII,* 2 vols., London, 1873.

Casady, E., *Henry Howard, Earl of Surrey,* New York, 1938.

Cavendish, G., *The Life and Death of Cardinal Wolsey,* edit. R. S. Sylvester, E.E.T.S., No. 243, London, 1959.

Chamberlain, J., *Letters written during the Reign of Queen Elizabeth,* edit. S. Williams, Cam. Soc., original set. vol. LXXIX, London, 1861.

Chamberlin, F., *The Private Character of Henry the Eighth,* London, 1932.

Cleaver, R., *A Godlie Forme of Household Government,* London, 1598.

Cobbett's Complete Collection of State Trials, edit. T. B. Howell in 33 vols., London, 1809-26.

Cokayne, G. E., *The Complete Peerage*, edit. V. Gibbs and G. H. White, 12 vols., London, 1910-53.

Cornwallis (Cornwallyes), W., *Essayes*, London, 1600.

Cranmer, T., *Miscellaneous Writings and Letters*, edit. J. C. Cox, Parker Society, Cambridge, 1846 (cited as *Writings*).

Crisp, F., *Mediaeval Gardens*, 2 vols., London, 1924,

Dekker, T., *The Seven Deadly Sinnes of London*, edit. H. F. B. Brett-Smith, Oxford, 1922.

Dictionary of National Biography, edit. L. Stephen and S. Lee, 63 vols., London, 1885-1900 (cited as *D.N.B.*).

Einstein, L., *Tudor Ideals*, New York, 1921.

Ellis, H., *Original Letters Illustrative of English History*, 11 vols., London, 1824, 1827, 1846 (cited as *Letters*).

Elwes, D. G. C., and Robinson, C. J., *A History of the Castles and Manors of Western Sussex*, London, 1879.

Essex Archaeological Society Transactions, new series, vol. XV, Colchester, 1921.

Fisher, J., *The English Works of*, E.E.T.S., extra ser. vol. XXVII, London, 1876.

Foxe, J., *Acts and Monuments*, edit. G. Townsend, 8 vols., London, 1843-9.

Friedman, P., *Anne Boleyn*, 2 vols., London, 1884.

Froude, A., *History of England*, 12 vols., London, 1872, 1875.

Fuller, T., *The Worthies of England*, edit. J. Freeman, London, 1952.

Garvin, K., *The Great Tudors*, London, 1935.

Gentleman's Magazine and Historical Review, vol. XXIII, new ser., London, March 1845.

Giustinian, S., *Four Years at the Court of Henry VIII*, trans. R. Brown, 2 vols., London, 1854.

Gosynhyll, E., *The Scholehouse of Women*, London, 1561.

Greene, R., *James the Fourth*, printed in A. Dyce, *The Dramatic and Poetical Works of Robert Greene and George Peele*, London, 1861.

Hall, E., *Henry VIII from The Union of the Two Noble and Illustre Famelies of Lancastre & Yorke*, edit. C. Whibley, 2 vols., London, 1904.

Harpsfield, N., *The Pretended Divorce between Henry VIII and Catharine of Aragon*, edit. N. Pocock, Cam. Soc., new ser. vol. XXI, London, 1878.

Harrison, W., *Elizabethan England*, edit. L. Withington, London, 1889.

Herman, V. (von Wild), *A brefe and a playne declaratyon of the dewty of maried folkes*, London, 1553.

Historical Manuscript Commission: see *Calendar of the Manuscripts of the Marquis of Bath.*

Hole, C., *English Home-life 1500 to 1800*, London, 1949.

Holinshed, R., *Chronicles of England, Scotland and Ireland*, 6 vols., London, 1807-8.

Holmes, G. A., *The Estates of the Higher Nobility in XIV Century England*, Cambridge, 1957.

Hooper, J., *Early Writings*, edit. S. Carr, Parker Society, Cambridge, 1843.

Howard, H., *Indication and Memorials, Monuments, Paintings and Engravings of Persons of the Howard Family*, Corbey Castle, 1834.

Hume, M. A. S., *Chronicle of King Henry VIII*, London, 1889.

Inquisitions Post Mortem: Calendar of Inquisitions Post Mortem. Journals of the House of Lords, vol. 1, London, n.d.

Latimer, H., *Sermons*, Everyman's Library, London, 1926.

Law, E., *A Short History of Hampton Court*, London, 1924.

Lees-Milne, J., *Tudor Renaissance*, London, 1951.

Letters and Papers, Foreign and Domestic, of the Reign of Henry VIII, edit. J. Gairdner and R. H. Brodie, 21 vols., London, 1862-1910 (cited as *L.P.*).

Leland, J., *Antiquarii de Rebus Britannicis Collectanea*, edit. T. Hearnii, 6 vols., London, 1770.

Lodge, E., *Illustrations of British History, Biography and Manners*, 3 vols., London, 1791.

Longland, J. A., *A Sermon Spoken before the Kinge, his Maiestie at Grenwiche, Upon Good Fryday*, London, I536.

Lords' Journal: see *Journals of the House of Lords*.

Lyly, J., *Complete Works* edit. R. W. Bond, 3 vols., Oxford, 1902. *Euphues and his England*, Arber's English Reprints, Westminster, 1900.

Machyn, H., *Diary*, edit. J. G. Nichols, Cam. Soc. original ser. vol. XLII, London, 1848.

MacNalty, A. S., *Henry VIII, a Difficult Patient*, London, 1952.

McNamara, F. *Miscellaneous Writings of Henry the Eighth*, Waltham Saint Lawrence, Berkshire, 1924.

Markham, G., *The English House-wife*, London, 1631.

Mattingly, G., *Catherine of Aragon*, London, 1942.

More, T., *English Works*, edit. W. E. Campbell and A. W. Reed, 2 vols., London, 1931. *Utopia*, Arber's English Reprints, London, 1869.

Sir Thomas More, edit. A. Dyce, London, 1844.

Moryson, F. *An Itinerary*, 4 vols., Glasgow, 1907.

Mulcaster, R., *Positions wherin those primitive circumstances be examined, which are necessarie for the training up of children, either for skill in their booke, or health in their bodie*, London, 1581.

Nashe, T., *Works*, edit. R. B. McKerrow, 5 vols., London, 1910.

Neale, J. E., *Queen Elizabeth I*, London, 1939.

Nicholas, H., *The Literary Remains of Lady Jane Grey*, London, 1825.

Nichols, F. M., *The Epistles of Erasmus*, 3 vols., London, 1918.

Nichols, J. G., *Narratives of the Days of the Reformation*, Cam. Soc, original ser. vol. LXXXVII, Westminster, 1859.

Notes and Queries: a Medium of Intercommunication for Literary Men, General Readers, etc., vols. CLIX, CLXVII, London, 1930, 1930,1934

Nott, G. F., *Works of Henry Howard and Sir Thomas Wyatt*, 2 vols., London, 1815.

Nucius, N., *The Second Book of Travels of Nicander Nucius of Corcyra*, J. A. Cramer, Cam. Soc., original ser. vol. XVII, London, 1841.

Original Letters relative to the English Reformation, 2 vols., edit. H. Robinson, Parker Society, Cambridge, 1846-7.

Ordinances for the Household at Eltham in the xviith year of King Henry VIII, ad. 1526 in A Collection of Ordinances and Regulations for the Government of the Royal Household, made in divers Reigns, Society of Antiquaries, London, 1790 (cited as H.O.).

Osborne, D., *The Letters of Dorothy Osborne to William Temple*, edit. G. C. Moore Smith, Oxford, 1928.

Paston Letters, edit. J. Gairdner, 3 vols., Edinburgh, 1910.

Pendrill, C., *London Life in the 14th Century*, London, 1925.

Perlin, E., *Description des royaulmes d'Angleterre et d'Escosse, 1558*, in *Antiquarian Repertory*, vol. IV.

Platter, T., *Travels in England, 1599*, trans. C. Williams, London, 1937.

Pollard, A. F., *Henry VIII*, London, 1934.

Prescott, H. F. M., *Mary Tudor*, London, 1953.

Proceedings and Ordinances of the Privy Council of England, edit. H. Nicolas, 7 vols., London, 1834-7 (cited as P.P.C.).

Raines, F. R., *The Derby Household Books*, Chetham Society, vol. XXXI, Manchester, 1853.

Register of Admissions to the Honorable Society of the Middle Temple, edit. H. F. Macceagh and H. A. C. Sturgess, London, 1949.

Roberts, H., and Godfrey, W. H., *London County Council Survey of London*, vol. XXIII, *Southbank and Vauxhall, the Parish of St Mary Lambeth*, London, 1951.

Robson-Scott, W. D., *German Travellers in England 1400-1800*, Oxford, 1953.

Roper, W., *The Lyfe of Sir Thomas Moore*, edit. E. V. Hitchcock, E.E.T.S., No. 197, London, 1935.

Round, J. H., *Studies in Peerage and Family History*, Westminster, 1901.

Rupp, E. G., *Studies in the Making of the English Protestant Tradition*, Cambridge, 1947.

Rye, W. B., *England as seen by Foreigners in the days of Elizabeth and James the First*, London, 1865.

Salzman, L. F., *England in Tudor Times*, London, 1926.

Smith, L. B., 'English Treason Trials and Confessions in the Sixteenth Century', *Journal of the History of Ideas*, vol. XV (October 1954), pp. 471-98.

Smith, T., *De Republica Anglorum*, edit. L. Alston, Cambridge, 1906.

Sneyd, C. A., *A Relation of the Island of England about the year 1500*, Cam. Soc., original set. vol., XXXVII, London, 1847.

Stapleton, T., *The Life and Illustrious Martyrdom of Sir Thomas More*, trans. P. E. Hallett, London, 1928.

Starkey, T., *A Dialogue Between Reginald Pole and Thomas Lupset*, edit. K. M. Burton, London, 1948.

State Papers during the Reign of Henry VIII, 11 vols., London, 1830-52 (cited as *St. Papers*).

Statutes of the Realm, edit. A. Luders, *et al.*, 11 vols., London, 1810-28.

Stow, J., *Annales, or, A General Chronicle of England*, edit. E. Howes, London, 1631.

The Survey of London, Everyman's Library, London, n.d.

Strickland, A., *Lives of the Queens of England*, 8 vols., London, 1852.

Strype, J., *Ecclesiastical Memorials*, 3 vols. in 6, Oxford, 1822 (cited as *Ecc. Mem.*).

Stubbs, W., *Seventeen Lectures on the Study of Medieval and Modern History*, Oxford, 1887.

Surrey Archaeological Collections, vols., III, LI, London, 1865, 1950.

Sussex Archaeological Collections, vols. XXIII, XLVII, XLVIII, LVIII. Lewes, 1871, 1904, 1905, 1916.

Third Report of the Deputy Keeper of the Public Records, London, 1842.

Thomas, W., *The Pilgrim: A Dialogue on the Life and Actions of King Henry the Eighth*, edit. J. A. Froude, London, 1861.

Victoria History of the Counties of England, History of Hampshire and Isle of Wight, edit. W. Page, 5 vols., London, 1900-12 (cited as V.C.H.).

Visitations of Cornwall, 1530, 1573, 1620, edit. J. L. Vivian, Exeter, 1887.

Visitation of Kent 1619-21, Harleian Society, vol. XLII, London, 1898.

Visitation of Norfolk 1563, Norfolk and Norwich Archaeological Society, edit. G. H. Dashwood, Norwich, 1878.

Visitations of Norfolk, 1563, 1589 and 1613, Harleian Society, vol. XXXII, London, 1891.

Visitations of Suffolk *1561, 1577, 1612*, edit. W. C. Metcalfe, Exeter, 1882.

Visitations of the County of Surrey 1530, 1572, 1623, Harleian Society, vol. XLIII, London, 1899.

Vives, J. L., *The Office and Duetie of an Husband*, London, 1553.

Wagner, A. R., *Heralds and Heraldry in the Middle Ages*, London, 1939.

Weever, J., *Ancient Funeral Monuments*, London, 1631.

Wilkins, D., *Concilia Magnae Britanniae et Hiberniae*, 4 vols., London, 1737.

Wilson, J. D., *Life in Shakespeare's England, A Book of Elizabethan Prose*, Cambridge, 1926.

Wilson, T., *The State of England, Anno 1600*, Cam. Soc., 3rd ser. vol. LII, London, 1936.

Wriothesley, C. A., *A Chronicle of England*, edit. W. D. Hamilton, 2 vols., Cam. Soc., new ser. vols. XI, XX, London, 1875, 1877.